HENRY COWELL
Selected Writings

Henry Cowell

Essential Cowell

Selected Writings
on Music

*Edited with an Introduction
by Dick Higgins*

PREFACE BY KYLE GANN

DOCUMENTEXT
McPherson & Company
2001

Designed by Bruce R. McPherson.
Typeset in Monotype Baskerville with Bembo titles.
Printed in the United States of America.

1 3 5 7 9 10 8 6 4 2   2002 2003 2004 2005 2006 2007

Library of Congress Cataloging-in-Publication Data

Cowell, Henry, 1897-1965.
    [Essays. Selections]
    Essential Cowell : selected writings on music / edited with an introduction
by Dick Higgins ; preface by Kyle Gann.
        p.   cm.
    Includes bibliographical references and index.
    ISBN 0-929701-63-1
    1. Music—History and criticism. I. Higgins, Dick, 1938-1998. II. Title.

ML60 .C85 2000
780—dc21

                                                        00-055904

₡

Publication of this book has been assisted by grants from
the Literature Program of the New York State Council of the Arts,
and from Furthermore…, a program of the J. M. Kaplan Fund.

₡

CONTENTS

5

Preface

Today it is high musicological fashion to find precedents for every musical innovation, to prove that no composer was truly original. The musicologist David Nicholls, however, after an intense search for such precedents, had to concede that Henry Cowell may be the one composer who seems to have come out of nowhere. When Cowell as a young teenager used enormous tone clusters in *The Tides of Mananaun*, when he invented new rhythmic notations at the age of 20 for dividing whole-notes into 11, 13, or 15 equal parts, when he notated fingernail sweeps up and down the wound piano strings in *The Banshee* of 1925, he seemed truly to have invented a world of music out of whole cloth, or rather out of the glorious sounds he claimed to hear in his head.

Henry Cowell remains a background figure in American music—little played, not routinely taught in schools—but one of the most important background figures any culture has ever had. One hears of him occasionally, hears his music less often, yet his influence on American music is more pervasive than almost anyone realizes. Print references to the seminal treatise of his youth—*New Musical Resources*—remain uncommon, and yet dozens and perhaps hundreds of composers read it when they were young and have continued carrying out its proposed experiments, often without acknowledging their source. Almost no one today uses the rhythmic notation Cowell invented, yet hundreds of American experimental works are based on the rhythmic premises it was developed to make possible.

Few realize how influential Cowell was because his influence was so indirect, and this was partly because *New Musical Resources* has spent so little of its existence in print—from 1930 to '35, then for a few years following 1969, finally republished by Cambridge in 1996. Yet Conlon Nancarrow bought the book in New York, retired to Mexico City with it, and spent his entire life composing according to Cowellian charts that still hung on his wall when he died. John Cage read the book, picked up certain attitudes toward rhythm from it, and may have taken it to Europe with him in 1952. Among the Europeans at Darmstadt, we know Mauricio Kagel read it because he wrote an enthusiastic report.[1] Karlheinz Stockhausen's celebrated 1955 article "...How Time Passes..." and Pierre Boulez's *Penser la Musique Aujourd'hui* of 1963 are suspiciously similar to Cowell's book in their attempts to apply new global procedures for the structuring of pitch and especially rhythm. Somehow, the rhythmic schemes Cowell had dreamed up as a teenager made their way across the Atlantic and were fed back to us poor Americans as The Latest Thing from Europe.

Harry Partch, La Monte Young, and Ben Johnston all read *New Musical Resources*, and all took Cowell's ruminations on the harmonic series as inspiration to go further in the microtonal pitch realm. In terms of numbers of composers, however, the real impact of Cowell's ideas is most evident in the composers who were born in the 1950s, who read *New Musical Resources* in its Something Else Press incarnation. Look at the rhythmic and pitch structures of John Luther Adams, Larry Polansky, Mikel Rouse, David First, Glenn Branca, Rhys Chatham, Ben Neill, Michael Gordon, Art Jarvinen, David Soldier, Evan Ziporyn, and myself, and you'll find Cowell's suggestions carried out on more levels than he could have hoped. Some of these people feel strongly indebted to Cowell, others don't realize that the ideas they work with first appeared in Cowell's writings. But taken altogether, they offer a vision of American music which would not be what it is without Cowell's prescient theorizing. Even more than the reclusive Charles Ives, Cowell seems at times the most American composer of all, the true Father of our American music.

If all this is true, why does Henry Cowell remain such a background figure?

Many of the answers to that question can be found in this book. And the most important one is that he chose to remain a background figure. When Cowell appeared on the scene, there was no such thing as an American music. Cowell realized that the creation of an American music could not be accomplished through composing music alone. Composers were at the mercy of critics, and every time an American composer did something original, the critics (especially in America) either dismissed it as noise or called it an imitation of some European like Schoenberg or Hindemith.

A pivotal such instance occurred in 1931, when Philip Hale of *The*

Boston Herald wrote about the concerts of American new music that Nicolas Slonimsky had conducted in Paris. Hale wrote that

> the composers represented were not those who are regarded by their fellow countrymen as leaders in the art, nor have they all been so considered by the conductors of our great orchestras. If Mr. Slonimsky had chosen a composition by Loeffler, [Edward Burlingame] Hill, one of Deems Taylor's suites, [Arthur] Foote's suites, or music by some who, working along traditional lines have nevertheless shown taste, technical skill and a suggestion at least of individuality, his audiences would now have a fairer idea of what Americans are doing in the arts.[2]

Likewise, a few days later, Henry Prunières wrote of Ives in the *New York Times,* "There is no doubt that he knows his Schoenberg, yet gives the impression that he has not always assimilated the lessons of the Viennese master as well as he might have."[3] The ignorance revealed in such critical reaction was probably the impetus behind the book Cowell edited, *American Composers on American Music.* Several of Cowell's own contributions from that volume—a major contribution to American music's self-understanding, both then and now—are included here.

Music is a social art, requiring for its operation a complex network of contributions—a network that, to this day, has never run as smoothly in America as it did in its native Europe. The critical reaction showed Cowell that to simply compose music placed an artist in at best a vacuum, at worst a hostile environment. Versatile and more verbal than most musicians, he was gradually seduced into social action on many levels: organizing concerts, publishing scores in New Music Edition, reviewing concerts for *Musical Quarterly,* discovering and describing connections between new American music and the "primitive" musics from outside Europe. In all these activities he became a composer focused outward, not on his own music but on that of his colleagues and of other cultures.

The transition toward this state is easy to see in the writings collected here, if they are viewed chronologically. The articles from the 1920s and early 1930s are aggressive, iconoclastic. Cowell writes unforgettably about his concert tour of Russia, and takes on a host of big musical issues: aesthetics, the importance of noise in music, the history of music as a gradual unveiling of the harmonic series. In all of these writings, he stands as the young genius out to set the world right, alone born to fix the time that is out of joint. Never afraid to be original, he throws over the past without fear or sentimentality; he is the inventor of tone clusters, the theorist of the harmonic series, and his own experiences are sufficient basis to extrapolate new rules applying to all corners of the musical universe.

By the mid-1930s, Cowell has met other figures with similar claims to originality; he has learned that an obscure figure named Charles Ives used tone clusters years before him, and for the rest of his life he will graciously cede precedence. He begins writing about colleagues: Ives, Varèse, Becker, Seeger. Even in these writings his own theoretical bent shines through: especially in the articles on Ives, where Cowell's own theories about folk and other non-notated musics are made the basis for considerable extensions of classical music practice.

Then, of course, comes the great dividing event of Cowell's life, his incarceration at San Quentin prison from 1936 to 1940 on a morals charge. During this prison stay he works on what could have become the most revolutionary music theory text of the century: *The Nature of Melody.* Unfortunately, as Dick Higgins notes, the book's brilliant passages give way to deeply flawed exegeses of traditional European practice. It's possible that Cowell might have come back to the book, cleaned it up, de-Europeanized its examples, and made the final chapters consistent with the bold opening ones. But either the book proved too deeply flawed to fix, or it reminded him too much of the most unfortunate years of his life. *The Nature of Melody* remained a fascinating but unpublishable torso.[4]

And finally come the articles of the 1940s, '50s, and '60s. In these, Henry Cowell the fiery young genius fades almost into the background. The articles are not the worse written for that; but where Cowell used to preach from above, as a genius laying down laws, he now documents and urges from below. He writes about his colleagues (even those he earlier chafed against and despised, like Antheil) carefully, and with respect. He seems more at ease, in fact, writing about musics from the Eastern world, and about his eye-opening experiences as musical advisor to America's war effort. His writing in these late years can become routine, but Higgins, a student in tune with his former teacher, has culled the best of Cowell's late writing and the most exciting of his early articles, maintaining quality as well as a consistent level of representation throughout the man's career.

What comes through most of all, though, in all periods, is Cowell's utter refusal to be hemmed in by, or overly impressed with, the past. In Russia he met the conductorless Persimfons orchestra, and was disappointed that they were playing old classics rather than eliciting new music for which a conductorless orchestra was required. He began listening to vinyl records, and expressed his displeasure that no new music was being written specifically for the recorded medium. "A record of a violin tone," he writes, "is not exactly the same as the real violin; a new and beautiful tone quality results."[5]

Cowell's openness to the new could be a boon to avant-garde young composers. One of his landmark articles, included here, takes seriously, though with a layer of good-natured humor, the early efforts of John Cage, Pierre Boulez, and Christian Wolff in 1952—at which time the last-named composer was only 18 years old. Refreshing in a particularly American way, Cowell viewed music as a limitlessly open-ended field. He has no patience for those who timidly want to add a drop at a time to The Great Tradition when vast new musical continents are available for habitation. Like John Cage, Cowell could say, "I can't understand why people are frightened of new ideas. I'm frightened of the old ones."[6]

Timidity toward the new Cowell saw as of a piece with the attitude that shunts music off into a corner as being a mere decoration of life. Over and over, in the articles on Russian and Asian music and elsewhere, one senses Cowell's envy of cultures in which music plays a central role in a people's social life. "We here," he complains, "are apt to regard music as a mere amusement." The quest to make music more than an amusement drew Cowell out of his role as a composer to make him a producer, publisher, theorist, critic, ethnomusicologist, and philosopher. As such, Cowell perhaps rendered himself unable to live the public composer's life his music warranted. But he gave us, in his writings, a vision for what an American music could be that has inspired young composers of every subsequent generation, and is likely to do so far into the future.

— KYLE GANN

1. Mauricio Kagel praised *New Musical Resources* in his 1959 article "Tone-clusters, Attacks, Transitions," in *Die Reihe*. V. Kagel calls the book "still relevant forty years after it was written," and says that "even today, Cowell's reasoning can be reconciled with the newest problem of serial music."

2. Philip Hale, "Mr. Slonimsky in Paris," *Boston Herald*, July 7, 1931, p. 14.

3. July 12, 1931, quoted in Charles E. Ives, *Memos* (New York: W. W. Norton and Co., 1972), p. 15.

4. I discuss *The Nature of Melody* in more detail in my article, "Subversive Prophet: Henry Cowell as Theorist and Critic," in *The Whole World of Music: A Henry Cowell Symposium*, David Nicholls, ed., Harwood Academic Publishers, 1997.

5. Cowell, "Music of and for the Records," *Modern Music*, VIII/3 (March-April 1931), p. 33; quoted here on p. 256.

6. Quoted in *Conversing with Cage*, Richard Kostelanetz, editor, Limelight Editions (New York: 1988), p. 207.

Introduction

H ENRY DIXON COWELL was born on March 11, 1897, in Menlo Park, California, to Harry and Clarissa Cowell. Harry Cowell, an anarchist poet, was the son of the Anglican Dean of Kildare Cathedral, Ireland, evidently the priest in charge of overseeing the parishes belonging to the Kildare Bishopric. Harry was sent by his father to manage a family-owned fruit orchard in British Columbia. Failing at this, Harry moved to San Francisco, and there he married Clarissa Dixon. The Cowell house was small but comfortable, and it remained Henry's home base until 1936. Henry's mother was a poet and novelist who separated from Harry Cowell in 1902, divorcing a year later.[1] Young Henry went with his mother (who was musical), living with relatives in Iowa, Kansas, Oklahoma and New York from 1907 to 1910, a period of extreme poverty for mother and son; but "HC," as we will henceforth call Henry Cowell (following his own usage), remained in close contact with his father. HC's musical memories of this period occur in *American Melting Pot* (1940). HC was given a violin in 1902 but he had to give it up because of a nervous condition which he developed at this time. He returned to California in 1910 and bought his first piano two years later with money saved from odd jobs. HC attended school only sporadically, but by 1916, when his mother died, he had composed over one hundred compositions. Working alone as he did, he paid little heed to the strictures and conventions of classical music, and felt at liberty to follow his own inclinations. Any free time was apt to be devoted to nature; in fact one way that HC earned money was to gather wildflowers and sell them to passengers on passing railway trains. Many of HC's pieces, both early and late, have a mimetic quality and seem to depict natural processes.

The key personality in HC's developing intellectual life was John Varian, an architect of some means who established a community, The Temple of the People, in Halcyon, California, near San Luis Obispo. How young Cowell met Varian or precisely when this happened is not known, so far as I know. However it was from Varian, not from his father (who was not musical), that HC developed a lifelong fascination with Irish myth and music, and this interest is reflected in the titles of such early piano pieces as *The Tides of Manaunaun* (?1912). Manaunaun was a pre-Christian, Neptune-like Irish figure, whose command of giant waves is suggested by the huge chords of the piece, played with the hand or forearms and forming the second-based chords which HC called "tone clusters." What the audience thought of HC's first public recital, in 1914, can only be imagined, as no reviews are known of this or of HC's first New York City recital two years later. There are also such pieces as the *Quartet Euphometric* and *Quartet Romantic*, composed in 1916 and 1918, in which Cowell's focus lies on flexible rhythms more than harmonics. The early piano pieces are among Cowell's best-known works, but it would be a mistake to imagine they are the only early pieces, since he wrote in many forms.

HC's formal musical studies began in 1914 when he was seventeen, with the composer and musicologist Charles Seeger, then teaching at the University of California at Berkeley. Perhaps it was Seeger who persuaded HC to study English with his colleague Samuel Seward at Stanford University. Seeger certainly influenced the theoretical text that Cowell wrote at this time, *New Musical Resources,* revised and published by Knopf in 1930, reissued by Something Else Press in the late 1960s and currently available in an excellent new edition edited by David Nicholls.[2] This book not only describes techniques which Cowell used himself, but many which have only been used subsequently, often by other composers.

HC enlisted in the US army and served from 1918 to 1919, but he was only stationed stateside, mostly at Camp Crane, near Allentown, Pennsylvania. There he played flute and was assistant director of an army band. Meanwhile, Seeger lost his job at Berkeley because of his radical politics and opposition to the war. HC kept in touch with him and remained an associate throughout his life. In the early twenties HC gave at least one all-Cowell concert in New York, went on tour in Europe for eight months (1923), accumulating fame and notoriety, and returned to New York for

his Carnegie Hall debut (1924), which received sympathetic reviews, such as one from Paul Rosenfeld in *The Dial*.[3] It was at this
point that HC, his composing career launched, began his second
career promoting modern music. He joined the board of the International Composers Guild and founded the New Music Society, which presented its first concert in Los Angeles on October 22,
1924. HC's views on music history and on the musical world around
him would remain a chief concern throughout his life.

It was also at this time that Cowell began teaching. As most
American artists did then, and now—ideas being more common
than dollars in their lives—HC lectured a great deal, and became
very good at it. That Cowell kept an eye on the terms and grammar of new music is evident in his early publication, "New Terms
for New Music" (1928).[4] In 1928 he first taught at what is now The
New School for Social Research in New York City, then at the
cutting edge of education, and he remained associated with it off
and on until 1964. Beginning in 1930 he taught oriental music at
The New School, leading to the essays which make up the third
section of the present volume.

For 1931-32 HC received a Guggenheim fellowship to work in
Berlin at the Hornbostel Archive. Erich von Hornbostel was a
wealthy German aristocrat wit a passion for organizing exploration parties, sending them off to the far corners of the earth with
cylinder recording to record non-western music. The records of
his demonstration collection, which HC brought back from Berlin, still exist and parts are available on record.[5] They can be con-
sulted if one wants to see world music before western popular music
became so widespread. It seems to have been a happy time for
HC. Sidney Cowell used to tell a story about Hornbostel and the
renowned musicologist Paul Henry Lang violently arguing over a
fine point of tonality, and finally asking HC which of them was
correct.[6] "Both of you," Cowell responded, proceeding to resolve
the issue in question. Also in 1931, besides studying Indonesian
music in depth with Raden Mas Jodjhana of Java (especially
gamelan music), and Indian music with Professor Sambamoorthy
of Madras, both living in Berlin at the time, he worked with Arnold
Schoenberg. However, the Cowell-Schoenberg relationship has not
yet been fully documented and explored.

HC first made the acquaintance of Charles Ives in 1927. Initially skeptical about Ives' work, HC evolved into a devoted champion and in 1932 published an article on Ives in *Modern Music*.[7] This led eventually to a book with Sidney Cowell on Ives, *Charles Ives and his Music* (1955). Without Ives' patronage neither HC's enthusiasm, nor his and his colleagues' ideas could have kept *New Music* and New Music Editions alive.

Nineteen thirty-two was an *annus mirabilis* for HC. In that year he invented the rhythmicon, which was built for him by Leon Theremin (1896-1993), inventor of the theremin, a musical instrument. The rhythmicon is a device which can play difficult combinations of rhythms—for example, four notes against thirteen, six against seven, etc. Once such combinations are heard, they become more possible to play, so the rhythmicon had a heuristic function. But Cowell being Cowell, he also composed music for the rhythmicon, notably a Concerto for Rhythmicon and Orchestra. The second rhythmicon which Theremin built still exists in the Smithsonian Institute in Washington, DC. Also in that year HC gave innumerable concerts; New Music Editions was perhaps at its first peak; and he edited and wrote much of *American Composers on American Music*, which was published the following year.

The late 1930s remained very active for Cowell, with another book drafted, "Rhythm" (1935?); but this period was brought to an end by HC's arrest on May 22, 1936, on charges of having sex with a seventeen-year-old boy. The irony here, we can say today, is that though he did have a few male lovers over the years, the boy was not among these. HC was poorly defended in court, and was far from helped by having Olive Cowell (HC's devoted second stepmother) throw herself onto the ground, beat her fists upon the floor and shout "Mercy! Mercy!" So it happened that from 1936 to 1940 Cowell's residence was San Quentin prison. Curiously, virtually everybody connected with Cowell's case died in the next few years, among them the judge, the secretary of the court, and the prosecuting attorney. But Olive Cowell and, among others, HC's friend, Sidney Robertson, a writer, photographer and folklorist, kept up a campaign for HC's freedom. Eventually the governor of California became convinced of his innocence and Cowell was set free in 1940 into the custody of Percy Grainger (1882-

1961) to be his "musical secretary." Grainger had a lifelong interest in new means and forms of music, but he is, alas, among the composers about whom Cowell wrote no serious text. As for Sidney Robertson, Cowell had known her since about 1931; they were married on September 27, 1941. The date is significant, because on the anniversaries of their wedding until his death in 1965 (and for other occasions as well) Cowell often composed small works, known as the "Cleistogamy" (a term suggested by Sidney) which they could perform together. These are among Cowell's most charming small works.[8] In 1942 Cowell received a full pardon.

Even while in San Quentin HC remained active and in surprisingly good spirits. When a neighbor, Buddy Welles, went to visit him in 1939, she was startled to find how little rancor he had.[8] He did complain, however, that it was too noisy in prison to compose original music, but that he could orchestrate, and here he did just that with some of the early piano pieces, making up *Tales of Our Countryside*, which should some day be among his most popular works.[9] HC also organized an inmates' band or orchestra at San Quentin (the program of one concert is in the New York Public Library). In addition, he wrote his *Dance Observer* articles during this time, speculating about "elastic form," pieces which could be assembled into various lengths. And he worked on yet another book, "The Nature of Melody" (1938?), still in manuscript though excerpted for this volume.

During World War Two HC served as senior music editor at the overseas desk of the Office of War Information. Some of his thoughts on the uses and, even more, the pitfalls of using music for propaganda are described in "Music as Propaganda" and "Shaping Music for Total War."

HC also continued teaching until 1963 at the New School for Social Research, at the Peabody Conservatory in Baltimore (1951-56), and at Columbia University (1949-65). His many students included John Cage, George Gershwin, Lou Harrison, Bert Bacharach, and Alan Hovhaness. I will speak more of HC as a teacher in the final section of this introduction. His energy continued unabated. Béla Bartók (1881-1945) was an old friend who had emigrated to the United States as a refugee from Hitler. HC learned of Béla Bartók's poverty and got him teaching work at

Columbia. Alas, Cowell never wrote a major essay on him.[10]

HC was now something of an elder statesman of American music, representing the United States at a number of important musical conferences, such as those at Tokyo and Teheran in 1956. This last led to several HC compositions, among these *Persian Set* (1957), which synthesizes traditional Persian and modern western compositional techniques, and *Ongaku* (1957), which works with materials from Japan's gagaku.

Then, suddenly, in 1957 HC's health failed and he had a heart attack. He recovered enough to teach and compose. At the time I knew him best (1958-60) he was subject to dizzy spells which would come and go mysteriously. If he was conversing and Sidney was present, she could spot HC's dizziness and would immediately take over. Then, a few minutes later, as he began to recover, she would gently draw him back into the conversation—"Well, you know, Mr. Cowell [this]" and "Henry says [that]" until he was back in reasonably good shape. HC continued to compose until the end came, which was December 10, 1965. In fact, until June 4, 1964, when he sustained a severe stroke, his composing program was almost as prolific as in his prime. The last pieces do not sound like the works of a sick man. He seems to have known pain all too well, but he could endure it. Sidney once told me HC wanted to live up to retirement age, to finish the teaching he had started at Columbia. He lived to be 65, but alas there were no golden years of retirement for him.

One issue which will have to be explored more fully is the relationship between HC's texts and Sidney Cowell. She ghost-wrote at least two pieces—reviews of books by Nicolas Slonimsky, *Music in Latin America* (1945) for *Notes*, and by William Malm, *Japanese Music and Musical Instruments* (1959) for *The New York Times Book Review*—and she had a hand in a few others, not always acknowledged in print. Knowing her qualifications, this is not necessarily a bad thing. Her opinions were very close to HC's.[11] But their way of working was utterly different; Henry Cowell seldom rewrote texts, while Sidney was a polisher, writing everything over and over again. This made collaborations difficult, even in the case of their highly successful critical biography, *Charles Ives and His Music* (1955), already mentioned.

It is hard to evaluate HC's music as such. Bruce Saylor's entry on Cowell in the Grove's *Dictionary of American Music* proposes a breakdown of Cowell's works into three periods: experimentation and innovation (1912-1935); folklike or traditional (1935-1950); and a synthesis of these (1950-65). We can go along with this only if we take it with a great deal of blurring. The music does not (as the writings do not) break down cleanly into sharply defined periods. Rather, they constantly extend: a strand from twenty years before is suddenly picked up and developed, then put aside again, only to return many years later. No technique is ever completely dropped. In the earlier works the focus is on the western tradition. By the 1930s the focus shifts eastward to the orient, but the west is not forgotten. From then on the problem at hand is to digest everything, to dissolve the seams, resulting in not a patchwork but a well-wrought whole.[12] HC is by turns avant-garde and conservative in his music. I shall return to this later.

It should be noted that with Cowell, even more than with other composers, a large-scale work is not necessarily a more major work than a small one. Several of the symphonies seem less impressive than some of the smaller works. This in addition to the sheer volume of work makes it hard to form a consensus concerning which are the most important pieces. Among my own favorites is a dance score written in 1941 for Erick Hawkins, "Trickster (Coyote)," a piano reduction of which I bought at a library sale for perhaps fifty cents; but I have never heard it live, never even heard of a live performance, though a slightly more polished version was printed in *Soundings* 11 (1981).[13] Given this kind of problem, it is sure to be some years before anything approximating a consensus of the key pieces can be formed, let alone an evaluation of HC's compositions as a whole.

One observation that has not been mentioned with regard to Cowell is that he was of the same generation as the New Critics in literature. Though HC was certainly no literary critic, and perhaps not even very aware of John Crowe Ransom, etc., many of their ideas were "in the air" in the twenties and thirties, such as an avoidance of personal specifics, an insistence on the Aristotelian genres ("this is suitable for this and that for that, and mix them at your peril"), and a mistrust of any vast theory, and anything approaching intermedia, at least in his own practice, in which media blur or fuse. Cowell's commitment was to music and to music alone. Thus, among HC's texts we do not find autobiographical statements, or historical and social parenthetical speculations. In only one text does anything like a self-portrait of HC in action emerge, namely "Playing Concerts in Moscow" (1931), written as Stalinism was becoming a problem for Soviet arts. Formal discussions are just that: formal discussions. They are presented as techniques, and their intellectual underpinnings are not explored as was later done, sometimes brilliantly, by John Cage, whose work (as of so many others) Cowell was the first to champion. He could appreciate criticism and near-music which differed from his own, but these lay outside his purview. As HC put it, "Music is my weapon."

II: *Musical History, World and Otherwise*

Cowell did have an overall view of the history of western music. It underlies the discussions of tonality and chord formation in *New Musical Resources*[14] but the only time it is explicitly written out and stated is in an early essay, written in collaboration with Robert L. Duffus, "Harmonic Development in Music." This article, published in Van Wyck Brooks's magazine *The Freeman* (1921), presents the theory that musical history proceeds by revolutions and that in the west this has been characterized by harmonic transformations, with new harmonies based on a progression of intervals becoming the basis of a new family of chords, moving ever upward through the overtone scale. Here we see music moving from harmonies based on the fourth and fifth to those based on the third, finally reaching those based on the second, major and minor. This last family of chords is, of course, the tone-cluster and it, and its accompanying theory of dissonant counterpoint, were as HC saw them, the basis of new music. What would logically lie beyond such chords? The music of noise, percussive and electronic. HC discussed percussion music in such texts as "The Joys of Noise" (1929), and wrote sympathetically about the appearance of electronic or tape recorder music.[15] HC composed several works for percussion ensemble, but he did not produce any major body of percussion music and never wrote any tape recorder music himself, so far as I know. Other theoretical articles HC wrote in the 1920s dealt with issues of creativity and the psychology of western versus non-western music—for example, "The Basis of Musical Pleasure" (1931), which is not in reprinted here—so there is no doubt that HC was well aware of the issues. But his primary concern was to make modern and world music accessible and familiar, for the sake of both people and artists; this was his primary mission.

By 1925 HC was ready to make his move toward this end. He involved himself on the organizational level with existing composers' organizations and he started New Music, as noted.[16] This took the form of a concert series from 1925 to 1936, in New York and Los Angeles and, later, San Francisco. The organization was somewhat amorphous, reflected in minor alterations to its name—"New Music Society of California," "New Music Society," and so on. Many of its concerts were conducted by Nicolas Slonimsky and, at least in the beginning, Cowell's closest associates in New York on the project were Edgar Varèse (Cowell prefers to use this form instead of the older "Edgard") and Carl Ruggles. The big quarrel in modern music at that time was between the French school (associated with Igor Stravinsky, Darius Milhaud, along with the various students of Nadia Boulanger, such as Aaron Copland and Virgil Thomson) and the more avant garde (and less popular) tendency which centered on American music, but whose European allies were Arnold Schoenberg, Alban Berg, Anton von Webern and a host of others (including Béla Bartók). The first concert which New Music presented took place on October 22, 1925, in Los Angeles, and it included works by Dane Rudhyar, Edgar Varèse, Carl Ruggles and Arnold Schoenberg.[17] Patronage was, of course, a problem; but somehow the series managed to keep afloat.

The second phase of Cowell's promotional activity was to establish *New Music Quarterly*, with the purpose of publishing four modern scores each year, starting with Carl Ruggles' *Men and Mountains,* an orchestral work. One of the early subscribers to the series was Charles Ives. Ives was, at that time, viewed as a wealthy eccentric by most of the music and intellectual community. Many a businessman who knew Ives slightly in a business context would note how shrewd Ives' judgment was, "but we didn't think much of his music." Jokes were widespread about how Ives' self-published *114 Songs* was a good size for children to sit on when they practiced the piano. However, Ives bailed out the deficit which arose from the cost of producing the first issue of *New Music Quarterly,* and his generosity with regard to the subsequent issues led to a close friendship between Cowell and Ives, and a deep understanding on HC's part of Ives' music. (New Music could not have survived the Great Depression without Ives' support.) Also in the mid-1930s, New Music produced New Music Quarterly Recordings, which undertook to bring to the public examples of the works from the New Music catalog. Though of variable quality, these phonograph records could go where the publications could not, and they too became an important contribution of the series.

The personal friendship between HC and Ives was severely shaken by HC's arrest, and though Ives slowly "forgave" the younger composer (as he saw HC), their closeness of the early thirties was never fully restored. Nevertheless, Ives willed the proceeds from one work, *The Unanswered Question,* to Cowell, and after Ives's death, HC and Sidney Cowell published their fine full-length study of Ives, *Charles Ives and his Music* (1955). It is not unfair to say that what Felix Mendelssohn did for us in rediscovering Bach, HC did for Ives.

Another area in which HC and New Music contributed is the field of Latin American art music. This had been pretty much ignored in North America, but HC wrote several articles on the subject, especially about Aléjandro Garcia Caturla, Pedro Sanjuan and Carlos Chavez; HC published works by each of these in *New Musical Quarterly.* He also was active in the founding of the Pan American Association (1927) which for many years was one of the few organizations which brought together the musics both north and south of the Rio Grande.

When Cowell was sent to San Quentin he turned over his position at New Music to the composer Gerald Strang.[18] Strang did yeoman's work reorganizing, eliminating the concerts and recordings, and focusing on the publishing program. Perhaps most importantly he moved New Music to New York City, where Ives continued to help with its support, and where it survived as a program until the mid-fifties. When Cowell himself moved to New York he did not resume his position at New Music, then held by Ray Green.

Cowell's new focus was on teaching, and, at last, on his own composing.

This, then, is the background of the remarkable series of articles which HC wrote from the twenties until his death. His preferred venue was *Modern Music;* the articles he wrote for them are all significant and hold nothing back. They never seem like simplifications. By the late forties he had begun an extensive series of articles (forty in all) in *Musical Quarterly.* These latter deal less with theoretical issues; they are instead a record of the significant musical events which HC witnessed—now a concert, now an interesting phonograph record, and so on. One might describe them as a sort of ongoing diary of sound events. They cover a large variety of musical performances, but do not cover all the composers and musics on whom one would like to have a text by Cowell. For instance, Cowell wrote only about the melodramatic "A Survivor from Warsaw" by Schoenberg, but produced no major essay on him, though he had several times cited Schoenberg as the greatest living composer.[19]

One aspect of HC's career as champion and crusader was his ability to communicate with all kinds of people. This is very rare among modern composers, who tend to be able to speak only with each other. Thus HC also wrote for trade magazines, for magazines of associations of one kind or another, for "hi-fi" magazines, in short, for anyone who seemed to him to need to hear The Word. HC's reviewing had to be somewhat curtailed after his 1957 illness, but even after that it was resumed sporadically.

As a teenager in San Francisco, HC lived for a while in a part of San Francisco which lay between Chinese and Japanese parts of town. Naturally, the Chinese knew Chinese music and the Japanese knew Japanese music—and HC knew both and his own besides. The Chinese considered the Japanese music strange, and the Japanese had the same attitude toward the Chinese music. It was HC who enjoyed them both and tried to figure them out, each according to its own code of values. Aware of the difficulty to many people of living with two or more kinds of music, he spoke of being "bimusical" or "multimusical." This led to his lifelong interest in non-western musics, what today is called world music. From the early 1950s Cowell had a radio series on Sunday mornings on WBAI-FM in New York, "Music of the World's Peoples," on which he played world music and commented on it. For a time even after Cowell's death in 1965 one could still hear every Sunday the old tapes of HC as a disk jockey playing world music and offering up insightful comments.

Already in his "The Impasse of Modern Music" (1927), reprinted in our collection, HC began to postulate a general theory of non-western music with western art music. The universality in his approach is extremely appealing, and must have been especially attractive to the political radicals of the time. As for Cowell's own overview, he reviewed non-western music along with the avant-garde in his *Musical Quarterly* articles, and always one is conscious of his taking non-western perspectives into account, especially Asian ones, in a non-patronizing way. We have already noted his study of Javanese and other Indonesian musics in Berlin. This finds its way into Cowell's own compositional practice, though nowhere nearly as much as in the music of his Canadian contemporary Colin McPhee, whom HC championed, or his friend, student and colleague Lou Harrison, whose involvement not only with the instruments of the gamelan but with the modes of Javanese music are an integral part of Harrison's achievement.

By the mid-1930s Charles Seeger was newly married and had settled on the East Coast with his bride, the composer Ruth Crawford. He had more or less abandoned his own musical composition by now, but as a musicologist specializing in world music he was increasingly respected. Seeger was also active in left-wing causes and was part of a circle which produced a magazine of leftist musical opinion, *Music Vanguard*. The Communist Party line in the early thirties was that the "vanguard of the proletariat" must provide leadership in all cultural areas including music, thus favoring experimentation and innovation of all kinds. However this position was shortly replaced by the "Popular Front" line, associated in the USA with Earl Browder, in which the artists must both follow and provide a broad base of popular art and culture. One of the most impressive of all Cowell's articles, "The Scientific Approach to Non-European Music" (1935), first published in *Music Vanguard* and included here, presents his ideas concerning world music in a way which would be fully acceptable to this Popular Front position. Seeger must have been pleased. HC was not, however, a highly politicized figure. Cowell was certainly a "man of the left," as his choice of texts for his "Proletarian Songs" (1930-1933) indicates,[20] but in "Music is my Weapon," his 1953 manifesto written for Edward R. Murrow's *This I Believe,* he asserts he is not a communist, and presumably he never had been a card-carrying member of the party. No doubt, but the early fifties was the period of McCarthyism and so Cowell's assertion might be taken with a grain of salt. Cowell was close to at least some communist circles, although he was never a true believer, and he was quite capable of objective criticism of the political situations in which he found himself.

After 1957 HC had to cut back on his writings, but he continued to publish articles from time to time. Often these were transcriptions of speeches given by Cowell. Saylor's bibliography of Cowell's writings lists only nine articles after 1957,[21] but one of these is "The Composer's World," a long speech HC gave at Teheran in 1961, in which he discusses what it means to be a composer. Another is "Music of the Orient," which in its first publication includes a splendid photograph of the aging but apparently happy HC playing a shakuhachi flute among a group of rapt onlookers. Even as an old man HC seems as committed as ever to "turning them on."

III: *A Personal Aside*

Perhaps it is appropriate for me to add a few remarks about what it was like to know and study with Cowell, in order to fill in the picture of the man and his teachings.

As a high school student I subscribed to the LP records by the American Recording Society which, in the early 1950s, brought out, among other things, a fine performance of Cowell's Fifth Symphony conducted by Dean Dixon.[22] This was the first Cowell work I heard, and when in 1956 my mother hired as a babysitter for my younger brother an erudite communist, who informed me that modern music was mostly garbage except for Henry Cowell's, I became very interested. I sought out all the records I could find of Cowell's music. A favorite was an a cappella version of "Hymn and Fuguing Tune Number Five."[23] I was a classical disk jockey at my college radio station, and I played that piece over and over. Moving to New York City in 1958, I enrolled at Columbia University's School of General Studies, in part to study with Cowell. But for me Columbia did not start until the autumn, and in the spring of 1958 there took place in New York the "25 Year Retrospective Concert of John Cage." I attended that concert and it awoke me to the complexities, implications and variety of Cage's achievement. I felt I *had* to study with Cage too.

So, starting the summer of 1958, I took Cage's courses in "Experimental Music Composition" and "Mushroom Identification" at the New School for Social Research. The Cage class met twice a week in the same classroom which Cowell used for "Music of the World's Peoples," and in the storeroom there was a large collection of oriental musical instruments. Many of the Cage class pieces were performed on those instruments, along with such nontraditional instruments as windup battleships, toy whistles and objects we made for our own use, such as the "schmatte-zereiser," a piece of cloth affixed to a sounding box and intended to be torn systematically. Out of the Cage class evolved Happenings and Fluxus, both of which I took part in, though that is another story.

The first time I actually saw Cowell was at the New School. There was to be a lecture by Vladimir Ussachsvsky on tape recorder music in that same room in which the Cage class met, and somehow we learned that Cowell would be there. I had talked Cowell up to my classmates, and several of us—myself, Al Hansen, and filmmaker Al Kouzel—chose to attend Ussachevsky's lecture, to see what was afoot. Too shy to introduce myself to Cowell, and fearful that if he knew we were sitting in on his class without paying he would send us away, we said almost nothing. But the impression which I formed of a smallish man, a cross between an Irish leprechaun and a Zen roshi, with a benevolent smile, a man who seemed to have heard more music than anyone else I had ever come in contact with, and who seemed to know what he wanted to say and do more than anyone else I had met. This image monitors my reading of his works, texts as well as music. Whatever else he was, HC was no naïf, and the descriptions one reads of the man which suggest a childlike persona do not accord with the HC I knew.

John Cage's first important music teacher was, of course, Henry Cowell. Cage had studied with him in 1930-31, until Cowell left for Berlin, and they remained close friends throughout their lives. Cage himself had a great charisma; he could not or would not argue a point, but would, instead, make one feel that one's disagreements were petty and reflected a lesser degree of nobility than Cage's point deserved. Cage persuaded with a smile. One felt outclassed. But I strongly recommend to anyone who studies with a powerful figure like Cage that, if possible, he or she also study with the powerful figure's teacher. Cowell, with whom I studied at Columbia in the fall of 1958 and the fall of 1959, provided the perfect counterweight to studying with Cage. He could and did discuss any issue in music, thus providing the ratiocination for any conclusion. Furthermore, one could not but become aware of Cage's tremendous debt to HC. In the Cage class, in speaking of any particular musical piece, the minimum unit of sound was the "event," with several events making up a "constellation." This terminology was also used by Cowell and may well have originated with him.[24]

Cowell's composition class at Columbia was under-attended both times I took it, with only four or five students. The reason for this became clear almost at once: each week one was expected to bring in a composition and perform it. Thus, the amount of homework was far more than most students could commit to. I dropped other courses (it delayed my graduation), but I was not about to give up my chance to study with HC. Each week we were given a specific problem to deal with in our compositions. For example, we were each assigned to write a German lied. I went home, fished out some Mahler and Hugo Wolf lieder, noticed that Hugo Wolf had set a number of the poems of Edward Mörike to music, found a Mörike poem I liked, and worked at my lied over the weekend. When class time came along I brought it to HC, whose first comment was "Hmm, this doesn't *look* like a lied at all. Too many syncopations, but—" and here he began to play "—it *sounds* like a lied." And he began to analyze my piece as if he had lived with it for weeks.

HC was right, of course; it sounded like Wolf but looked like the transcription of a calypso song. The lesson I learned from that was invaluable. To look and sound the same became an objective for me. Another assignment was more theoretical: to write the most expressionistic piece possible. My solution to that one was hopelessly grotesque—unintentionally funny. But then, so were the pieces that my fellow students turned in. However, my annoyance with myself stayed with me, and years later, when I was active in Fluxus, I composed *Danger Music No. 17* (1962) with Cowell's assignment in mind—a sustained and loud scream, kept up until the screamer is exhausted. It is perhaps my best-known piece and a photograph of myself doing it is on the cover not of one but of two books.

One never knew exactly what a Cowell class would cover. For dissonant counterpoint and the logic leading up to it, HC showed the pathways in Schoenberg, Seeger, and others who, independent of one another, arrived at the same point. HC argued that because these several routes had been used, the development of dissonant counterpoint was inevitable. He demonstrated how chords were based on the overtone structure. He played us his composition "The Banshee" correctly and, to show us what would happen, then with several perfectly logical wrong approaches. If anyone suggested that HC was an experimental composer, he would say: "Listen harder—I am also conservative." Never "traditional," since he was well aware of the innovative tradition, but he liked to call himself "conservative." Or, if they would say he had become too conservative, straying too far from his innovative roots, off he would go again: "Listen harder—there's just as much innovation there as ever." He must have been saying that for some time, since once in the Cage class, when someone complained about Cowell turning into a composer of jigs and reels and no more, Cage smiled and suggested: "Listen harder—"

Occasionally, the class would move to areas that were far from its official purview, as when HC brought a shakuhachi flute to class, which he maintained was best played in a meditative state, relaxing the lower lip; thus making it a suitable instrument for Zen Buddhist purposes. And in another class I mentioned my fondness for "Gärdebylåten," a Swedish walking song which was on one of Cowell's "Music of the World's Peoples" records, and this led to a long discussion of the function of the piece: in the Swedish mountains the men worked the valleys while the women and children were in the hills, so on weekends the men would play walking songs when they marched into the hills to join the women. "Gärde-bylåten" is such a "gångsång." HC called himself a nationalist in music—a nationalist of whatever music or country he found himself in. And he spoke of Irish fiddling, and how fiddlers would compete with the dancers and attempt to trick them by skipping a beat now and then. Why? To keep them alert, of course. In other words, function was a part of music too, function and context. Function suggested meaning, and meaning was very important to someone in my generation, coming as we did after abstract expressionism and therefore looking for forms of meaning other than the normative ones or, as some seemed to, rejecting meaning altogether. It was a challenging and valuable class, and the "A" I received from HC for my Concerto for Trumpet in D and Orchestra, my term project, meant more to me than just about any grade I ever received.[25]

In the summer of 1959 I decided to hike to Canada, choosing Woodstock, New York, as my starting point. I knew that the Cowells had a home at Shady, a hamlet of Woodstock. It was a very wet summer. Every morning I would leave the boarding house where I was staying, head off across Overlook Mountain and then, on the other side, I would be caught in a rainstorm. The nearest shelter? The house in Shady where the Cowells were residing while work on their own house was completed. They received me graciously and I would spend a while with them, then hitchhike back to Woodstock and my boarding house. After a week it was clear that this was not the year for me to hike to Canada. So I stayed on a few more days, gathering wild mushrooms, visiting once or twice with the Cowells, who patiently put up with my arrivals and my questions, looking over the mushrooms, HC commenting on whatever music I had been working on (as every night I did), telling marvelous stories that were always to the point and making useful comments. Then I returned to New York.

I saw less of HC after 1960. I invited the Cowells to my wedding (May 1960) but they could not come. I graduated from Columbia and went to printing school, was involved in Fluxus and, later, Something Else Press. I saw the Cowells a few times at concerts, at the premier of the Cage *Theater Piece* (1962) on which occasion David Tudor played some Cowell piano works. But I did not see them socially. One day in December 1965 I heard over the radio that HC was dead. I had not even heard that he was ill. Still, as I have mentioned, his broadcasts of "Music of the World's Peoples" were played over WBAI-FM on Sunday mornings. It felt strange to hear him talking posthumously about the difficulties of finding authentic Hawaiian music or flute players in New Guinea. Finally these broadcasts stopped, and I learned from a friend who worked at the station that the tapes had been erased because they needed them for reuse.

One day in particular comes back from that summer of 1959. I was hiking down to Shady. The daily storm had passed, and I was drenched and shivering in spite of my poncho and two sweaters. As I came into the valley I heard a perfectly dreadful caterwauling as if a herd of pigs were being slaughtered—or so it seemed to me. Shortly I realized that the sound was coming from the house where the Cowells were staying. I walked around the house and there was Henry with a dozen or so neighbors and musicians, quite amateur. He had set them to playing some piece of his. The resulting dissonance was quite amazing, but the expression on HC's face was angelic and radiant. Clearly he was listening through the mistakes and dissonance and, without ignoring these, hearing through to the over-piece,[26] perceiving and enjoying the hidden melodies and patterns. That is, of course, how many of Cowell's tone-cluster pieces are constructed. One listens carefully and finds, concealed inside, a simple hymn tune. One must *perceive* what is going on actively, so that every element becomes transparent and the over-piece is revealed. Watching HC hear his piece—that is how I prefer to remember him.

1. For my discussion of Cowell's early life I am indebted to Bruce Saylor's entries on Cowell in Stanley Sadie, ed., *The New Grove Dictionary of Music and Musicians* (20 v. New York: Grove Dictionary of Music [Macmillan], 1980) and H. Wiley Hitchcock and Stanley Sadie, eds. *The New Grove Dictionary of American Music*, 4 vols. New York: Grove's Dictionary of Music, 1986, where the entry on Cowell is in vol. 1 pp. 520-529; and also to stories told me from time to time by Sidney Cowell and to a small display of well-captioned photographs at the Henry Cowell Festival in April 1987 at the Catskill Conservatory of the State University of New York, Oneonta, New York. There is also information on Cowell's development in Lichtenwanger (1986) pp. xiii-xxxvi (*see* Bibliography).

2. Cambridge: Cambridge University Press, 1996. Hereafter cited as *NMR* (1996).

3. Lichtenwanger (1986) xxviii. See also Manion (1982) for reviews from this time.

4. "New Terms for New Music." *Modern Music* V/4 (May-June 1928) pp. 21-27. Most of HC's terms are either too well known to justify printing the list, have subsequently acquired different meanings or new terms have supplanted HC's proposed terms.

5. *The Demonstration Collection of E. M. Hornbostel and the Berlin Phonogramm-Archiv...* 2 records. Ethnic Folkways Library FE 4175.

6. Sidney Cowell told me this part of the story when last I saw her, in November 1995.

7. A selection of these has been recorded by Kenneth Goldsmith, violin, and Terry King, cello, as Music and Arts CD 635. The Cowells played them on recorders or recorder and piano, but for these works that is unimportant.

8. This is per a conversation with Ms. Welles in July 1996. She was a friend of Cowell and neighbor of the prison. Her husband was Ralph Emerson Welles who wrote the text for the experimental stage work *Fanati* (1935), which was attended by, among others, Lou Harrison, who wrote about it as a seminal experience for him in a letter to Sidney Cowell, quoted in Lichtenwanger's catalog (1982) p. 145.

9. "Tales of Our Countryside" is the title suggested by Leopold Stokowski who felt "Four Irish Tales," Cowell's original title, was too narrow. The work was recorded by Stokowski and the All-American Symphony in 1942 and released by Columbia Records as a 78 RPM 2-record album, Columbia Masterworks Set X-235. It has never been reissued, alas.

10. HC's other essay on Bartók is a short one, "Bartók and his Violin Concerto," printed in Boosey and Hawkes's house organ *Tempo* 8 (September 1944) pp. 4-6. The full Bartók-Cowell relationship will have to be explored via the letters and other documents.

11. Sidney Cowell's account of this is in her article "The Cowells and the Written Word," in Richard Crawford, R. Allen Lott and Carol J. Oja, *A Celebration of American Music: Words and Music in Honor of H. Wiley Hitchcock* (Ann Arbor: University of Michigan Press, 1990) pp. 79-91.

12. Saylor's entry on Cowell appears in *The New Grove Dictionary of American Music* (1986) pp. 520-529, with the classification on p. 522. The last text in our book, "A Composer's World" (1961), shows how close Cowell's ideas remained to his earlier ones—for example, "The Process of Musical Creation" (1926). A transcription of a lecture given at Teheran but published in Professor J. H. Kwabena Nketia's occasional periodical *Music in Ghana* 2 (1961), it shows Cowell attempting a synthesis of many of his ideas on world music, the composition process, and the art of teaching. The result is, however well it may have worked as a speech, a bit of a patchwork; to succeed fully in print it would need to be a whole book.

13. See *Soundings* 11 (1981) pp. 2-17 and Lichtenwanger (1986) 182-3.

14. *NMR* "Part One: Tone Combinations" pp. 3-40 and "Part Three: Chord Formation" pp. 111-139.

15. See Cowell's review in "Current Chronicles" from *New Musical Quarterly*. There is also a fine article, "Composing with Tape," *Hi-Fi Music at Home* I/6 (January-February 1956), pp. 23, 57-59.

16. These activities are extraordinarily well documented in Rita Mead, *Henry Cowell's New Music[:] The Society, the Music Editions and the Recordings* (Ann Arbor: UMI Research Press, 1981). Hereafter cited as Mead (1981).

17. Mead (1981) p. 36.

18. Mead (1981) p. 356.

19. For example, in "Who is the Greatest Living Composer," in *Northwest Musical Herald* VII/5 (January 1933) p. 7. Cowell also did not write anything major on Stefan Wolpe (1902-1972) or on Schoenberg's followers. His articles on his close friend, the composer Wallingford Riegger (1885-1961), are also somewhat perfunctory.

20. Lichtenwanger's catalog (1986) pp. 140-141 gives the titles of these songs as "Canned," "Free Nations Unite!" "Move Forward!" [untitled proletarian song], "We can win together," and "Working men unite, we must put up a fight!" The songs are in rough form and would need some creative editing to prepare them for publication or performance.

21. Saylor (1977) pp. 34-5.

22. Dean Dixon, conductor. Vienna Symphony Orchestra. Reissued on Desto D405 and more recently as a CD by Bayside Cities BCD 1017.

23. David Randolph, conductor, with the David Randolph Singers, issued on LP as Concert Hall Society LP CHC 42.

24. HC used these terms in class if not in his writings.

25. My concerto, some of my other pieces from the Cowell class, and some of my notes are now in the Archiv Sohm in Stuttgart, Germany.

26. This concept, which we used in the Cowell class, I have described more fully in my essay "Underpiece/Overpiece," in my book *Horizons: the Poetics and Theory of the Intermedia* (Carbondale, IL: Southern Illinois University Press, 1983) pp. 64-70.

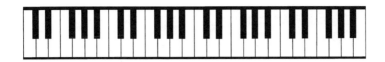

PART ONE

HC in Person

Playing Concerts in Moscow

Moscow is musically conservative. My music is usually considered radical, on account of its innovating a new and fulsome kind of piano resonance, and some new modes of piano technique. This tale is an account of the unheard-of ups and downs I encountered in playing concerts of my own music in Moscow, on the invitation of the Soviet government through its vehicle, the Society for Cultural Relations.

It should be clearly understood that the unusual features of my music are to blame for a good portion of the curious happenings; but it was not exclusively a matter of unique Soviet methods. Yet probably the music would not have had a similar reception, nor would details of a government invitation be carried out in the same way, in any other country in the world; and it seems paradoxical that advanced tendencies in American music, acceptable here, should prove too radical for Russia. Yet that is just what happened, as far as the official Soviet music committee is concerned. Other groups, however, took up the music with eagerness, and it is the resultant war between the two factions which made my experiences sufficiently novel to be worth relating.

Every detail of my trip, of the carrying out of plans, of the giving of concerts, included some unbelievable contrast in the behavior of different officials, from greatest enthusiasm to utter lack of interest.

Just when the heavy miasma of Stalinism was settling over the arts in the Soviet Union, Cowell was invited to perform in Moscow. This is his account of the experience, originally published in Musical Courier CII/21 *(May 21, 1931) pp. 6, 30-31. Besides its interest as an account of the Soviet Union at the time, it shows Cowell's irrepressible spirit. How many other composer pianists would have slept on a park bench or faced official opposition with such equanimity?*

35

I first received an invitation to go to Russia and play under Soviet auspices in London in 1926. The invitation had several unusual aspects. In the first place, it was utterly unsolicited. Usually so grave a matter as an official invitation to do anything whatsoever must be made the subject of voluminous correspondence before being decided, and in the case of a musician it might be assumed that his manager had worked under cover on the matter for some time before such an invitation would be forthcoming. In my case there was no such thing. After my playing a London concert, a gentleman introduced himself to me backstage, and informed me that he was a consul from Soviet Russia. He forthwith and without parleying, asked me to appear in Russia under official auspices. On inquiry, I found that it was one of his regular duties to investigate any unique artists who came to his attention, with a view to an official invitation to go to Russia if they proved sufficiently interesting. The idea intrigued me greatly, as we unfortunately do not instruct our consuls to foreign lands in this fashion.

I agreed to go to Russia at that time, but had no sooner made all final arrangements with the London consul than all Soviet delegates were returned home by Great Britain. I could not find the address of the consul through whom I had made arrangements; letters to him sent to England were returned to me. I wrote to every Russian official in Moscow who I considered might know something of the arrangements, but not one of my letters was answered. So I did not go to Russia; and this was the first example of my oscillation between unexpectedly hearty interest and utter indifference.

Early in 1928, when I knew that I would be on tour in Europe during 1929, I thought it would be interesting to visit Russia, and tried to re-open the invitation to play there. I wrote again to the officials in charge of musical affairs there, and to a number of private musicians to whom I had letters of introduction. Only one of these letters was answered. One musician wrote "It would doubtless be interesting if you gave some concerts in Russia; why don't you give some?" It will be seen how meaningless this was, when it is understood that there is no way to play concerts in Russia except by government invitation.

Being disappointed in getting a renewal of my invitation to

play in Russia, I applied for a visa to go there as a casual visitor.

I made the application from New York in February, 1929. The application was to be considered, and the answer given in Berlin. When I got to Berlin in April, the visa was not granted; no reason was given.

I made an interesting discovery in Berlin. This was that the Soviets have in Berlin a certain official who has entire charge of all invitations to be tendered to foreign musicians to play in Russia. By the recent arrangement no one can go to Russia as an official musician except by his approval. In all my correspondence with Russia no one had told me of this important fact, and I only learned of it by chance. Most Russian officials, in fact, do not seem to know of it; it was entirely unknown at the Society for Cultural Relations in New York, for example. This official, who has the fates of all foreign musicians in his grasp, is not primarily a musician, but a doctor of chemistry. I was told that he was especially chosen on this account, because it was thought that a musician in this position would be biased, and not carry out the policy of the Soviets, which is this: they do not wish to be bothered by having sent to Russia any conventional performers on musical instruments, no matter how fine. Their attitude is that they have in Russia, among themselves, very fine performers, and the only difference would be one of individual interpretation. This they are not particularly interested in. They wish to invite to Russia only musicians who have made some definite innovation, who have added something new to music which is not known in Russia. A musician, they feel, would be apt to become moved by fine playing to such an extent that he might send in a mere good performer, while a scientist would be more likely to preserve cool judgment. So they chose Dr. Ernst Chain, a chemist with a great avocational devotion to music.

I had the good fortune to meet and please Dr. Chain, and he and some of the Russian embassy to Germany were inveigled into attending my Berlin concert. Several of the members of the embassy became wildly excited, said my music was something Russia must positively hear, and telegraphed Moscow to grant a visa and arrange concerts at once.

It was then the very last moment that I had time to go to Russia before playing in other parts of Europe, and the only train I could get was the weekly train which goes through from Paris to Vladivostok. The train was filled mostly with people going through beyond Moscow, and one could not get a sleeper. Nor could one find a seat; in fact it would have been a problem to find a place to put one's feet to stand. I had some misgivings as to whether I could stand from Berlin to Moscow, and then step off the train and play a concert immediately. But Dr. Chain was horrified that I should ever have considered so unpleasant a possibility; "of course, we will get a private car for you," he said, "at least as far as the Russian border!" I was not at all prepared for a private car, which I would have considered far too elegant for Soviets to consider. I thought it augured well, however, and began to have visions of an official reception committee, and of being housed in state, perhaps in some former palace, once I got to Moscow.

When I arrived in Moscow, though, no one met me and no provision had been made for me to sleep, which is a serious matter there, as I found, for the hotels were filled for many days in advance. With great difficulty, as I know no Russian, I made my way to the home of Samuel Feinberg, a composer whom I had met at Dr. Chain's in Berlin.[1] He succeeded, after telephoning a great deal, in finding that a concert was being arranged for me, and had been announced; and that the Cultural Relations Society's music committee was in charge of it. I visited the music committee, who, as a polite gesture, invited me to play for them. When they heard the music, however, they behaved strangely. Instead of saying anything to me, they congregated in a corner of the room and whispered. The result of the whisper was soon made known to me. They were profoundly shocked at the radicalism of my music, which they considered would be too advanced to be understood in Russia, and they therefore felt obliged to cancel my concert. So after being hauled in state to Russia in a special car, I still had nothing to do, once I got there. And still there was no provision for my being housed. The committee did not feel any responsibility in housing me, and the Cultural Relations people promised sweetly to do their best, but nothing ever came of it. Feinberg telephoned for me to every hotel, big and small, in Moscow and we found one hotel which might possibly have a room in some weeks. A private room was out of the question, as everyone is very crowded in Moscow. I tried to make myself comfortable on a park bench, when word came through an American newspaper man that he had been able to get permission for me to sleep in a room which was to be sublet for a few days. It was a horribly costly, but most grateful shelter.

When the music committee canceled my concert I gave up hope of presenting music in Moscow, but thought only of availing myself of the opportunity to visit Russia. Yet as it proved, the committee's refusal was the best thing that could have happened, as far as making me known musically in Moscow is concerned. For all circles are not musically conservative there, and when it became noised about that there had come from America a young musician who was so radical in his music that he had been boycotted by the conservative committee, then for the first time there was interest about me in more important musical circles. It being a rash thing to go counter to any government decision, the first invitations I received to play for well known musicians in Moscow privately were somewhat surreptitious. If I proved to write really dangerous music they could then withdraw their interest and no one would be the wiser.

My first invitation was to play for Constantin Igumnoff, director of the Moscow Conservatory. He also invited a few trusted members of the faculty. My music was received by all of them with wild acclaim, and they took a vivid interest. Igumnoff declared that the committee who turned me down was wrong, stodgy and over-cautious, and said that he would buck them, and present me himself, in concert. This was the equivalent of declaring a musical war, because the committee which turned me down was official, and official decisions are not usually contravened; yet Igumnoff's position is very distinguished, and he has legal authority as the government's head of Russia's greatest musical institution. Within the conservatory, Igumnoff had final authority, so it was there that he first presented me, with [the] assistance of Feinberg and of Nicolas Shiliaeff, one of the faculty, who was very enthusiastic.

The conservatory at Moscow is probably the greatest university of music in the world, for all private music teaching is obsolete in Moscow. All the former music teachers are at the conservatory, and all the talented music students from all over Russia are sent to it, or to similar schools in other large centers. There are thousands and thousands of music students in the Moscow institution, and almost as many teachers in the faculty as there are students in most conservatories.

I first played for the faculty of the conservatory, and created so much interest and discussion that I was asked to play for the students, which I did in three relays, there being no available hall that would hold them all at once. The student concerts were exciting and extraordinary. They began at four o'clock in the afternoon, and were supposed to last an hour. For the first of these concerts I made the mistake of preparing an hour's program, but this arrangement proved utterly futile. After I played my first number for them, there arose from the hall an indescribable roaring and bellowing, like Niagara Falls and a touchdown at a football game combined. Yells, shouts, clapping, and stamping of feet jumbled into one mighty din. The noise indicated neither approval nor disapproval, I think, but intense interest. The noise showed no sign of abating, so I raised my hand, and when there was quiet, I began to play the second number on the program. Upon which, the noise began again, and rose to such a wild pitch that I was forced to stop. The students sent a delegate onto the stage who could speak German (in which language I did most of my conversing in Russia) to ask if I would please be good enough to play the first composition over. I did so. The same sort of roaring followed, and I again tried unsuccessfully to start the second piece on the program. They sent up the delegate again to ask if I could please consider playing the first piece a third time. I did so; and it was only with reluctance that I was then finally permitted by the students to begin the next number. Its reception was the same, and after I had played it four times in succession I was permitted to go on and play the third piece. The third piece, as it happened, contained some very unusual methods of playing the piano, and it created such excitement that I had to play it through no less than seven times! In other words, I had to devote a half an hour, or half the supposed length of the whole program, to repeating one piece alone.

After I had been playing for about the full hour which was supposed to be the entire length of the program, I began to think longingly of an intermission. So after the final repetition of the third piece on the program, I began sneaking off the stage, hoping to reach the safety of the green room for a moment's rest before my absence from the stage was noticed. But this was not to be. As soon as I tried to escape from the stage a more frightful roar than any before went up, and the familiar delegate came up to ask me if I didn't realize that an intermission would be a great waste of time. This was the only opportunity of these students to hear me, and they were all greatly interested and wished me to continue. "Besides," the delegate said, "the time is very limited, as there will be another concert at eight-thirty in this hall, and we can only use it until about eight-fifteen." The time was then a few moments before five o'clock. The upshot was that I played right through from four until eight-fifteen, repeating every work not less than three, nor more than seven times. When we finally had to abandon the hall because of the next concert held there, the students all gathered about me and said what a pity it was that the hall had to be used, and that we couldn't go on with the concert.

I played the same sort of concert, lasting from four to after eight o'clock, on three successive days. The psychology of these Russian students is particularly interesting, on account of being so very different from that of our audiences here. If an encore is demanded of an artist here, and he is forced to play a piece over, it is a sure sign that the auditors were pleased with the music and understood it. Among the Russian students the pieces which were at once understood were taken for granted, while the more abstruse compositions were the ones they wished to hear over the most times; they were unwilling to let a piece go by without understanding it as nearly as they could by repeated hearings. And in America, an average auditor may walk out of a concert hall in the middle of an abstruse work, not even taking the trouble to hear it clear through once.

Many of the students, I was told, wrote down some of my music from memory, after hearing it so many times. They were all very eager to get hold of foreign new music, because, owing to the Russian ruble having no value in foreign countries, no foreign music can be bought by the students, and they are pathetically eager to get possession of it.

The government officials in general do not approve particularly of giving the students a great deal of foreign new music for study, for fear they will become too much influenced by the mode of expression of "bourgeois" nations. One government group has decided that in order to be communistic, music must be liked at once by the people. This was found to limit the music not only to well known types of melody and harmony, but to actual tunes that are known, and resulted in much playing of well known folk tunes. Another government group is not so extremely conservative as the first, but feels that there should not be individual expression on the part of a composer—he should express not himself, but the commune. A result of this has been that any new or individual tendencies have been discouraged on the part of young composers, and they are asked to model their music more to a general style.

There are a large group of composers now composing in Moscow, whose work can hardly be told apart, it is so similar in style; and this is just what they are aiming at. A rather small group, with some government support, tries to sponsor radical music, and claims that the government must have a new sort of music as its expression. Chief among these composers is Mossolow;[2] but his music does not belong to a new order of radicalism but to a sort which we in other lands have passed through about fifteen years or more ago, and represents the use of discords in a crude and uncalculated way, with childishly inadequate form, and constant repetitions of the same material. His most interesting work is *Machine-Music*, which has Honneger's *Pacific 231* as a model.

So it can be stated that in musical composition, Russia is mainly conservative, and that its minority of radicals are passing through a stage of development already passed through in other countries. This is perhaps because none of them realizes that there is unconsciously springing up in Russia a real new musical expression— not among musicians, but among the people themselves. I noticed this in the delightful music which is improvised on the spur of the moment to the also improvised plays, performed by workers in the evening at their working places. They build up a stage, supply a general rag-bag from which any one may pick up a costume, and then have a perfect lark making up their parts as they go along, and burlesquing anything and everything. The music which is improvised to fit the action of the play at the moment, which is not written down, and has never yet been considered seriously by any Russian musicians, seemed uniformly delightful to me; and burlesquing anything and everything else, as well as one particularly induced, it seemed to me, by the exigencies of workers' conditions in Russia today.

There are many concerts of the more formal type in Moscow. There are three symphony orchestras, I was told; although I heard only Persimfons, the great leaderless orchestra, which plays with surprisingly good ensemble and refinement. Then there are three opera companies, and the many concert halls are constantly filled. Musicians from other countries come occasionally but are still somewhat rare.

To resume my personal experiences—after I had played at the conservatory, I was invited to play for the jury of the State Publishing Edition. All the music published in Russia is now under the auspices of this edition, and the way they choose their music is interesting. Instead of having music-readers examine a score which comes in for consideration, as our publishers do, the government supplies an orchestra and all other necessary musicians, and the music is actually performed for a jury, which is made up of a number of Russia's most distinguished composers, as well as former publishers, such as Jurgenson. Miaskofsky is the chairman of the jury.[3]

I played for the jury, and they were very excited and asked permission to publish some of my things in the State Edition. I was very pleased, of course, and accepted at once. I was then served a glass of tea (an essential part of any Russian social or business transaction) and before the tea was finished, the treasurer presented me with a large roll of bills. I was most astonished, because here one's royalties, if any, begin to dribble in after a year or more. But in Russia they pay advance royalties on the first 500 copies right away. When I had recovered from my stupefaction I asked the treasurer how it had been decided in such a few minutes just how much royalty to tender me. That was very simple, I was told: "We pay ten kopeks per quarter note for all our music!"

Since the Soviets have no international currency, I have arranged for all future royalties to be paid in barter—the State Edition will send me music in payment, instead of cash. One transaction of this sort has already taken place; I have received two huge packages of musical scores in return for an article on American composers, which they accepted and translated into Russian for their music magazine, "Music and Revolution." It was a very agreeable surprise to find any country in the world where a composer of music of the more serious sort is paid for his work as a matter of course.

Following playing for the State Edition, I played for the State Department for the Science of Music.[4] The work done by this department is fascinating and important; in fact it probably leads the world in this field, but its accomplishments are of too technical a nature to describe here. I found it of great interest, though, that the Soviet government finances a huge department for music science, a subject almost unknown to us, employing several hundred workers, and fully equipped with scientific apparatus.

Finally comes the most extravagant experience of all. The conservative committee who first cancelled my original concert in Moscow came forth and said that they wished, after all, to give me a concert in Moscow. They spoke of it as a postponement of the original concert. I accepted, and it was only later that I learned that the concert was not arranged in good faith. Underlying the matter was much politics. I had been successful in almost all musical quarters in Moscow, and there was open controversy between the musicians who took my part and those who had refused me a hearing; there was even a concerted movement on foot to disqualify the members of the conservative committee, on the ground that they had made a vital mistake in my case. So the committee set themselves about to show that a concert as originally planned would have been a failure, and that even if I had been successful with musical groups I would not be so with a general audience. So the committee definitely made arrangements for the concert they gave for me to be a failure, so as to vindicate their position. I learned this secretly from one of the committee members, who thought it outrageous and opposed the other members; and who therefore confessed that all the arrangements against the success of the concert were made deliberately.

All concerts in Moscow are held in the evening, as a rule. Muscovites eat dinner at about six o'clock. My public concert arranged by the committee was announced for five o'clock in the afternoon, with the idea that it would begin late, and the audience would all leave for their dinners a little after I began playing, and it could be said that they were disgusted with the music and walked out. Then there was a deliberate halting of the beginning of the concert, to anger the audience.

At five o'clock promptly I appeared behind the scenes, ready to begin the concert, and was seen there by the audience, as I was quite visible. The audience wanted me to begin, and began applauding; but although I wished to begin I was not permitted to do so. I must wait for a certain official who would open the concert, I was told. The audience, however, was told that I was having an artistic tantrum and temperamental outburst, and refused to start. At six o'clock, just an hour late, the official, who proved to be Mme. Kameneva (sister of Trotsky) came and opened the concert. The audience all remained. I started the concert. There had been no programs, but instead an announcer was specially instructed how to announce my pieces, each piece being announced during the applause from the former selection. This had the effect of stopping the applause instantly, as the audience hoped to hear better; and also no one knew what I was playing, as the words were drowned out by the applause. When the applause stopped, the announcer would not repeat his statement. So during the entire program, the listeners were in ignorance of what I was playing. As a final gesture, the committee arranged that twice during the performance, while I was actually playing, a flash-light photographer slowly set up his apparatus on the stage behind me, deliberately waited in readiness to set off his flash until the entire audience was in a state of nervous excitement, and then he set off a super-charge behind my back. The first time this happened I was utterly unprepared, and was sure a bomb had been thrown. The audience, to the dismay of the committee, began to see through these childish attempts to make the concert fail, and all remained to give the music a tremendous ovation at the end. The people of the audience and other Moscow musicians were also so stirred against the committee that they presented the matter to higher Soviet authorities; and since such sabotage is not, of course, the general policy, but was only resorted to as a final measure by this particular committee, I have been told since leaving Russia that the committee referred to lost its official sanction on account of the episode.

Whether this is true or not, probably more unexpected things may happen in concerts in Russia than anywhere else in the world. Such a condition may be partly due to unusual political situations, but I believe that it is largely because of the vital part that music plays in the lives of Russians. We here are apt to regard music as a mere amusement. To the Russian music is a deeply ingrained necessity for the outpouring of his feelings. This is the cause of the possibility of such dramatic outbursts concerning music as are here related; for the Russian, treating music as seriously as he does, will take action for or against it according to his feeling as to its validity, with the same fervor that he deals with his political policies.

1. According to Richard Kostelanetz in a personal letter (September 1, 1996), Feinberg's recording of Bach's "Well-Tempered Clavichord," played on the piano, is among the best. However, none of his compositions is currently available (1996).–DH
2. We have kept the original spellings of names. Alexander Mosolov (1900-1973) is best known for his work *Iron Foundry*, an instrumental depiction of the sounds of an iron foundry.–DH
3. "Miaskofsky" is Nicholas Miaskofsky (1881-1950), conservative in his own work but friendly to Cowell.–DH
4. Today we would say "musicology" for "Science of Music."–DH

Music Is My Weapon

I BELIEVE IN MUSIC: its spirituality, its exaltation, its ecstatic nobility, its humor, its power to penetrate to the basic fineness of every human being.

As a creator of music I contribute my religious, philosophical and ethical beliefs in terms of the world of creative sound—that sound which flows through the mind of the composer with a concentrated intensity that baffles description, the sound which is the very life of the composer, and which is the sum and substance of his faith and feeling. When he offers a composition one should remember that it is complete, concrete, and full of dynamic force in his mind and consciousness; and that a performance is only a run-through of the music for the benefit of those who listen, those who the composer hopes will respond. Yet this presentation will, if successful, so impregnate the listener with the philosophy of the composer that it is shared both in the realm of feeling and that of intelligence.

Since I am more used to expressing ideas in music than in words, I find that the latter seem inadequate, and do not have the drive, positiveness and persuasiveness that I should hope for in a musical presentation; but here are what words I have: My belief is that the Golden Rule is the supreme guide in human relations. I do not

In mid-century the famed radio newsman Edward R. Murrow hosted a broadcast series called "This I Believe" in which prominent people were invited to present statements about life or faith. Many of the statements were published in a two-volume work. This one appears in Edward R. Murrow, This I Believe, *Vol 2, ed. Raymond Swing (New York: Simon and Schuster, 1954), pp. 40-1. Note Cowell's expressed abhorrence of Communism, a reflection of the effect of McCarthyite anti-communist hysteria of the era. Still, HC had close associations with progressive causes and people.*

believe that any race or people is better or worse than any other.

I believe that each human being should have the liberty to be an individual, and that everyone who wins the right to act in his own way must, in return to society, behave ethically. I used to be almost totally uninterested in politics; but it becomes increasingly clear to me that ethical individualism cannot flourish under radically extreme political conditions. Thus I abhor communism, under which individualism is impossible and expression of liberal thought is punishable; and I abhor its right-wing counterpart under which innocent liberals fear persecution and reprisals of various sorts if they express their sincere ideas for the betterment of the government. My own belief is in a regard for individual rights according to the letter and spirit of the United States Constitution. This I fight for by creating music which I hope will reach and touch all who listen so that they will be thereby encouraged to behave according to their own highest possibilities. Unexpected inner response to the power of music dedicated to human integrity might reach dictators more easily than an atom bomb.

In any event I believe that a truly devoted musical work acts to humanize the behavior of all hearers who allow it to penetrate to their innermost being.

This is why I am a composer.

PART TWO

Contemporaries

Charles Ives

CHARLES E. IVES IS THE FATHER of indigenous American art-music and at the same time is in the vanguard of the most forward-looking and experimental composers of today.

Many composers before Ives tried to utilize American folk-material; such men as Stephen Foster practically composed folk-songs. But some of their music yielded to banal European influences, because they invariably altered the original rhythms (often fascinatingly irregular) so as to fit the current European mode, which was nothing but 2/4, 3/4, 4/4, or 6/8 meter, and in note-lengths nothing but whole, half-, quarter-, eighth-, sixteenth-, or thirty-second notes, or, at the wildest, eighth-note triplets. Also, all the slight deviations of pitch in the musical scale of the American village folk, wrought in deepest musical ecstasy, were (and still are by most arranger-butchers) altered so as to suit the conventional European mode of tuning of the major or minor scales. And, perhaps worst of all, a schoolbook harmonization like a hymn in four-part harmony was given to all alike. Thus the process of squeezing out all the original life and fire of the music was complete.

Ives was born in 1874 in a small Connecticut town where native music lived. His father, a musician, conductor of the band and experimental enough to be interested in acoustics, was evidently a splendid influence. He did not try to narrow down or standardize the views of his son, but allowed him to hear all the native music in

Apart from HC and Sidney Cowell's Charles Ives and His Music *(1955), now available in a fine new edition edited by David Nicholls (1996, see bibliography), this is Cowell's fullest appreciation of Charles Ives (1874-1954), written at a time when few people regarded Ives as a serious composer. Earlier versions of the text appeared in* Disques *III/9 (Nov. 1932) pp. 374-377 and* Modern Music *X/ 1 (Nov.–Dec. 1932) pp. 24-33. This version first appeared in* American Composers on American Music *(1933) pp. 128-145.*

its charming and naïve entirety, and encouraged him to think for himself. This led into a scientific-musical understanding, and to the ability to sort and utilize his many impressions and to build from them a new musical structure. Such a structure is what Ives has created.

As a child, Ives heard the village band. Not all the members played exactly together; there was always a player or so a fraction either ahead or behind the rest. The pitch of the notes was not always the same with all the instruments; some played a bit sharp, some a bit flat. Sometimes the bass tuba would be an indistinguishable pitch, almost a percussion noise. Perhaps the trumpet, or rather the cornet, would feel jolly enough to play his addition to the whole quite independently, so that his part would be altogether different from the rest of the orchestra; yet he would eventually find a way to get in with "the bunch."

Or perhaps Ives heard the fiddling to a dance. The fiddler not only did not play in tune with the conventional notion—he did not want to, and it would have been wrong if he had. His idea of music was quite different, and through slips and slides, and slightly off-pitch tones, which could go loosely under the title of "quarter-tones," he created the right and proper music for the village dance. Kreisler and Heifetz are masters of their art, yet neither one of them could play the fiddle in an old American dance. They would not know where to accent, where to "dip" and "pull" the tone, where to be deliberately and joyfully "off-tune"! The old village fiddler is as much master of his craft as they, although neither can excel in the system of the other.

Ives was also influenced by the village church music. With a wheezy and often out-of-tune-to-the-point-of-discord harmonium playing simple hymn concords as a base, the congregation sang soulfully and nebulously around the supposed tones of the tune. The so-called unmusical of the congregation sang along behind the tune in both rhythm and pitch, either a bit flat or those with great self-assurance over-aiming at the note and sharping on the high pitches! And in the hands of some of the organists, the harmonium would sometimes play the tonic chord through a passage where the dominant tones were sung in the hymn, or vice versa. Yet the singing was intense in feeling, as well as spontaneous.

Such native characteristics exist all through American village and country music. They are typically American, and are the distinctions between American folk-music and the folk-music of the Europeans from which we spring. Yet the "cultivated" musicians who collected and published these songs of our people unconsciously and without question weeded out all such irregularities and the result was that there is not the slightest suspicion of an original, indigenous, or truly American feeling left in the published versions of these songs. The sad part is, also, that the village children in the schools have learned the songs from the notes, and sing them in the narrow, stiff way they are written down, losing all the native beauty and charm of the unwritten variations, the fine spirit of minstrelsy in the songs and dances. The children naturally take for granted that their elders sing badly and that the notes taught in school are correct; whereas the truth is that the notes are a miserable and vain attempt to preserve the living art of the older folk. Thus the spontaneous way of folk-singing is being rapidly lost.

All of the elements of backcountry New England music were assimilated by Ives, on whom they made a deep impression. Having too good a musical ear and general perception to do as the others have done and remove in the cultivated version of this music all the characteristic and charming irregularities, Ives began early to build himself a music in which he could include all these mooted elements. Working with musical feeling deeply rooted in the spirit of the music rather than from a purely intellectual point of view, he found that it was necessary to build his whole musical structure from the ground up. It was impossible for him to confine himself to the known scale, harmony, and rhythm systems brought from Europe.

He therefore found it essential to form a new and broader musical architecture, a scheme of things which, founded on American folk-music, permitted the use of all the elements to be found in it. He did not discard any elements of known musical culture (except irrelevant pedantry); all of them are present in his work; but he also included the extra-European elements of the folk-music as actually performed, and made a new solid foundation on this music, which permits infinite development and cultivation. With breadth of concept, and beginning from the rock-bottom of American soil, he proceeded to write one work after another, each one going farther than the last; and through feeling rather than a mechanically thought-out plan he created an individual musical style. This style contains an astonishing number of elements to be found in no other music. In the end, the music goes far from its folk-foundation into symphonic works of length and complexity. As Burbank created a world of unsuspected optical beauties in flowers by the selection and cultivation of undeveloped tendencies in plants, so Ives took apparently slight elements of American folk-music, and by diligence and sympathetic cultivation found new musical beauty.

The style of his finest music is a style of richness and outpouring, of warmth and largesse. It is humanitarianism applied to sound. No element of music, no matter how unpopular, is left uninvited—all possible elements are included, and not only included but made warmly welcome in the musical fabric. It is a music not of exclusion but of inclusion, and is the most universal in its use of different materials and shades of feel ing of any music which I have ever heard. Ives is a wizard at taking seemingly irreconcilable elements and weaving them together into a unity of purpose and flow, joining them by a feeling of cohesion, as well as through the logic of his system, which, as I have indicated before, is wide enough to bring together elements of many different sorts. In the hands of many, such free combinations would result in a hodgepodge; with Ives they result in grand music. There is great similarity, artistically, between Ives and Walt Whitman.

To try to give in words an impression of the feeling of any music is futile—one must hear the music itself. Let it suffice to say that Ives's music contains endless shades of profundity and ecstasy, humor and sadness, commonness and exquisiteness. That which can with more interest be spoken of lies in the analysis of the means used and a survey of what actually takes place in the music.

As a beginning toward an analytical understanding of Ives's works, one must take into consideration his point of view. He believes in music as a vehicle of expression, not so much a personal expression of himself, the composer (although this is included also), but a general human expression. He regards a musical composition almost as though it were a living organism, of which the composer gives the germ, the performer adding to its growth by widening the initial concept. For this reason, although there are always certain delicately balanced sounds about which he is very particular, he gives the performer unusual freedom in playing his works. He does not believe in laying down an absolutely rigid pattern for performers to follow, but believes that if the performer is great and adds his creative fire to the composer's in the rendition of the work, new and unexpected beauties will be born and the concept of the work will grow and flourish. This view has made it difficult for Ives to find the best way of writing down his music. There are always passages which he feels may be played in any of several different ways, depending upon who the performer is and how he feels at the moment, without injury to the composition, since the composition is a germ idea which may develop in any of a number of different directions. Therefore, if he writes down one certain way, he fears that the form of the piece will become crystallized, and that players will fail to see the other possibilities. This idea has led him to pay particular attention to the manner of writing down works, and has resulted in a number of characteristic features of his scores. For instance, he gives directions in a certain place for the performer to play very loud if his feelings have been worked up sufficiently; if not, he is to continue playing more softly. Very frequently, also, he gives a choice of measures. When the player comes to a certain place, he chooses between two or three different measures, according to how he feels. The same idea is also carried out in individual notes: there will be very full chords written, with a footnote stating that, if the player wishes, he may leave out certain notes or, if he wishes, he may add still more! In many places it is indicated that certain measures may be left out at will. In other places, measures are given which may be added at will. In still other places, certain parts may be repeated at will. Many other similar and characteristic directions may be found.

The same fear of hampering the freedom or cramping the feelings of the performer has resulted in his creating very independent parts for each of the men in his orchestral works. Each player, with a very strong feeling for the general whole, has his own quite individual part. The result is a full polyphony, as each one is apt to have his own melody, and all may be sounded together; yet the whole synchronizes into a rich unity of sound. Individual players are often rhythmically independent also, and are asked to play a different rhythm of their own across entirely different rhythms of the rest of the orchestra, but coming out together with the rest at some specified point! In several instances he writes for two orchestras at once, each playing something different—different in harmony, melody, and rhythm. Sometimes they come out together; but I remember one case in which one of the orchestras ends somewhere in the middle, and the other goes on, the winner of the contest. The second orchestra is requested to play, not in a certain specified cross-rhythm against the main orchestra, but in an independent rhythm having nothing to do with the other; and it is indicated that they may find themselves ending anywhere within several pages in relation to the main body of the music, which is taken by the "first" orchestra. This idea came from hearing two bands passing each other on the march, each playing a different piece. Ives was marching with one of the bands; consequently the other seemed to rise in strength as it came near, and die away as it drew further away.

A good example of the Ivesian individual-part writing is in the latter part of "Washington's Birthday," in which the orchestra changes from an Allegro to a slow movement. The viola, however, is still full of the feeling of the Allegro, so continues to play an altered version of it against the rest of the orchestra's Adagio! In the same work, in the Allegro, the flute-player feels that the tempo should be faster; so he plays it faster than the rest of the men, and his measures come out a sixteenth-note shorter than those of the rest of the orchestra on this account. One can find such examples throughout Ives's music.

Ives notates many things which are unusual and not to be found in any other music, together with some things which are very common in performance, but which it is unconventional to write down. An instance of this is shown in his *Concord* Sonata, in which he writes six whole notes and a quarter-rest in 7/4 meter. This indicates the actual length of each tone, which is to be held over with the pedal, one note overlapping another. This is very frequent in practice, but I know of no other instance of its being notated. Ives recognizes, as I have said before, that the notated form of music is only a skeleton about which the performer wraps the flesh and blood of the living being of the composition. Ives does not, however, believe in presenting in the written form only the cut-and-dried conventional outline. He believes, probably quite rightly, that this form of notation does not in the least stimulate the imagination of the performer into finding the subtle deviations which give real life and character to the music. Ives tries to induce the performer to share in the creation of the work he is playing by showing, in the written-down form, one way of really performing the piece, carefully worked out, and written down as nearly as possible in the way it actually sounds. This has led him into placing on paper rhythms which are sometimes actually performed but which have never been seen on paper before. From this as a beginning, he also developed rhythms which have never been used before but which he found ways of writing down.

Similarly, in melody, if he wished to suggest the feeling of a country fiddler who plays music with scales tuned unconventionally, he did not write down the tones of our scale which are close and let it go at that, but attempted to write down the exact shades of pitch. This increased his interest in quarter-tones and other intervals of less than a half-step which are to be found in many of his works. In the same way he wrote down the actual lengths of tones held by the pedal. Writing down a scale with the pedal held, he found that all the tones of the scale had to be written as a chord. Such a chord had never been seen on paper before, and was a great sensation; yet similar chords are actually sounded by every pedaler of Chopin. Seeing these chords on paper led to their use later as a new and independent sort of harmony. Ives has also taken special interest in refinements of tone-quality, in which he desires certain overtones to come out, and in delicacies of dynamics, which he puts down with care.

Thus his original notations cover all known fields of musical materials and are in themselves an indication of his covering of all fields, of his musically overflowing in every conceivable direction, of the wealth and fertility of his invention.

An analysis of some actual examples will give a clue to the style which he has developed, the materials he uses, and the way he has of fusing into a musical and emotional unity the riff-raff of cheap, discarded musical materials, the complete gamut of materials in good general standing, and the innumerable materials which he has personally added to the world's palette of possibilities.

All the developments which will be shown in the examples here are original with Ives, not influenced by other composers. Ives attended practically no concerts whatsoever at the time that he was developing his materials and style, and certainly none in which "modern" usages were shown; also it must be truthfully said that Ives in some of his works came before his more famous European contemporaries, Schoenberg and Stravinsky, in the use of materials which they are credited with having been the first to use. Not that they were influenced by him, of course. They had no more heard of him than he of them. Apparently it was the right time for such things to develop, and they sprang from several sources almost simultaneously. In any case, Schoenberg began writing in the dissonant style that made him famous in 1909, and the first completed works were made public in 1910. It was at the same time that Stravinsky threw off the shackles and branched out independently.

Ives began using experimental materials in his music about 1895. At first they were more or less impressionistically employed— the sound of drums by sounding a number of bass notes together on the piano, or the impression of two bands playing at once through playing chords in differ ent keys together, and by using at least two rhythms at once. But gradually the sounds thus conceived became more and more interesting to Ives as a musical medium in themselves, and he used them to wider advantage. Tone-clusters, polyharmonies, polyrhythms, strong dissonance, atonal passages, rapid metric change, jazz-rhythms, and many other materials supposedly dating from a later period were freely used by Ives between 1895 and 1907, and then were further developed until about 1916 or 1917. Before the twentieth century these materials were utilized by him tentatively and occasionally; from about 1901 onward they became a fundamental part of his style. All his larger works were written before he had ever seen or heard any music by either Stravinsky or Schoenberg.

Sometimes his findings are surprisingly similar to those invented later by others; sometimes they are in directions not yet explored by others but which will unquestionably be further utilized in the future, as they are inevitable in the line of historical musical development.

The bar below shows the sort of ejaculatory rhythm for which Stravinsky later became famous, a rhythm of off-beats sharply accented, with the same dissonant harmony always continued. These things are shown perfectly in the excerpt from "Putnam's Camp" written long before.

Ex. 1– Charles Ives, "Putnam's Camp" from *Three Places in New England.*
© 1935 Merion Music, Inc. Used by permission.

The next example shows a sort of syncopation and accent which is associated with jazz, a type of rhythm which has only very recently been adopted in "serious" music, and which has been considered to be original in jazz. It is a recent mode in the orchestral works of Gershwin, Copland, and Gruenberg. Roy Harris in his article speaks of such rhythms as characteristically American;[1] that he is right is all the more proved by Ives' use of them in his symphonic work, Second Orchestral Set, near the beginning of the century. The jazz part of this set was written about 1902 or 1903.

Ex. 2– Charles Ives, Orchestral Set No. 2. © Copyright 1971 by Peer International Corp. International Copyright Secured. All Rights Reserved.

Specially characteristic of Ives is the remarkable rhythm scheme in these bars from "The Housatonic at Stockbridge." Such a rhythmical fabric as is shown here is not an unusual case, but the sort of thing that is to be found throughout Ives' music. It is an interwoven texture of rhythm. Rhythms are used against each other at the

Ex. 3- Charles Ives, "The Housatonic at Stockbridge" from *Three Places
in New England.* © 1935 Merion Music, Inc. Used by permission.

same time, forming harmony of rhythms in the same way that
tones are used together to make the more familiar harmony of
sound. Just why the idea of a harmony of rhythm has remained
practically undeveloped with us, or why there has been so much
prejudice against the idea of different simultaneous rhythms, is very
hard to say. They sound magnificent, and are in current use among
all peoples of the world, with the sole exception of the conventional music of Europe. In Ives' works such different rhythmical
harmonies are very varied, and it can be said with certainty that
nowhere in the world have such rhythms ever been written down
before. Ives goes farther in rhythmical development than any other
composer either of today or of yesterday. In the measures on the
opposite page one finds as a rhythm-harmony different parts moving simultaneously in 20, 17, 8, and 5 notes to the measure, with
other parts in figures taken from rhythms of 12, 10, 6, and 4 to the
measure. It is specially notable that Ives' use of cross-rhythms is
through long experience so free that one seldom finds a simple
underlying rhythm mechanically thumped out on every beat. The

rhythms are all or in part varied by means of figures or patterns within the realm of each rhythm-system, and by means of accents and phrasing. With anyone else, a rhythm of 17 against 20, for instance (if one could find anyone else audacious enough to go that far!), would mean 20 against 17 equal and unvaried notes. In the example shown, the 17-rhythm is varied by the second and third note being tied together; the 20-rhythm also has the second and third notes tied, and is divided into groups accented in tens. The accent does not fall on the first beat of the 20 but on the third

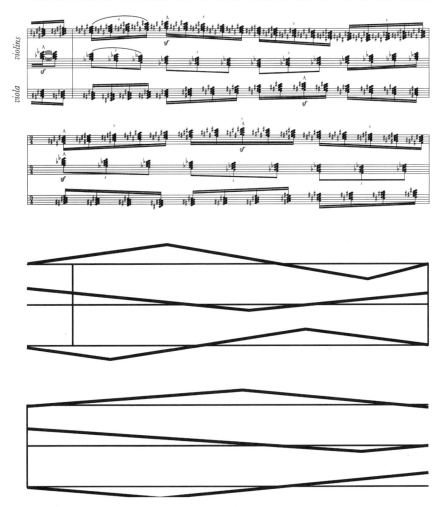

Ex. 4 – Charles Ives, "The Fourth of July." Copyright © (Renewed) by G. Schirmer, Inc. (ASCAP). International Copyright Secured. All Rights Reserved. Reprinted by permission.

note before the measure. The group of ten notes goes through the bar-line, so that the eighth note after the bar is again the accented note; then another ten; then three notes before the end of the measure falls the last accent; and so forth. Such schemes give enormous rhythmical interest and diversity. It will be seen also that the rhythm of eight is divided into fours, and that the first note of the four-group is one eighth-note before the bar-line, so that the fourth and eighth eighth-notes are accented, instead of the first and fourth, as would otherwise be the case. This way of straddling the groups across the bar line is now to be seen in much music; before Ives used it there is hardly an example to be found. I have heard of one or two isolated instances, but no one has ever been able to tell me just where! It will also be seen how the rhythm of five is phrased in two's, again across the bar-line.

Such a rhythm-polyphony makes a polyphonic style absolutely essential in the sound also. It would be hard to find greater polyphonic freedom than in the combination of melodies in Ives's works; yet there is also a harmonic feeling which binds all his melodic parts together and makes them sound almost homophonic. It is evidently necessary in a style so diversified both rhythmically and melodically that there should be a strong harmonic unity. Otherwise the whole structure would fall apart, and chaos would be the result. Ives's style has a powerful harmonic surge, and sounds far less complex than it looks on paper.

The graph (p.61) shows melodic lines in counterpoint against each other for the first violin, second violin, and viola.[2]

Ives has developed "polyharmony" very strongly; one finds chords of contrasting tone-systems placed against each other even in his very early works of the late 1890's. In many cases polychords are used one after the other.

Ives was the first to make any extensive use of tone-clusters, or harmonies built on major and minor seconds instead of thirds as in the conventional system. Example 4 shows an instance of how he has employed such clusters of tones in running chord progressions along scale lines, in such a manner that there is always a different set of actual intervals (that is, a different relationship between the major and minor seconds within the cluster) in each successive cluster. There are three sets of clusters, each in a different key system, so that one also has an example of polytonality. There are seven tones used in each cluster, making twenty-one different independent parts! Yet they are made quite clear by the simplicity of the outlines. Each of the three cluster-lines has an independent rhythm and melodic curve. The counterpoint of these curves against each other is shown in the graph following the example. Such clusters are used for many measures in "The Fourth of July," as an accompaniment figure, and are considered as lines of sound. Sound itself, as being a musical element no less important than melody, harmony, and rhythm, is an important view of Ives. Musicians often stupidly assume that the same written note must always mean the same thing, forgetting that in our way of writing music the same note is often used to indicate many different sorts of sound.

Melodically, Ives also has something unusual to say. With true courage, he is not afraid to utilize melodies so simple that other modernists shun them; or, on the other hand, to use occasionally some very complex melodic structure. Such a melodic structure is seen in the development of the theme E flat, D flat, C, B flat, B, C in the Second Pianoforte Sonata. The variations are made by widening the distance between the notes into different octaves. In the final form, a span of five octaves is reached! A truly pianistic idea, as the piano is the only instrument on which tones so separated hang together melodically. One can follow the melody perfectly in this instance. Like atonality, this idea of using wide melodic skips, usually credited to Schoenberg, was used first by Ives.

Countless other examples could be given of things which have been developed by Ives, as his fecundity seems never to be exhausted; but perhaps those already given will serve to show the many different directions in which Ives has experimented farther than any other composer, and in directions which he has found either before other composers or at the same time quite independently. I hope I have shown also that an interest in materials as such is not his main interest. His finding so many new musical resources is the result of his powerful musicality, which demands freedom of expression. He is not content, like many superficial radicals, with merely tearing down known standards. If Ives finds it necessary to reject an older standard, he never rests until he has created a new structure to take its place. Such creations he has made and still makes in every field of music, and the result is a wonderfully universal, rounded-out whole, not technical, but deliciously and fascinatingly human and charming, and with an emotional but not a sentimental basis.

Recently, Ives has had very favorable reviews from some of the world's most famous critics, and is beginning to come into the recognition he so richly deserves. Yet as a whole, particularly formerly, he has been subjected to absurd misunderstanding and stupid criticism. If he wrote four whole notes in 4/4 meter because he wanted each tone held a whole note with the pedal on the piano, musicians would ask whether he knew the difference between a whole note and a quarter-note. He was snickered at because he suggested that a row of tone-clusters should be played on the piano with a board of certain length and properly cushioned, for the reason that there are too many notes in the cluster to play with the fingers. Perhaps because they were not practiced enough to play them, musicians laughed also at his rhythms without making the slightest attempt to examine them earnestly and to find out what was really meant by them. More recent criticisms have also sometimes been equally superficial. It is complained that his texture is too thick. That is, of course, because the style, now, is to have thin music. There is no reason why music should not also develop in richness. Those who believe in rigidly fixing every note, in making an absolutely exact and crystallized form for music, complain of his minstrel-like qualities and of the freedom he permits his interpreters; yet there is no reason to suppose that music will not develop in freedom as well as in precision. Again, it is complained that in his orchestration certain parts will not "come out." These parts are not meant to come out, but to alter slightly and delicately the color of the tone, an acoustical flavoring!

All these criticisms are due to the fact that some of the aspects of music which Ives has developed are momentarily out of style. Many of these aspects, however, are now growing into general recognition, and one can predict that his work will come more and more into public favor. Public favor comes slowly to those great enough to be independent. Ives is independent, and is truly great; both in invention and in spirit he is one of the leading men America has produced in any field.

II

IVES WROTE OF EMERSON, "As thoughts surge to his mind, he fills the heavens with them, crowds them in, if necessary, but seldom arranges them along the ground first." This statement might apply with equal force to the composer of the *Concord* Sonata. It is a work bursting with overlapping celestial magnificences, tonal and philosophical. Its four movements take more than [three quarters of an hour] to play; they are filled with deeply felt, highly original music, alive with new ideas of form, melody, harmony, counterpoint, rhythm and tone-quality. Yet, characteristically, the work is based on a theme deliberately taken from another composer. Ives says, "There is an 'oracle' at the beginning of the Fifth Symphony—in these four notes lies one of Beethoven's greatest messages." Ives uses this most famous of musical motives without ever quoting it exactly, building about it a thousand musical and philosophical connotations unsuspected by Beethoven.

When Ives distributed copies of the first edition of this sonata (privately printed in 1920) to anyone he thought might be interested, the general reaction among conservative professional musicians was expressed by ribald comment. Only a few intrepid souls, such as the late Henry Bellaman and the famous pianist, E. Robert Schmitz, reacted favorably and Schmitz played at least part of it in Paris in the early 20's. Ives had privately printed, also in 1920, a little book written to accompany this work, entitled *Essays Before a Sonata*. It carried this inscription: "These prefatory essays were written by the composer for those who can't stand his music—and the music for those who can't stand his essays; to those who can't stand either, the whole is respectfully dedicated."

Charles Ives (by now he was seldom using the middle initial on programs) was still more discussed than played. Therefore it was essential that when his music was published, the scores should be reviewed. It would have been bad form for Cowell to review publications for which he was responsible to any extent, but the Second Pianoforte Sonata No. 2 "Concord Mass., 1840-1860" was reissued with corrections in 1947 (New York: Arrow Press, 1947 [68 p., $4.00]) and Cowell could discuss it and explain why it was an important work. The review appeared in Notes *V/3 (Jun. 1948) pp. 412-413 (Music Library Association).*

Charles Ives has always lived so entirely outside of the professional musical world that each admirer of his music in turn believes himself to be its discoverer. I am generally credited with the first wide dissemination of Ives' music, through publication and concerts here and in Europe, but actually I was anticipated by both Bellaman and Schmitz. Almost the last thing Lawrence Gilman did before his death was to "discover" Ives when John Kirkpatrick gave the first complete performance of the *Concord* Sonata in New York in 1939. Gilman's review declares unequivocally that the *Concord* Sonata is the greatest American work for the piano.

Arrow Press performs a valuable service in printing this new edition, as copies of the first edition, never on public sale at any time, have not been available for many years. It is unfortunate that Ives' note, *Prose,* originally set in parenthesis at the top of page 1, and *Verse,* at the top of pages 5 and 8, should have been eliminated in this edition. *Prose* at the top of page 12 is retained. If one thinks of the first section of the Emerson movement as being in the form of prose narrative, it makes it easier to follow a structure which does not (as most musical forms do) rely on repetition for its balance and design. Both editions contain copious quotations from Ives' book, so that one can obtain a very good idea of Ives' philosophy as well as his music.

III

A GROUP OF FIVE miscellaneous short orchestra works by Charles Ives has been used by Balanchine as music for the new ballet *Ivesiana* at the City Center. Quite aside from the value of the dance as such, some of the pieces are heard in live performance for the first time in New York, and none of them has before been in any repertory, so that one could hear several performances. The ballet uses "Central Park in the Dark," "Over the Pavements,"

Next, from The Musical Quarterly *XLI/1 (Jan. 1955) pp. 85-89, we have Cowell offering a critique of the Ives works used by choreographer George Balanchine in his modern ballet* Ivesiana.

"In the Inn," "Hallowe'en," "The Unanswered Question," and
"In the Night." These were not originally composed as a set to go
together, and we understand that some will be changed about for
next season; but the order works very well, and it is strictly according to Ives's usual practice that the final movement should be a
slow one. Leon Barzun conducted an excellent and relaxed performance, meeting with equanimity the difficult rhythmical problems of the pieces that conductors used to say couldn't be performed. The ballet is original and somewhat daring, even if not
always very closely related to the music or to Ives's philosophies.

    "Central Park in the Dark" (Ives added the words "Some Forty
Years Ago" to the title when it was published recently) was suggested by a walk along a pathway that Ives knew very well, since
he lived near the Park. He could hear sounds of others walking
without being able to see them; it is not the mystery of loneliness
in the dark, but of, the dark seething with unseen activity. The
path runs close to a merry-go-round, and in the middle section
there are superimposed fragments of an old ragtime song in jerky
syncopation above the calm-flowing basic dissonances. The latter
win out in the end, however, and the quiet melodic first theme
returns.

    "Hallowe'en" is an amusing scherzo, based on the flying about
of small children, each busily engaged in his own trick-or-treat
activity. There are tricks or treats in the simultaneous keys of C, B,
D-flat, and D, all scampering about in the strings, mostly dashing
up and down scalewise, against a piano which encourages with
syncopated polychords. "Hallowe'en" is meant to be played through
several times, and Ives has directions: "If played four times" and
"If played three times" (in the latter case–"First time: Allegretto–
pp. second violin and 'cello, until two measures before the D.C.
which all play. No piano. Second time: Allegro–*mf.* All strings, piano may play; if so–*pp.* Only upper and lower notes in each hand;
or piano may not play at all this time. Third time: Presto–*ff.* All
play all notes and coda"). Ives then adds: "P.S. A bass drum or a
drum during the last time may play the total rests in measures 3, 4,
5, and 8, and from there on may add his own part—impromptu,
or otherwise." Nothing could be more typical of Ives's attitude to
the performance of his works. For the close, Ives makes believe

Ex. 1. Charles Ives, "Hallowe'en." © Copyright 1949 by Bomart Music Publications: copyright assigned 1977 to Mobart Music Publications, Inc. Reprinted by permission.

that he is going to end in C major and then fools one by dashing up in chromatic triads to E flat instead.

Ex. 2. Charles Ives. "Hallowe'en." © Copyright 1949 by Bomart Music Publications: copyright assigned 1977 to Mobart Music Publications, Inc. Reprinted by permission.

"Over the Pavements" was first suggested by the nervous, restless pacing of city pavement-walkers, who seem always to be in a hurry, but never get anywhere. Later Ives incorporated some of the ideas into *In the Cage,* to suggest the thought of an animal pacing back and forth. The music continues an energetic *ostinato* in 3/8 and 5/8, with the tonality bouncing back and forth from C to F sharp.

"In the Inn" describes the feelings of one standing outside in the dark and listening to ragtime being played in the inn. Although this was written well before the advent of the Charleston or of the popularity of the rumba, the characteristic rhythms of both may be found here, as well as a great many more syncopations, both basic and complex. Even today, if there is any other piece with as many varieties of syncopation, it is unknown to us. The secundal chords in the introduction have tremendous rhythmical bite (Ex. 3a) while the main theme preserves a lyricism of spirit that seems in extraordinary contradistinction to the 32nd-note syncopations against a background of 3/8 superimposed on changing meters of 3/4 and 2/4 (Ex. 3b). Example 3b shows several such miscellaneous syncopations, of which there are many, many more of the same nature sprinkled throughout the work. In the City Center the orchestra version was used, but "In the Inn" is also incorporated into the First Pianoforte Sonata as a scherzo-like section.

Ex. 3a and 3b. Charles Ives. "In the Inn," measures 1-3 and 22-34 from
First Piano Sonata. Copyright © 1954 by Peer International Corporation. International
Copyright Secured. Printed in USA. All rights reserved. Used by permission.

"The Unanswered Question," which has been performed once before in New York and may be heard on records, seems on its way to becoming a repertory piece. The idea is original, the result moving, the form simple and understandable. A string section plays long-sustained open-spaced triads; when they have got well started, a trumpet (or English horn or oboe or clarinet) sounds the Question against the strings in biting dissonance. This stirs up what Ives calls "the flutes and other human beings" to find the "invisible

answer." This they do with a scurry and a flurry, again in dissonance to the strings, which continue, without paying any attention
to the goings on of the wind instruments, in their quiet and aloof
concordance. At the end, in spite of the wildest efforts of the flutes
to find the Answer, the Question is still asked again by the trumpet, and the strings remain to give a sustained triad of G major at
the close.

Ex. 4. Charles Ives. *The Unanswered Question.* Copyright 1953 by Southern Music
Publishing Company Inc. Copyright © 1984 by Peer International Corporation.
International Copyright Secured. Printed in USA. All rights reserved. Used by permission.

"In the Night" is a short nocturne composed of a dark inter-
weaving of low, slow-moving voices, each with its own rhythm and
melody. Against this impressionistic fabric a snatch of familiar hymn
tune sometimes emerges, as though sung in free rhythm, or as
though heard in one's mind rather vaguely. It dies away without
coming to any very definite conclusion, a sort of ending very beloved of the composer.

Since the death of Ives in May 1954, there have been, as might be anticipated, a number of performances of his works, and a new surge of interest in them. Yet in spite of everything he continues to be a controversial figure. In America he is more and more becoming a real influence among younger composers, perhaps more in his philosophy than in his musical practice; yet for this to operate there must be a prerequisite of appreciation of transcendentalism and a certain acceptance of informality. The American followers of the more modern schools of Paris and Vienna are apt to be very critical of his position in American music, even though musicians in both these centers have responded with great interest to his compositions. All in all, however, there can be no indifference in any camp to the uniqueness and fervor of Ives's works, in comparison with most other American composers' products during his most fertile period—about 1893 to 1914.

1. Roy Harris (1898-1979) contributed an article, "Problems of American Composers" to *American Composers on American Music* (1933) pp. 149-166. Cowell also included an article, "Roy Harris" (pp. 64-69) not included in this book.—DH
2. This example is printed without any identification whatever in the 1933 book. For its identification we are indebted to H. Wiley Hitchcock.—DH

Charles Seeger

CHARLES SEEGER IS THE greatest musical explorer in intellectual fields which America has produced, the greatest experimental musicologist. Ever fascinated by intricacies, he has solved more problems of modern musical theory, and suggested more fruitful pathways for musical composition (some of which have proved of great general import), than any other three men. He has rarely been given public credit for the ideas which he has initiated, since with a perverse humor which is very characteristic of him he always presents his important new ideas in such a way, at such a time, or to such people that they are never accepted at first; later when the ideas have proved to be singularly adaptable, their users often forget the source.

While Seeger has worked out some of his findings himself, his greatest importance lies in his subtle influence in suggesting to others both a new musical point of view and specific usages in composition. Few modern composers, either in America or abroad, are entirely uninfluenced by him; yet most of those who use his ideas do not know his name and believe themselves to have originated the ideas, so delicately does he work! He has a new idea—he imparts the idea to a few important acquaintances, usually in such a way as to cause instant repulsion on their part and to irritate them

Little information is available concerning the early activities of Charles Seeger (1886-1979), Cowell's most important teacher and the husband of the composer Ruth Crawford, a Cowell protegé. Most studies focus on his contributions as a musicologist. Cowell's text, too, glosses over at least two aspects of Seeger's work: his experimentalism in the period around World War One which led to Parthenia, *a sort of proto-Happening, and his long identification with progressive political causes. This last led to the loss of his teaching position at the University of California, Berkeley, in 1919. This text on Seeger appears in* American Composers on American Music *(1933) pp. 119-124.*

greatly; but Seeger does not mind irritating: he knows that if he irritates his subject enough, the idea will be remembered, and passed on. And this is what actually happens. He springs an idea which is so unpopular and unprecedented as to cause absolute outrage, in California. One of the insulted listeners, who travels a great deal, goes to Germany, and in an aggrieved manner relates the idea, perhaps as an example of idiocy. Next season a new and unprecedented type of music will be shown to the world by a young German composer. So it has gone. He not only has no credit but often has to fight against personal irritations which he has sometimes aroused through his methods of presentation, in people who do not understand his witty but cynical way of getting results.

He is personally a bundle of contradictions; but where a majority of people are self-contradictory without suspecting themselves of it, he knows it of himself and is satisfied! All his vagaries are quite self-conscious. He is outstandingly (and to many people obnoxiously) intellectual, but with a leaning toward sentimental outpouring. Here again he sees the tendency in himself plainly, but instead of frowning on it as a thing to be hidden, he takes prankish delight in it. He is rigidly conservative in many ways, never accepting thoroughly anything until it has been entirely proved, believing in precedent, training, even bookishness. Yet no one else has taken as great an interest in the new, the unexplored, the modern. He is aristocrat and radical, but nothing between.

As a composer Seeger has produced little, but all he has produced is of importance in the history of indigenous development in America. From the standpoint of precedent, one must concede to him the position of being the second in time to create works which are genuinely dissonant from beginning to end, and which in other respects are thoroughly experimental. The first is Ives, who started quite independently on such explorations about 1897. I have no knowledge of anyone else before Seeger, who, about 1912, broke away from the imitative style of his early songs and began a series of nervy experiments which resulted in his *Parthenia* music for two public productions at the Greek Theater in Berkeley. A veritable wealth of examples of fantastic dissonances, curious rhythms, new melodic structure, and form, are to be found in these works, to say nothing of the orchestration! A germination bed for musical ideas. They are, however, not focused; they are scattered, and do not stand up as musical compositions. After their creation, Seeger became so self-critical that it was for many years virtually impossible for him to complete a work. He has discarded music which almost any composer in the world would have been proud of, because of some infinitesimal fault which no one but he himself would have knowledge enough to mark. Thus the intellectualism which is one of his predominating features became so rigid as to quench the creative spark; that is, almost. Not quite.

During this period he composed a few works, which he will never show, and pretends he does not have. These works are short, and are all but absolute perfection. Nothing in music surpasses, for instance, his Solo for Clarinet in exquisite delicacy, in beauty of tracery, in unity of idea, in unbelievably developed melodic line. It is far more than an intellectual experiment. It is great music! It is an etched cameo, and in it he completely eradicated the fault of his earlier music, which was to try out too many things at once!

To return to Seeger's ideas. It may be asked, What are some of them with which he has influenced composers?

When the whole world thought Stravinsky and Schoenberg both insane, Seeger found them the most important new composers of their time. They were. He at that time, when the average musician could see no difference between the two, predicted that Stravinsky would become popular with the general concert public and that Schoenberg would be beloved by musical intellectuals. This has come to pass. Before Schoenberg eschewed thickness of sound and wrote the economically outlined *Pierrot Lunaire*, Seeger worked for the downfall of over-voluptuousness and a return to thin lines of music. This at a time when, under the influence of Strauss, music was thought to be good inasmuch as it was full and thick, and to call music thin was to damn it utterly. Now the return to thin line has penetrated every circle of composers.

At a time when Debussian impressionism was the rage, Seeger advocated sharp definiteness of line. Now this definiteness is attempted by nearly everyone, and impressionism has all but disappeared. Before the idea of piling one chord on top of another as being the only line of musical development had lost its sway, Seeger suggested a return to counterpoint. The return has been made.

Before Hindemith produced his works in dissonant counterpoint poured into a Bach mold, Seeger suggested this very idea, and created a system for such a counterpoint, worked out to the last detail of what the intervals should be and how they might move. Hindemith and Schoenberg both came out later with works embodying the principles of Seeger's suggestions. Long before Stravinsky supposedly led his group of followers into "neoclassicism," Seeger predicted the whole development of this return, or attempted return.

At a time when it was generally considered unaesthetic to use unresolved dissonances, Seeger predicted that in a very short time all possible dissonances would be freely used throughout all new music. They are. Away back, Seeger insisted on being enthusiastic about very ancient music; no one could see what possible musical value it had. Seeger also pointed out that it has similarity with modern music, in point of view; at that time no one could see the resemblance—people as a whole saw modernism as a "bunch of discords" only. Today, nearly all modernists have developed an interest in very old music, and the relationship between the very old and the very new is recognized.

Seeger pointed out the possibility of analyzing certain modern complexes as polychords, long before the word was generally known. He has often taken special interest in the works of certain composers who at the time were relatively unheard of, and insisted on his students studying them. A few years later, there has invariably been a wave of public interest in the direction of these composers. Monteverdi, Bruckner, and Stravinsky are examples.

One could go on indefinitely and not exhaust the number of subjects in which he has been a pioneer. Probably his most important standpoint, however, is his open advocacy of the intellectual point of view in approaching music. This he started at a time when such a thing was utterly inconceivable —when it was considered that music had value only if it had nothing to do with the intellect, that the most damning thing that could be said against music was that it was intellectual, and that *thinking* about music not only has no value but destroys the musical impulse. Seeger almost proved this old-fashioned notion to be right by allowing over-intellectualism to stultify him. But he has brilliantly recovered, and has renewed activity in a great new outburst of fertility. And, as in the other cases, the public is gradually following him in this, his most important stand. There has been a reaction against "sentimentality," against gushing; a movement which is gaining strength is openly opposed to "expression" as the aim of music (Seeger suggested this long ago). Although the name intellectualism is still in bad repute in musical circles, actual intellectualism is in full power. The very ones who rant against intellectualism are the most eager to discuss music, to talk about it. This very attitude, of course, denotes the intellectual approach. So things are going his way; but paradoxically (he is always paradoxical) he also strongly advocates not talking so much about music, but letting it talk for itself. The intellectual elements which he most admires are those contained within the materials of the music itself, not so much questions concerning the philosophy of music.

Seeger has always advocated an interest in "musicology," or the study of all things pertaining to music scientifically. His latest activity is the editing of the new edition called *American Library of Musicology.*

How long will it be before the lethargic musical public learns the ecstasies of investigating this alluring field?

Edgar Varèse

EDGAR VARÈSE WAS BORN in France, but has become an American citizen. For many years he lived in New York, and through his vehicle, the International Composers' Guild, he was the first to introduce modern music to America with any degree of consistency. Thus he has been an influence in the development of new musical ideas in America; and his fostering of many American composers and his presentation of their works were the only things which encouraged them in maintaining a modernism of style which prevented them from being performed elsewhere for a long time. Many of these are now recognized as of importance.

Varèse's own music has nothing in particular to do with America otherwise. It was originated in Europe under the influence of his teacher, [Ferruccio] Busoni, and was also affected by the Italian "futurist" school of percussionists. However, his best work, *Arcane,* was written in America, and his longest work is called *Amérique,* indicating very well just what the work is—a Frenchman's concept of America! His music is acrid and telling, with a magnificent hardness of line which used to irritate our naïve listeners greatly, as did also his investigations in the field of emphasis on percussion sounds.

In making his music Varèse breaks no rules of ordinary harmony; they do not come into consideration at all, as they do not pertain to that different art which is his aim. This does not mean, however, that he follows no rules. To attain his ends, he is forced into certain limitations which one might call rules of his own making, as will be seen.

Here we have a brief, largely analytical account of the music of Edgar Varèse (1883-1965), with whom HC had worked closely in the twenties. One wishes it were a fuller account. An earlier version of this apiece appeared in Modern Music V/2 *(Jan.-Feb. 1928) pp. 9-19 as "The Music of Edgar Varèse" This version first appeared in* American Composers on American Music *(1933) pp. 43-48.*

In order to make technical references, it is necessary here to expand the meaning of certain musical terms. Let us assume that the word melody refers to any succession of single tones, without reference to whether or not it is immediately pleasing, follows certain curves, or is contained within a key. The word harmony will refer to any group of tones played simultaneously. And any succession of accents, note-values, or rates of speed will be considered as rhythm.

One key to a comprehension of Varèse's music is the fact that he is more interested in finding a note that will sound a certain way in a certain instrument and will "sound" in the orchestral fabric than he is in just what position the note occupies in the harmony; except, of course, in so far as its harmonic position will pertain to its "coming out" in the scoring.

One must consider that besides the harmony of notes, which with Varèse is somewhat secondary, there is at any given time also a harmony of tone-qualities, each of which is calculated to sound out through the orchestra. For example Varèse will use a certain chord. Superimposed upon this chord, and more important than the harmony itself to Varèse, is the harmony resultant from the tone-qualities of the instruments owing to their particular sound in the register in which he scores each; so that, while the chord might be found in many a modern composer's work, it assumes a character found only in Varèse when we see it in his particular scoring.

I have frequently noticed that when Varèse examines a new score, he is more interested in the orchestration than in the musical content, although no amount of brilliant scoring will interest him in a work in old-fashioned style.

Just as harmonic combinations of sound qualities are emphasized above harmony itself by Varèse, one finds that dynamic nuances on the same note, or repeated tones, often take the place of melody. He very frequently does away with melody entirely by having only repeated tones for certain passages. Removing from the listener's ear that which it is accustomed to follow most closely, sometimes almost to the exclusion of everything else, naturally induces a keener awareness of other musical elements such as rhythm and dynamics. Varèse, however, is always careful to supply the ear with subtleties of dynamic change which take the place of melody in certain passages. Owing to his reliance on specific tone-qualities and dynamics for the very essence of his music, there are dynamic markings and directions as to quality applying to nearly every note in Varèse's scores. Sometimes a single note will have a number of signs, as for instance a certain note in the trumpet part of *Octandre* which is marked *sf, diminuendo, p, crescendo, sfff.* I have heard Varèse express great contempt for composers who do not use many expression marks. "They do not know how they wish their music to sound," he says.

Sometimes Varèse cuts out melody to call attention to the rhythm rather than dynamics. The opening of the second movement of *Octandre* is a long flute solo, of a type which would ordinarily contain a long melodic curve. Varèse uses only repeated tones, with two or three grace notes to relieve the monotony of pitch. This introduction is in the form of five rhythmical phrases, all different, and separated by longer notes.

In *Hyperprism*, page ten, we find a good example of the discontinuance of the melody (partly by repeated tones and partly, as in the flute and trumpets, by continued repetition of a figure) for the purpose of calling attention to the cross-rhythm between the parts. There is a combination of two, three, and four against each other, and in the center of the last measure a quarter-note triplet of particular interest, since it begins and ends on a weak beat, running through the strong beat; the second note, being accented, almost but not quite coincides with the third beat of the measure in an extremely unusual manner. Varèse evidently realized that these rhythmical subtleties would be lost on the listener, were his attention to be diverted by melodic interest or harmonic change.

It is perhaps this desire to focus the interest on harmonies of sound-quality alone—without the distraction of harmonies of pitch—or on chords of rhythms, that has led Varèse to develop his emphasis on the percussion instruments. He probably uses more such instruments, proportionately, than any other composer. For example in *Hyperprism* there are seventeen percussion as against nine melodic instruments. Sometimes he uses percussion passages alone, but more often the percussion is in connection with some of the other instruments. His *Ionization* is for battery alone.

In *Hyperprism*, page eight, there is a good illustration of a simple chord combination of tone-qualities. First a chord composed of the qualities of Indian drum, bass drum, tambourine, and cymbal against each other moves to a chord of snare drum, crash-cymbal, tam-tam, and slap-stick, which in turn progresses back to the first combination—a sort of four-part harmony. On page sixteen, measure two, there is an example of rhythmic harmony, as each instrument has an independent rhythm.

An analysis of the rhythms throughout *Hyperprism* reveals a great variety of rhythmic figures. On the first page alone there are thirty-two different rhythmical manners of filling a measure. Through the whole work there are surprisingly few rhythmical duplications. It has been said by those who perceive a minimum of tonal, melodic, and harmonic changes in his music that Varèse lacks invention; yet undoubtedly for the development of so many different figures of rhythm one must concede as great inventive fertility as is usually recognized in the field of pitch.

Varèse does not ignore melody and harmony, but merely does away with them on occasion. He limits himself almost exclusively to harmonies containing strong dissonances, i.e., minor seconds or ninths, and major sevenths. One may therefore say that he has developed for himself a rule that such dissonant intervals are requisite for the harmonic fabric he desires. To introduce a consonant harmony would remove the sense of implacable, resilient hardness, and create a weak link in the chain; the let-down would be so great that the whole composition might fall to pieces. Varèse's chords are obviously not haphazard, but belong to a special category in which he is careful to have certain general proportions of different sorts of intervals.

Melody, when Varèse uses it, is often characterized by wide skips, broken sometimes by chromatic passages, as, for example, in *Hyperprism*, flute part, page five. Sometimes the wide skips are broken by repeated tones, as in the voice part of "La Croix du Sud," page three, from *Offrandes*.

One rhythmical innovation used by Varèse is his metrical marking of 3/4 and a half, 1/4 and a half, 4/4 and a half, and so forth. The extra one-half represents in each case an added half-beat, or eighth-note, at the end of the measure. Some musicians claim that

1/4 and a half time is really the same as 3/8 time, since it contains the same number of eighth-notes in a measure. There is, however, a great distinction in the rhythmical feeling between these two signatures, as 3/8 is smooth-flowing, and is conducted in three movements of the baton, while 1/4 and a half is irregular, and is led by one longer followed by one shorter stroke of the conductor's stick.

There is a dramatic and incisive element about Varèse's music which causes it to stand out on a program, and to "kill" any work standing next to it by brute force. This does not mean that the music is better or worse; but it is unquestionably telling. And if stirring auditors to an almost unendurable irritation be taken into account, then the music can be said to be highly emotional. While he lacks melodic invention and harmonic succession, Varèse is in other respects unique, and deserves the highest place among European composers who have become American.

II

DESERTS, BY EDGAR VARÈSE, had its first American performance at Bennington College on May 17. This is the first new work, by one of the world's most extraordinary composers, to be heard in many a long year. Varèse is not very prolific, and aside from a shorter piece for flute alone, his fame rests on a rather small number of unique, belligerent-sounding compositions for orchestral instruments (including many percussion) written in the early 'twenties and before. Nearly all of these have, in their way, become classics. Their particularized use of rows of percussion sounds melodically, and their drive towards maximum intensity of dynamic dissonance on wind instruments in particular, form an entirely distinctive style; and while this has been influential, it has never been exactly imitated. He is the only composer connected with the fu-

---

Finally, we have a review of Varèse's Deserts, *from* The Musical Quarterly *XLI/3 (Jul. 1955) pp. 370-373. (A review of a work by Jan Meyerowitz, absent here, leads off the article.) Generally Varèse's* Deserts *received terrible reviews. The music historian, Beekman Cannon, whose Yale course in music history I was taking at the time, told his class it was the most disagreeable and unfocused piece he had ever heard. Cowell disagrees.*

turist manifesto written at Milan in 1913 who has achieved a position of importance in modern music.

Deserts was begun at New York in 1952, and finished November 1954 in Paris, where, on December 2, its European premiere took place at the Théâtre des Champs-Elysées performed by the Orchestre National under the direction of Hermann Scherchen. It was given again in Hamburg December 8, and in Stockholm December 18, conducted by Bruno Maderna.

The Paris performance was received "in a deluge of vociferations and applause, and this collision of enthusiasm against indignation resulted in pandemonium, or what the French call 'un scandale.'" One critic said, "Music always lags behind the other arts. Only today has its revolution finally burst: with Varèse." Another: "Certain belligerent listeners took the work as a direct assault on their stupidity and protested noisily." A third: "The furious rush of sound invades the desert of the human brain. We are powerless before its onslaught; it takes possession of us, staggering us with its formidable punch."

Varèse says:

> *Deserts* was conceived for two different media: instrumental sounds and real sounds (recorded and processed) that musical instruments are unable to produce. After planning the work as a whole, I wrote the instrumental score, always keeping in mind its relation to the organized sound sequences on tape to be interpolated at three different points in the score. I have always looked upon the industrial world as a rich source of beautiful sounds, an unexplored mine of music in the matrix. So I went to various factories in search of certain sounds I needed for *Deserts* and recorded them. These noises were the raw materials out of which (after being processed by electronic means) the interpolations of organized sound were composed.
>
> The score of *Deserts is* made up of two distinct elements: 1) an instrumental ensemble composed of 14 wind instruments, a variety of percussion instruments played by 5 musicians, and a piano as an element of resonance; 2) magnetic tapes of organized sound transmitted on two channels by means of a stereophonic system to provide a sensation of spatial distribution of the sound sources to the listener. There are four instrumental sections of different lengths and three stereophonically trans-

mitted interpolations of organized sound introduced between the first and second, the second and third, and the third and fourth instrumental sections. Of the music given to the instrumental ensemble, it may be said that it evolves in opposing planes and volumes, producing the sensation of movement in space. But, although the intervals between the pitches determine these ever-changing and contrasted volumes and planes, they are not based on any fixed set of intervals such as a scale, a series, or any existing principle of musical measurement. They are decided by the exigencies of this particular work. Of the interpolations it should be noted that the first and third are based on industrial sounds (sounds of friction, percussion, hissing, grinding, puffing) first filtered, transposed, transmuted, mixed, etc. by means of electronic devices and then composed to fit the pre-established plan of the work. Combined with these sounds as a structural and stabilizing element (especially in the third interpolation) are fragments of instrumental percussion, some already present in the score, others new. The second interpolation is for an ensemble of percussion. It will be noticed that the shorter the section the higher the intensity, the music rising to a climax in the third interpolation and fourth instrumental section, finally fading out in a long *pianissimo*.

Deserts is not in a totally new style; it resembles very much the earlier Varèse manner known to all followers of modern music. It is, however, more integrated and expanded. The number of elements used is greater, the form more understandable although on a larger scale (the bridge passages are especially worthy of notice, since they bridge "from the human being to the industrial machine and back again" in quite an uncanny way). The sense of climax is more pointed; there is a feeling that each section arrives at at least a partial conclusion, and this conclusion is not, as in some of the earlier works, arrived at mainly through reiterated notes.

Of the seven sections, Numbers 1, 3, 5, and 7 are actually played on wind and percussion instruments; Numbers 2, 4, and 6 are interpolated, and are on magnetic tape. The real performance leads to the tape sound, and the tape sound to the live players by gradual degrees which surprisingly bridge what might be a wide gap in tone quality, but which is handled expertly to form a real tonal splice. The tone-qualities employed on the tape are apt to be percussive, but with many new sounds on definite rather than in-definite pitches (not necessarily in equal temperament). Some of the new qualities are sustained, others explosive in nature; this differ-ence is also maintained in the live-performed portions of the work, and is one of the means of preserving a feeling of unity between these and the tape sections.

It may be of interest here to compare *Deserts* with the works of some others who work with tape in America. Luening and Ussachevsky, working together, use many human-voice sounds, changed in range and out of original context. Varèse uses none. They also use familiar instruments which are greatly changed in range—for instance, a flute that originally played high C may be lowered to a bass low C, but retaining a flute quality. If Varèse employs any such means we failed to detect it. Luening and Ussachevsky, in their Louisville Concerto, used tape sounds as the solo voice, against actually performed orchestral sounds. Varèse alternates these sounds so that they never are heard together.

Deserts builds to a tremendous climax dynamically and in in-tensity towards the end. Varèse develops his old interest in maxi-mum resonances of combined instruments in *fortissimo,* and wields a biting percussion group which has less going on at once than in his older works (such as *Ionisation),* but in which each rhythmical rapier-thrust counts so that the counter-rhythmical patterns are more vividly clear.

This is the best work, the most mature, the largest and the most integrated, by a composer who holds a unique position among the world's creators. We predict that *Deserts* will be held as a master-piece by those who follow tape and percussion music with devotion.

John J. Becker

T HE MIDDLE WEST HAS produced many composers of attainment. In many cases, however, these composers have fled from the Middle West at the earliest possible moment and no longer acknowledge it as their home. Ruth Crawford and Vivian Fine, for example, come from Chicago; now they have both become seasoned Easterners.

The liveliest composer who still retains the Middle West as his home is John J. Becker. He makes his home not in Chicago, the supposed center of Middle Western activities, but in St. Paul; and such is his energy, and so many and so diversified are his activities, that it is a question if he does not carry the center of interest in modern creative music in the Middle West with him wherever he goes. He composes experimentally, fervently. He is still in the process of building his own musical style, which is forming gradually toward a certain combination of principles of ancient polyphony, not of the Bach but of the Palestrina type, with the dissonant intervals which have come into use in modern times. He aims at independent parts, at development through polyphonic devices, at loftiness, majesty, and at sincere straightforwardness in expression. These objectives he succeeds more and more in attaining with each new work; and his selection of dissonances, always biting and unyielding, becomes more and more resourceful with each new composition.

Sometimes it seems as if Cowell thought of modern music as a monolithic organization with representatives dispersed throughout the land. If so, then his man in the Midwest was John J. Becker (1886-1961), a highly skilled conductor and composer whose work was second to none in quality and degree of innovative thinking. What impressed Cowell most seems to have been Becker's ability to digest materials from the history of music and to create a new whole. This all-too-short article first appeared in American Composers on American Music *(1933) pp. 82-84.*

85

His earlier works, while showing a modern tendency, are commonplace. Through experimenting over a period of years, he has little by little replaced the commonplaces with more interesting materials and philosophy. His music never follows conventional lines, either new or old. Perhaps for this reason his work is often very much underestimated. He does not please the conservatives, or even the part-conservatives, as his works are drastically dissonant; he pleases only the more open-minded of the radicals, because his works never follow any particular fads or styles of modern writing. He is, however, becoming recognized on account of his knowledge and technique as well as his staunchness of spirit, both in his personality and in his work.

Aside from his own creative work, Becker is a fighter. He plunges directly into the most conservative quarters and emerges with victory and plunder in the shape of having stimulated new ways of thinking, and openness to new ideas. He works for the most part in Catholic colleges, which, although always emphasizing music, are apt to be extremely conventional. He lectures not for one such college but for many; he travels every week to Duluth; he goes to Milwaukee; he is known throughout the middle Northwest. He tears down moth-eaten conventions, and suggests a different position for all cultural and artistic activities, specializing, of course, on music. He lectures on music and the arts; he conducts orchestral and other concerts of new music in St. Paul and other cities; he writes articles for leading periodicals. The more he is criticized the more grimly he battles. He is a crusader—perhaps the only one among American moderns who could undertake the Herculean labor of overcoming the prejudices of people who are almost entirely ignorant of contemporary arts, and that in a locality where he is quite alone, has not the support of a group who work with him!

If Becker has his way, he will make St. Paul and Minneapolis into leading centers of contemporary culture. And if St. Paul does not hinder him by making him occupy too much of his energy in fighting its doubts, he will war with his personal problems of composition until he takes his place among the leading contemporary composers.

II

JOHN J. BECKER's Concerto for Horn in F was performed for the first time anywhere in the series of orchestral programs conducted by David Breckman in Cooper Union. This series was devoted to novelties, and among them Becker's Concerto surprised a critical audience with its substantial values.

Becker was one of the first, if not the very first, to sponsor dissonant music wholeheartedly in the Middle West. Certainly no one else has so consistently fostered unfamiliar kinds of new music in the Chicago and Minneapolis areas. He has been responsible for a number of first performances of contemporary works by such Americans as Ives, Riegger, and Ruggles, both in Chicago, where he now lives and is active with the local ISCM chapter, and in St. Paul, where he conducted an orchestra for several years. Now 67 years old, he looks back over thirty years of pioneering with difficult music before skeptical groups who found it hard to understand, disagreeable, and even annoying. Becker sat them down and made them listen anyway. He became resigned in time to the thanklessness of his role as gadfly in Middle Western musical circles and so was astonished when, at Ernst Krenek's first radio interview after his arrival to teach at Hamline College in Minneapolis, Krenek declared that if there was now an audience for his music and a place for him as a teacher in that region, it was because of the stubborn pioneering spirit of John J. Becker. Later the two men met and became friends. Krenek learned Becker's Piano Sonata and has played it several times in concert. When Krenek left Chicago, Becker succeeded him in the principal chair of musical composition at the venerable Chicago Musical College.

Becker has also worked to improve the level of Catholic music in this country. He has taught at Notre Dame in South Bend, at St. Mary of the Springs in Columbus, at St. Thomas College in St. Paul, and he has been composer-in-residence and professor of music at Barat College, near Chicago, since 1943. He is tireless in com-

---

Here Cowell reviews Becker's lyrical and impressionistic Concerto for Horn in F. It appeared first in The Musical Quarterly *XXXIX/3 (Jul. 1953) pp. 426-432.*

bating the natural conservatism of musicians in the Church, vigorously upholding the idea that while nineenth-century music may be largely of the flesh, the best a twentieth-century music returns to spiritual values through a dissonant counterpoint that is related in a way to the sixteenth-century choral style of Palestrina and the other great Catholic masters. This point of view lies behind his editorship of a new series of brief lives of great reli gious composers, each written by a composer of the twentieth century. (The first of these, on Ockeghem by Krenek, has just appeared.) Last year Becker was invited by the Vatican to represent American music as delegate to the First International Congress of Catholic Artists—the first gathering of its kind in the history of the Church. In the committee meetings on music, the Pope's recent declaration that modern music should not be excluded from the life of the Church led to much dis cussion about what modern music in this sense is, exactly. There was strong opposition to any idiom more recent than that of the late nineteenth century, but when Dr. Becker pointed out the parallel between sixteenth-century and twentieth-century styles and intentions, discussion died out and his views were incorporated in the resolution presented to the Congress by the committee on music.

As a composer, Becker has worked out his own way of applying the principles of sixteenth-century counterpoint to modern atonal dissonance. He arrived at a style related to that of Hindemith, Riegger, Berg, and Ruggles, but his music is rather more serene, even gentle, and it is devoid of voluptuous elements. The Horn Concerto, one of his best works, represents this style, colored with Impressionistic accompanying figures. The piece opens with a dramatic proclamation delivered by the horn alone (Ex. 1)

Example 1. John J. Becker, Concerto for Horn in F.
Copyright © 1936 New Music Edition. Used by Permission.

after which a dissonant murmuring figure is set up in the high woodwinds (Ex. 2); this is used with pizzicato strings, against a further development of the declamatory melody. The second theme changes from dramatic prose to lyric poetry. The melodic qualities of its medium low register are explored by the horn, while the murmuring figure is transferred to strings. The continuation of this figure, falling along new chord sequences, brings the first and second themes into the same formal plan, and is the unifying fac-

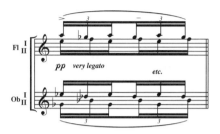

Example 2. John J. Becker. Concerto for Horn in F.
Copyright © 1936 New Music Edition. Used by Permission.

tor in the change of mood. After some orchestral development, the second theme is recapitulated and developed.

The movements are not separated; instead, an episode leads directly into a scherzo section called "A Satire," in which the horn player has virtuoso double and triple tonguings as fast as he can play, in duet with a trumpet, with occasional staccato exclamations from the rest of the orchestra. A more lyrical passage leads without pause into "A Song," which plays the role of the slow movement. It is built on an extension of the middle portion of the poetic second theme of the first movement (Ex. 3). A few scraps of the scherzo lead into a quiet, dignified chorale fugue: the horn

Example 3. John J. Becker. Concerto for Horn in F.
Copyright © 1936 New Music Edition. Used by Permission.

sounds the chorale melody, and there are three fugal string sections against it, with the answer in the major seventh rather than in the conventional fifth. The fugue leads to a recapitulation of the first two themes, followed by the coda. The form is thus one large movement with cyclic return; its beginning is in essence a sonata allegro form, followed by a scherzo, a slow movement, and a fugue, and with a return to the essentials of the first movement in lieu of the conventional last allegro. All the materials in the later sections are developed from the first and second themes. The general impression is not at all startling; Becker does not use his dissonances harshly, but emphasizes their lyric and impressionistic possibilties.

His other best works, notably a string quartet and *When the Willow Nods*, an opera with text by Alfred Kreymborg (existing also in the form of an orchestral suite), are in this general style. Becker himself has been so sure that no audience would like this style that he has often done his reputation the disservice of offering conductors and performers pieces written in a style that attempts unsuccessfully to compromise with tonality, something he has never handled with the same skill and con viction. He has only now come to discover that his dissonant music written twenty or thirty years ago no longer shocks or surprises. From the standpoint of musical enjoyment, the Horn Concerto bridged the gap between sophisticated and unsophisticated members of its audience. The musicians took satisfaction in the fact that the work is competently written, integrating several contrasting elements successfully, and that the instrumentation is handled in a thoroughly experienced manner. The lay auditors were pleased to be able to follow the melodies, for the Impressionistic dissonances did not bother them. The Cooper Union Auditorium was packed, with a mixture of experienced composers and critics who came to hear new works, the usual eager but somewhat vague students, and the lonely souls who are usually found at the Union, some of whom come in off the streets to take a little nap in a clean warm place. This disparate group enjoyed the Concerto and gave a rousing reception to it.

Roldán and Caturla of Cuba

Two of the most colorful and exciting composers of the Western Hemisphere, Amadeo Roldán and Aléjandro Garcia Caturla, both Cubans, died unexpectedly in their prime during the year 1940. Their general outlook was similar; they were above all interested in developing the extraordinarily vivid native musical resources of their country. Although both composers wrote chiefly for symphony orchestra and smaller chamber combinations, and both had a sound European training, their work produced quite different results.

Roldán, born in 1900, was educated in Madrid as a violinist and composer. At the age of nine he won first prize as composer, and in 1916 first prize in violin-playing at the Madrid Conservatory. He returned to Havana in 1921, where he organized the Havana Chamber Music Society. In 1932 he became conductor of the Havana Philharmonic Orchestra, a post he held until his death.

He had enough Negro blood to be stirred and interested by Afro-Cuban rhythms of the natives. It was Roldán who introduced large numbers of native percussion instruments and the African-style counter-rhythms and accented off-beats into symphonic scores. Nowhere else in America has the native African rhythm been so well preserved as in Cuba, and no other composer has made so significant a development of these ritualistic and secular rhythmic modes. Roldán's best music sounds like an almost literal enlargement of genuine native performance. It preserves that spirit through

Cowell's favorites in Cuba were Pedro Sanjuan (1886-1976) and his students Aléjandro García Caturla (1906-1940) and Amadeo Roldán (1900-1939). Roldán's magnum opus is said to be the folk and percussion ballet La Rebambaramba, *while Caturla, who also studied with Nadia Boulanger, is all-too-often remembered by his dramatic death: murder by a criminal who was out on bail. This article appeared in* Modern Music *XVIII/2 (Jan-Feb 1941) pp. 98-9.*

the use of characteristic rhythms and instruments. In my opinion, no composer has ever succeeded better in capturing the feeling of native music in symphonic works.

Aléjandro Caturla, born in 1906, studied a short time with Nadia Boulanger in Europe. His technic of composition was less secure from a formal standpoint than that of Roldán, but the self-education which followed his work with Boulanger resulted in great originality of scoring, form and harmonic material. In contrast to the professionally elegant Roldán, he appears a talented amateur. Whereas Roldán introduced actual Cuban rhythms and instruments, Caturla tried to use the more conventional instruments (with some additions) to imitate the sounds of Cuban music. Thus his symphonic works give an impression of Cuban music, rather than of being native in style. Caturla inevitably invented many unusual orchestral effects and developed a unique treatment of conventional instruments. His music is brilliant and dashing, with much atmosphere of dissonance, which is used to give the impression of native sounds rather than as a necessary part of the harmony. Although less close to genuine native music, Caturla's orchestral works are more telling and effective as show pieces than those of Roldán. His glittering orchestration, dashing rhythms (even though not always really faithful to those of the original tunes) and rapier-like discords create a sharp and memorable sensation. At times he has used native themes, adding discordant notes not to be found in native scales. Roldán, on the other hand, often used actual native melodies, preserved as accurately as possible, and composed original melodies in native style which are almost impossible to tell from the really indigenous ones.

Although the music of Roldán and Caturla has been occasionally performed by leading orchestras of the United States, neither has attained quite the United States reputation of other Latin American composers. Yet the actual values in their music will stand beside those of any better-known Spanish Americans. The death of these men in their prime is a loss to both North and South America.

Carl Ruggles

WHEN I FIRST MET Carl Ruggles in 1917, there was none of the present confusion and hypocrisy about accepting the free use of dissonance in music. Today, the fashion is for musicians to reject new works unless they have some dramatic dissonant punctuation, and to reject even more vehemently, as passé, any musical style containing continuous dissonant polyphony. But no style can be said to be passe, outmoded, before it has become the intimate aural possession of the average composer. It is easy to prove against the critics of dissonance that they have not 'lived through' this style as they claim to have done. Try them; they cannot name by ear the notes in a dissonant chord, not even if you name a note for them to start with; nor can they name a succession of tones in the type of melody used by composers like Ruggles. In 1917 the issue was clear; musicians universally disliked dissonant music, because they disliked free dissonances, and they had not yet learned not to say so loudly and firmly.

Looking back, it is hard to realize that at that time, after following every clue which might lead to a musician who liked 'modern' music, I had found only two who shared my intense delight in exploring free dissonance: Charles Seeger and Leo Ornstein. Carl Ruggles was to make the third. His raucous and rugged enthusiasm on finding a "magnificent," "superb," new dissonant chord was as catching as a prairie fire, not in the least damped by the fact

One of the most difficult American composers to come to know well is the Vermont Yankee Carl Ruggles (1876-1971). His music is extraordinarily dissonant but does not follow any of the usual methodologies. Lou Harrison (1917-) wrote a technical essay on Ruggles's music, published as About Carl Ruggles *(Yonkers, NY: Oscar Baradinsky at the Alicat Bookshop, 1946), and on pages 1-3 of this chapbook there appears this warm and personal article on Ruggles by Cowell, subtitled "A Note," which complements Harrison's more analytical article.*

that he himself was the only composer he knew of who invented them.

Ruggles was then in the process of evolving very fastidious and focussed standards for the way he wanted chords, melodic lines and polyphonic texture to be. Since few other composers used any such material at all, and on the rare occasions when they did use it they handled it rather differently, it was natural for Ruggles to assume that he was the only man who could write decently. It is only fair to add that when he found a hint in the works of others that they had a sense of the same thing he aimed for in his music, he was always pleased and enthusiastic. He noticed these tendencies in some of my works, and accepted them and me delightedly; for my part I had, from the beginning, a profound admiration for his fresh and glowing yet perfected use of dissonances, at a time when any use at all of free dissonance was very rare, and it was rarer yet to find anyone aiming at its thoughtful and exact employment.

On my first visit to Ruggles he took me immediately into his living room and began unwinding a huge roll of pieces of butcher's paper, pinned together with safety pins to make a whole which almost covered the entire floor of the room. Drawing his own huge staves, he had written down his ideas, borrowing his baby son's colored crayons for that purpose, each on a separate piece of paper; then he had pinned them together. This carpet of musical creation was spread out over the floor and we got down on our hands and knees to study it. He had begun to write on this Gargantuan scale at a time when he was having trouble with his eyes and couldn't see notes smaller than tablespoons; after a few years of this it somehow seemed silly to return to ordinary notes when his eyes improved.

Along the margins and over the staves Ruggles was accustomed to comment with vigorous crayon scribbles, and he added a few more adjectives ("Superb!" "Stinks!" "Putrid!" "Sublime!") each time he went over his work. When he sent off the manuscript of *Toys* to H. W. Gray for publication, he neglected to erase these comments; the engraver faithfully placed them on the proofs, and added a polite note to inquire whether they had to be printed to match the color of the crayon originally used.

My visits to Ruggles were a weekly event for many years. I

arrived the first thing in the morning. We looked at new chords, argued over where to include this note or that and fought over the best way to continue one melodic line or another. Ruggles can be violently concerned about the exact ranking of composers in terms of their historical importance, and so we spent many hours trying to decide whether Tchaikovsky was a thirteenth- or fourteenth-rate composer, and why.

Ruggles has always been far from reluctant to make public his dislike for other composers. His reasons for this are always good, from his point of view; they do not depend on the personality of the individual at all, for nine times out of ten Ruggles has never met the man, nor on his public reputation; but rather they are the result of Ruggles' close and considered examination of a score, an examination which usually results in a verdict one way or the other from which there is no appeal.

On the famous occasion when he lectured on composers at the Whitney Museum, he took along his lecture, written out carefully on an armful of the familiar butcher's paper which he deposited in a heap on the grand piano. It was with some difficulty he made out what he had written, but he determinedly and painstakingly read out sizzling criticisms which called composers names and by name. The presence of Mrs. Hadley in the audience did not deter him from opening his lecture with this remark: "I thought that music had reached the lowest possible point when I heard the works of John Alden Carpenter. Now, however, I have been examining the scores of Mr. Henry Hadley!"

Ruggles' exaggerated brusqueness does not always make enemies for him, however. Many admire it. When the great London publisher Kenneth Curwen came to America, he invited both of us to lunch. Ruggles arrived from Vermont in rough boots and mountain clothes. He had never met Curwen before. In greeting, he said as man to man: "I really didn't want to come down Mr. Curwen, but my wife told me that it would be the politic thing to do, to come down and try to make a hit with you. Our idea is that maybe you would publish one of my works." This Curwen later did, rather to the surprise of everyone concerned.

Ruggles is not really conceited; he thinks his own music is the best only because no one else writes according to his standards.

He is quick to call attention to positive values as he sees them.

Carl Ruggles is irascible, lovable, honest, sturdy, original, slow-working, deeply emotional, self-assured and intelligent. He is without question an important composer. If history slights him, it will be not because he has not made magnificent works (each one of them has real magnificence), but because he has composed too small a body of works altogether. A bit of work, once written, is never complete in his mind, but is something to keep on perfecting the rest of his life.

One morning when I arrived at the abandoned school house in Arlington where he now lives, he was sitting at the old piano, singing a single tone at the top of his raucous composer's voice, and banging a single chord at intervals over and over. He refused to be interrupted in this pursuit, and after an hour or so, I insisted on knowing what the idea was. "I'm trying over this damned chord," said he, "to see whether it still sounds superb after so many hearings." "Oh," I said tritely, "time will surely tell whether the chord has lasting value." "The hell with time!" Carl replied. "I'll give this chord the test of time right now. If I find I still like it after trying it over several thousand times, it'll stand the test of time, all right!"

II

WHEN STOKOWSKI RECENTLY performed Carl Ruggles' *Organum* with the Philharmonic for the first time anywhere, the warm and glowing performance created great interest and excitement. Rather to the surprise of both composer and conductor, the work achieved a real popular success. Audiences have gained wide experience since the Twenties, when all dissonant music sounded alike and horrible to them. Nowadays, the audience of the New York Philharmonic discriminates. It hissed and tore paper resoundingly this winter at the rather cerebral dissonant music of Anton Webern; but it applauded Ruggles vociferously. The differ-

---

Unlike the preceding remarks, Cowell's remarks on Carl Ruggles' Organum, reprinted from Musical Quarterly *XXXVI/2 (April 1950) pp. 272-274, are not anecdotal but extremely analytical and precise.*

ence obviously lies in the fact that Ruggles's web of chromatic, atonal sound is felt fully and vitally by the composer, to a point of extraordinary contagion; the music is full of verve. It is rich, full-blooded, super-romantic, urgent.

Pure calculation does not enter into its composition, but there are nevertheless embodied in it a number of principles that the composer loves to ponder and discuss. Ruggles does not use a 12-tone row, but he prefers not to have the same note repeated too soon in a melodic line, all the same. Twelve tones, however, seem to him too many. He likes from 7 to 9 different tones, with the rest of the 5 to 3 remaining tones free. Another moot point with Ruggles is the doubling of the same notes in a chord at different octave levels. He will ordinarily no more use an octave doubling (except of a whole line) than a harmony instructor would use consecutive octaves in a harmony exercise. But he will argue for hours about occasional specific instances in which he thinks such a doubling is desirable-usually in a final chord. Its chief justification in such a case comes, of course, from the universal sense of a more concordant closing chord. No matter how dissonant the fabric, the final chord must be less dissonant.

Another subject that comes in for a great deal of discussion with Ruggles is melodic continuation. Ruggles likes to start his long melodic sweeps with a germ of a motif which grows and expands. The opening of *Organum* shows such a continuation in simplest terms. The germ is the interval of a semitone; the first melodic fragment is formed by inverting this after a leap of a major third.

Carl Ruggles. *Organum.* © 1947 New Music Editions. Used by permission.

The intervals are small, the melody forms the sort of curve dear to the hearts of all well-grounded polyphonists. In measures 3-4 there is expansion by the addition of another major third; then the melody bursts its bounds, the intervals widen more and more, and seconds change to sevenths. The full range of the melody's total expansion is four octaves and a third, which is typical of Ruggles. In dissonant counterpoint, many old contrapuntal principles are preserved but are applied to dissonance instead of to consonance as they once were. So Ruggles often begins sustained tones which are to become consonants by preparing them as dissonances first:

Carl Ruggles. *Organum.* © 1947 New Music Editions. Used by permission.

These technical points, though they contribute to the consistency of texture of *Organum,* are unnoticeable in listening to the vital, surging, ever-growing work, a work in which there is enough material, in highly concentrated form, for a complete symphony. Ruggles occupies in American music a position similar to that of Webern in modern Teutonic music: both have written a rather small number of short, condensed, highly finished pieces of dissonant texture. Ruggles, however, preserves a dynamically continuous flow in his melodic outlines, while Webern deliberately separated his melodies into disjunct fragments.

Joseph Schillinger

Overture to the Schillinger System

THE SCHILLINGER SYSTEM MAKES a positive approach to the theory of musical composition by offering *possibilities* for choice and development by the student, instead of the rules hedged round with prohibitions, limitations and exceptions, which have characterized conventional studies.

If a creative musician has something of importance to say, his need for studying the materials with which he must say it is acknowledged as a matter of course. No great composer has ever omitted the study of techniques. Musical theory as traditionally taught, however, has always been a profound disappointment to truly creative individuals. Such men have invariably added to the body of musical theory with researches of their own. Invariably, also, they have not followed the "rules" laid down in conventional textbooks with any consistency. If these rules had been based on something inevitable in the nature of music, composers would have had no reason to disregard them.

Actually, musical theory has dealt with no more than a small part of the potential musical materials; its assumptions concerning the science of sound have often been based on misapprehen-

Joseph Moievitch Schillinger (1895-1945) is best known for his system of musical composition based on mathematical relationships and methods. That he was also a composer of remarkable music is often forgotten. Cowell was an enthusiast for Schillinger, co-founded a Schillinger Society (now defunct), and wrote four articles about him and his work, two of which have been selected.

In his brief introduction to Schillinger's The Schillinger System of Musical Composition *(1946) pp. ix-x, Cowell places the Schillinger system within the larger matrix of music, defending him from the charge made by the young Elliott Carter and others, of leaving no room for musical intuition.*

sion, and the rules it lays down often reflect the personal taste of a certain theorist, or they may be based on the study of a single composer or of some one historical period. The resulting generalizations are far from being objective, but they are nonetheless imposed upon the student in the form of "rules". Writers on theory have not been scientists, and no scientist has tried to make a complete and co-ordinated system of musical possibilities.

Joseph Schillinger is the single exception: he was superbly competent in the two fields of musical composition and science. His monumental *System of Musical Composition* represents a lifetime of work in research, co-ordination and creative discovery. The synthesis he achieved has resulted in an entirely new point of view about the function of theory studies.

In the course of the research which led to the formulation of his system of musical composition, Schillinger took all known facts concerning the nature of musical materials from conventional theory studies, and added to the discoveries and speculations of modern and less conventional theorists such as Schoenberg, Conus[1] and myself. By applying the laws of mathematical logic as developed by modern science, he found that he could co-ordinate all of the seemingly diverse factors. He found also that he could open further untried possibilities for the development of new materials. A glance at his Table of Contents will show an extraordinary number of aspects of music here organized for the first time for inclusion in the theoretical approach to the study of composition.

The idea behind the Schillinger System is simple and inevitable: it undertakes the application of mathematical logic to all the materials of music and to their functions, so that the student may know the unifying principles behind these functions, may grasp the method of analyzing and synthesizing any musical materials that he may find anywhere or may discover for himself, and may perceive how to develop new materials as he feels the need for them. Thus the Schillinger System offers possibilities, not limitations; it is a positive, not a negative approach to the choice of musical materials. Because of the universality of the aesthetic concepts underlying it, the System applies equally to old and new styles in music and to "popular" and "serious" composition.

Schillinger is sometimes criticized on the basis that his system reduces everything to mathematics and that musical intuition and the subjective side of creativity are neglected. I have never been able to understand this criticism. The currently taught rules of harmony, counterpoint, and orchestration certainly do not suggest to the student materials adapted to his own expressive desires. Instead he is given a small and circumscribed set of materials, already much used, together with a set of prohibitions to apply to them, and then he is asked to express himself only within these limitations. It has been the constant complaint from students of composition that their teachers fail to make clear the distinction between the objective and subjective factors in music. A young composer is constrained, as things are now, to spend several years following rules deduced or assumed from the works of his predecessors, but as soon as his works begin to be heard he is reproached, and rightly so, if they sound like somebody else's. He has not been shown what possibilities there really are in music in any objective, scientific way, nor has he been trained in the manner best calculated to develop an original talent, by exercising his own taste and judgment in choosing from among these possibilities the materials best suited to his musical intention.

Whether or not one agrees with Schillinger's great personal interest in the scientific realities of music, it is nevertheless true that no composer is well equipped to express himself subjectively until he has so profound a knowledge of musical materials and their relationships that, consciously or unconsciously, he seizes on just the right ones to use for whatever he wishes to say in music. He can be trained to do this if he will subject himself to the disciplines inherent in musical materials themselves, as they are set before him by the Schillinger System.

II

The Schillinger Case:
Charting the Musical Range

T HE DIFFERENCE BETWEEN the sounds produced by a trained
composer and by a gifted child at play among the piano keys
lies in the fact that the composer sets his sounds in order, organizes
them in accordance with some definite scheme of relationship.
Innumerable starting points exist for a musical composition, of
course, and each initial musical idea is susceptible to organization
in more than one way. Whatever skill is involved is developed by
conscious examination of the possibilities and by practice in handling them.

A composer functions in still another way, however, avowedly
mysterious: he makes a series of choices among these possibilities.
Each choice is a creative act; in this the composer shows himself to be
an artist. The selection of his initial idea may be perfectly unconscious, but once this starting point has been established, the composer must again function as an artist, make decisions about keeping some things, discarding others. The reasons for his choice can
never be more than partly objective, but the range of possibilities
offered to him may surely be entirely so.

Joseph Schillinger's *System of Musical Composition* (Carl Fischer,
Inc., 1946), which explores these possibilities, begins by applying
the element of rhythm to time duration in the familiar way. He
then extends it to all other phases of composition: to the way in
which block harmonies change, to intervals in scale and melody,
entrances of counter-themes in counterpoint, distribution of parts
through a score, and other processes of composition. For the first
time, complete theories of rhythm and of melody writing are

When Schillinger died in 1945 the new edition of his System of Musical Composition *had not yet appeared. Cowell not only wrote the introduction to it, but he
and Sidney Cowell reviewed the book in* Modern Music *XXIII/3 (Summer 1946)
pp. 226-228. Interestingly, their favorable review was followed with an attack by
Elliott Carter, "The Fallacy of the Mechanistic Approach," which contradicted many
of the things Carter is associated with today.*

offered. Schillinger systematizes musical relationships by expressing them methodically in mathematical formulas. Nicolas Slonimsky has said of him that he has done for music what Mendeleyev did for chemistry: he has provided an exhaustive periodic chart of all its elements, making possible the discovery of those that have not yet been used. The principles which Schillinger establishes can be made to cover all styles of music known. The theoretical systems of Hindemith and Schoenberg are now seen to be equally logical and find their places within Schillinger's organization of musical theory, along with the tonal systems of India, Persia and Africa, sixteenth century counterpoint, classical harmony, dissonant counterpoint, harmony based on fourths or on seconds.

Einstein has turned our world into something about whose reality scientists believe we can know nothing final. We cannot know *what it is* but only *how it acts*. Nature then consists of movement and relationship, that is to say, of rhythm. Any natural phenomenon becomes an event in this modern rhythmic conception of the universe; Einstein found that the only objective way of studying these events was to chart their periodicities, with their reinforcement or interference, on a graph. Schillinger believed music might be included among the natural phenomena which can be examined in this way. His system uses a comparatively simple form of Einstein's graph, with its time-space co-ordinates.

If the arts consist of a series of relationships, then their patterns might be expected to reproduce the actual process of nature: growth, motion and evolution. And since mathematical formulas are the expression of these patterns and their performance, Schillinger wondered whether mathematical analysis of great works of art would not show that they imitate natural processes very closely. Confirmation was dramatic, for he actually found in works of the masters the same patterns, expressible in the same formulas which are used to describe the formation of crystals, the ratios of curvature of celestial trajectories, and the division and multiplication of cells, for instance. He concluded that great artists had intuitively realized the mathematical logic of structure and movement, just as early philosophers and scientists had prefigured intuitively the Einsteinian concept of the universe.

The prime advantages of the graphic method of presentation for music are, first, a clarity and exactness which cannot be approached by any other method of notation and, second, its capacity for infinite orderly expansion to conform to systematic phenomena. Since a graph is no more than a symbol which stands for the behavior of things, however, music is not written out graphically by Schillinger pupils except to simplify a problem. Instead, the formulas are used as a kind of shorthand which may be translated into ordinary score writing at will. The composer produces a plan for a composition whose parts *cannot* be anything except logically inter-related. He need do only the actual creative thinking; a copyist trained in certain elementary aspects of the method can accurately follow the formulas, in which every detail is implicit, and clothe the composer's skeleton in conventional notation.

A talented student of composition will inevitably want to select his own material, to use it in ways of his own devising. Until now there has been no method to enable this natural tendency of the creative mind to function successfully, while at the same time pursuing the objectives commonly held by teachers of composition. The study of technique should inform the composer about the extent of possible musical materials and how they may be classified and used. He cannot expect to learn to handle every possibility. But he does need to be shown a plan by which he may discover, organize and use whatever type of material it pleases him to investigate. It is just such a plan that Schillinger has devised.

Many have criticized the confusion of style and taste with "law" in music, as being a holdover from nineteenth century religious thinking. Schillinger felt the trouble lay in a limited and faulty idea of what music is, which resulted in the old anachronistic dichotomies of art and science, art and life, art and nature. Once these sets of apparent opposites were understood to share the pattern-in-movement, or rhythmic, nature of things, the arts fell into their natural place. Schillinger's perception of this, and the exceedingly comprehensive and practical application he made of so broad a philosophical concept, must have a revolutionary effect upon the relationship between composers and their craft.

1. Presumably Julius Conus (1869-1942).—DH

Nicholas Slonimsky

YOU MAY BELONG TO THAT comfortable group who as students of an instrument were taught the forms of the major and chromatic scales and, with some difficulty, three forms of the minor scale. Probably nothing thereafter led you to suspect that your practical education in these matters was not complete. It is usually assumed by the few who have vaguely heard of other forms that only musicologists need to understand the intricacies of the Greek and ecclesiastical modes, that nobody but an odd modernist would be interested in whole-tone or other specially constructed scales, and that pentatonic and similarly exotic scales could be important only to a folklorist.

The average musician, then, will hear with shocked surprise that a dictionary of scales may be of real use, and that there are enough different scales to form such a volume as this *Thesaurus* in the first place.

Slonimsky's definition of a scale is "a progression, either diatonic or chromatic, that proceeds uniformly in one direction, ascending or descending, until the terminal point is reached." This means that a large number of tonal progressions not previously thought of as scales are treated as such in the *Thesaurus*: certain arpeggios, for example, or any progressions such as those used in

Nicolas Slonimsky, composer, conductor and close associate of Cowell, was one of the most erudite men of music of his time, or any other. Feeling the need for a major critique of the music of Latin America, he produced the large study reviewed here by Cowell, who notes almost waggishly Slonimsky's passion for seeking out curious and strange facts. Slonimsky's Thesaurus of Scales and Melodic Patterns *[New York, Coleman-Ross Co., Inc., 1947; xii, 244 p.]is the only book of its sort, basically an encyclopedic reference work on different scales and modes intended to be used by composers. Cowell notes the problems with this in his review, published in* Notes *IV/2 (Mar. 1947) pp. 171-173.*

Hanon's finger exercises for pianists, where a "scale" in ascending form may start out by going downward before it betrays its intention of moving generally in an upward direction. Any nonconformist notes in such a progression are penalized by being christened "infrapolated" tones. If you wish to be in a position to converse freely and easily at cocktail parties about sisquitone, quadritone, quinquetone, and diatessaron scale progressions, or to engage in profound discussion of, let us say, the sesquiquinquetone progression of an equal division of eleven octaves into twelve parts (p. 136 in the *Thesaurus* if you are inclined to look it up), Slonimsky's *Thesaurus* is an absolute *must* for your library.

From the standpoint of theory, the *Thesaurus* is in accord with the modern idea that the student should be presented with all possible combinations within certain limits of classification, be shown the musical relationships involved, and then be permitted to make his own selection, instead of having a teacher or a harmony book decide for him what is "good" and what is "bad" in the old way. Any student or composer who prefers to select his own material may look up in the *Thesaurus* any scale now in use within the scope of the twelve tones of the chromatic scale; he may also discover, in the systematic arrangement of all orderly progressions within this definition, hundreds of scale progressions which are unexploited but which could without question be put to fine musical use. In addition, Slonimsky presents a large number of musical patterns which, through some irregularity in their structure, he cannot classify as scales, and from these, too, composers might draw an overwhelming amount of useful melodic material.

It is easy to see that many stubbornly introspective composers will prefer to continue to compose in an old familiar scale, or, if they should happen to need a new one, will prefer to invent it themselves out of the whole cloth. Fair enough; but they are warned here that they must not be unduly horrified if their "invention" is later pointed out to them in the teeming pages of the *Thesaurus*. Creative activity in music is being driven toward selection and organization of materials, rather than their invention, by the logical extension of familiar musical elements which men like Joseph Schillinger and Slonimsky now offer us.

One of the "palindromic canons," for instance, which occurs

in the *Thesaurus* simply as one of a series of orderly classifications, turns out to have been used *in toto* by Arnold Schoenberg in his *Ode to Napoleon*. Slonimsky pointed this out to Schoenberg and obligingly sent him some other similar palindromic canons as well. Some composers would have been extremely annoyed, but not Schoenberg, who was pleased by the whole episode and who commended the cleverness of a system which arrived by pure logic at the same themes which he as a composer had hit upon in his own way.

Slonimsky particularly enjoys inventing new terms, and when his system leads him to the discovery of unfamiliar materials, he performs the service of naming as well as classifying them. But it seems to me an excess of enthusiasm which leads him to include the intervals of $4\frac{1}{2}$ tones and $5\frac{1}{2}$ tones, for example, as among those not in the system of historic scales (for which new terms have had to be coined. I was under the impression that those very intervals had long had a respectable existence in the "historic system" under the names of major sixth and major seventh respectively, and am not entirely convinced that such terms as sesquiquadritone and sesquiquinquetone are an improvement. To a man who learned English by reading and memorizing the dictionary, as Slonimsky did many years ago, such elaborately compounded tongue-twisters probably seem simplicity itself.

What gives this writer the gravest cause for concern, however, is the dire plight one foresees for the unsuspecting young composer, who goes to a lot of trouble to perfect his own newly-invented scale, only to find that Coleman-Ross Co., Inc., already owns the rights to it! It looks as if the Music of the Future will have to stick to major and minor and the old modes which are safely in the public domain, if—as it would appear—Coleman-Ross now owns all the scales in the *Thesaurus*.

Colin McPhee

T HIS SEASON HEARD for the first time Douglas Moore's crisp
Symphony in A (his second), Virgil Thomson's one-movement
work called *The Seine at Night,* a piece of formalized impressionism,
and two of the three movements of Colin McPhee's fabulous symphony, *Tabuh Tabuhan.* The instrumentation of *Tabuh Tabuhan* was
reduced by the composer for performance by the CBS orchestra,
but it retained the two pianos, the celesta and marimba, and the
other instruments that give the scoring its characteristically fresh
and ringing sound.

The Balinese word *tabuh* means to strike; *tabuhan* indicates the
striking of several different things at once. So McPhee's title is appropriate to rhythmically polyphonic music,[6] music in which lots
of things happen, as they do in this score. With the exception of
two Oriental gongs, loaned by the composer, which give the work
a special tonal feeling, only instruments of the Western orchestra
are required. Yet since McPhee uses actual Balinese themes and
methods of variation, and of course the Balinese modes, the work
reproduces to an astonishing degree the sound of gamelans, the
great Indonesian orchestras of tuned percussion instruments: gongs,
gong-chimes, metallophones, and drums. McPhee's knowing use
of different Balinese modes, together with the characteristic rhythmic polyphony and melodic contour and embellishment, shows
that these are the important elements for this music's authenticity,
of far greater significance than the variation in tuning between
Indonesia and the West which produces intervals of different sizes
in the two cultures. Comparative musicologists have been accustomed to make a great fuss over differences in tuning between the

---

*Cowell, ever tuned in to gamelan music, here reviews work by Colin McPhee (1901-
1964).* The Musical Quarterly *XXXIV/3 (July 1948) pp. 410-412.*

East and the West; actually, in more than one musical culture a tuning is considered correct within a surprisingly wide range of variation, and Indonesian music is a particularly good example of this. Because gamelans in Bali offer a great variety of tuning, and also of instrumentation, McPhee's music has been accepted without question by Indonesians themselves. Javanese who danced to music by Colin McPhee at a Ballet Society concert were heard to comment with especial favor on the use of pizzicato 'cellos and violas to replace the Oriental high tuned drums. One feels that if a Balinese composer were to acquire Western technique, he might write in this manner.

No Western composer has probably ever known the music of another culture so thoroughly as McPhee does the Indonesian, so that when he writes in this style he is able to retain the characteristics that are most important to Indonesian culture and at the same time most attractive to us. The result is music of fine taste and restraint. It was not, of course, the composer's intention simply to reproduce Balinese music as a *tour de force,* but rather to write music of the sort that at the time lay closest to his heart. *Tabuh Tabuhan* is not, therefore, an ethnological document, but rather an invigorating illustration of what may happen when a highly trained Western musician of distinction and imagination is drawn into close contact with a sophisticated and appealing music from another world.

The opening of the first movement (marked *ostinato*) starts in the 2nd flute with a 4-note theme along a 4-note scale, played within a rhythmic scheme that takes five notes to complete; it is repeated four times, producing a different rhythm each time. Such

Example 1. Colin McPhee. *Tabuh Tabuhan.* Copyright ©1956 (Renewed) by Associated Music Publishers, Inc. (BMI). International Copyright Secured. All Rights Reserved. By Permission.

schemes are also to be found in American popular music. McPhee develops his initial idea through much syncopation, and adds complexity to complexity until there are at least eight different 4-, 5-, and 7-note scales going at once; amusingly enough, parts of *Tabuh Tabuhan* were mistaken for boogie-woogie by the learned instrumental body of the CBS orchestra.

Ex. 2 shows one of the 5-note scales in the first movement. It is typical of much of McPhee's music, as well as of Indonesian usage, that the notes with a parenthetical flat above them are used

Example 2. Colin McPhee. *Tabuh Tabuhan.* Copyright © 1956 (Renewed) by Associated Music Publishers, Inc. (BMI). International Copyright Secured. All Rights Reserved. By Permission.

freely either flattened or not—it is considered the same scale either way. Typical, too, is the use of deliberately out-of-key low and medium-pitched gong-like tones which give an unearthly quality to the sound.

For this particular symphony McPhee took themes of temple chants, street dances, trance music, *legong* ballet, and sacred tunes heard only at cremations; it contains no themes composed by himself.

Several other men, of whom Henry Eichheim is the most familiar example, have tried to write Eastern music for Western orchestras. The reason Eichheim's music gives so curiously false an impression is partly that he mixed Eastern and Western instruments in such a way that the best values of each are lost, and partly that he never did understand the system that underlies Eastern music and is responsible for its special organization. McPhee, on the other hand, is so thoroughly at home with the music of Indonesia that he was actually able to take over one of the native instruments and play with a Balinese orchestra.

Because it seems to me certain that future progress in creative music for composers of the Western world must inevitably go towards the exploration and integration of elements drawn from more than one of the world's cultures, I think *Tabuh Tabuhan* will prove to be an important landmark. The kind of acculturation I foresee is already going on at second hand among the composers who draw on the African elements in American popular music for their symphonic works. More direct attempts have usually resulted in tasteless hybrids. *Tabuh Tabuhan,* however, is an entirely successful combination of Eastern and Western elements into a finely balanced and integrated music of warmth and brilliance.

Virgil Thomson

WHEN RECENTLY Virgil Thomson's Symphony on a Hymn Tune and *The Seine at Night* were played over for friends, one of the group asked: "How does it happen, Mr. Thomson, that you have two such widely different styles? The Symphony is so stark and plain, the new tone-poem so delicately impressionistic in color?" "Oh," said Thomson blandly, "the Symphony on a Hymn Tune was written to present Kansas City to Parisians, and The *Seine at Night* is intended to describe Paris to people from Kansas City." The latter work is dedicated to the Kansas City Philharmonic Orchestra. In his youth Thomson played hymns as an organist in Kansas City. In Paris he found appreciation of the bareness of Protestant hymns, the French capital being then rather bored with impressionism. In Kansas City he found appreciation of the touches of chromaticism, the polytonal suggestion, and the gentle dissonances with which he decorated the succession of triads that is the basis of *The Seine at Night*. This is well calculated to appeal to a city that considers the folk-hymn singing tradition of the nearby Ozarks crude. In New York, neutral ground, Thomson finds both aspects of his music are admired.

And one listener, at least, finds them to be fundamentally alike in style. It is only the facade that is different. At first it seems odd to find music of Thomson's sounding even vaguely like French impressionism, for this is something he has most carefully avoided—perhaps because he has lived so much in France. He is fond of unadorned major and minor triads, and equally unadorned major (sometimes minor) scale passages. He has also been attracted by the most extreme dissonance. The use of these elements with un-

Virgil Thomson (1896-1989). This review of Thomson's The Seine at Night *first appeared in* The Musical Quarterly *XXXIV/3 (July 1948) pp. 413-5.*

yielding consistency throughout whole sections of his music has produced a really glaring simplicity, a simplicity that has often proved hard for listeners to understand. His music is only now, after many years, being received in general with real warmth and understanding.

Thomson has always abjured secondary seventh chords, with their easy appeal. The fundamental chords in *The Seine at Night* are triads, and they move in Thomson's familiar block formation, as is shown in the low strings in Ex. 4. This is later developed into longer lines of block triads. The relation of the melody to the chords,

Ex. 4. Virgil Thomson. *The Seine at Night.* Copyright © 1940 (renewed) by G. Schirmer, Inc. (ASCAP). International Copyright Secured. All Rights Reserved. Reprinted by Permission.

however, suggests a series of minor seventh chords, although the melody itself, for the first six measures, uses only four different tones in what might be a primitive scale. Actually, this is the same scale used by Colin McPhee in the opening of *Tabuh Tabuhan*. It is only in the seventh measure that Thomson lets the cat out of the bag: the A sharp in the chord of the second measure really did have some relation to the melody, after all, for by the dramatic insertion of the A sharp the melody changes from a primitive mode to the ecclesiastical Dorian. So the plain triads may be said to be decorated with a seventh chord-producing melody. A simple downward-moving scale is introduced as early as p. 7 of the score. By p. 16, m. 2, it is decorated by having five low wind instruments run down the scale at different levels simultaneously, each in its own rhythm. The last beat winds up 2 against 3 against 4 against 5 against 6. The next page brings a variety of scales skittering against each other in every direction. There are only two directions in music but crossed parts and counter-rhythms make it sound as though there were at least five!

On p. 24 a 5-note melody derived from the opening theme bounces up through the strings and lands on a plain triad in high flutes, celesta, and harps—the plain triad here decorated by means of unusual orchestral color. By the end of p. 29, the upward-running passage, which has become more and more chromatic as it goes along, finally turns into a plain chromatic scale in the flute. This passage winds up with a succession of three triads, to each of which one dissonant note has been added in the celesta, answered by a chromatic scale in the oboe which leads to a similar succession of triad chords in the string body, in harmonics. So the diatonic scale is decorated into a chromatic one, and the triads are consistently decorated by the addition of a single dissonant second. Without abandoning any characteristics of the style for which he is known, Thomson has, by the simplest embellishments, produced a work apparently far more conventional in richness of perfumed sound than usual. In reality the change from his plainest writing is very slight indeed. This is a lovely piece, and it is easy to predict that it will be more played than others of his works in which the severity of manner is more obvious to the ear.

II

THE METROPOLITAN has never produced a successful American opera, perhaps because those it has staged were written with its grandiose 19th century manner in mind. Americans of Anglo-Saxon and Celtic origin prefer understatement, and have never produced a school of tragic opera. Both the English and Americans have been far more successful in the witty genre of *The Beggar's Opera*, the cheerful Gilbert and Sullivan repertory, or more recently in Douglas Moore's *The Devil and Daniel Webster* and Menotti's four Italo-American excursions.

Virgil Thomson's The Mother of Us All, *his third collaboration with Gertrude Stein (1875-1945) has never had the cult following which came to his and Stein's earlier* Four Saints in Three Acts. *However, when staged, as it was in 1947 at Columbia University, it has been much admired. Cowell's description sounds convincing, though we only know the suite from the work. He also stresses the essence of Thomson's style—extreme simplicity. This review appeared in Notes V/2 (Mar. 1948) pp. 260-262.* Virgil Thomson: The Mother of Us All, an Opera. Text by Gertrude Stein. *New York: Music Press, Inc., 1947, 157 p.*

Virgil Thomson has succeeded in establishing single-handed a basic variant of this tradition. *The Mother of Us All*, produced last spring by the Opera Workshop at Columbia University, conducted by Otto Luening, had a notable popular success. It is sure to delight any English-speaking audience, chiefly on account of a sophisticated modern simplicity of manner, now suggested elsewhere only in the other Thomson-Stein opera: *Three Saints in Four Acts*. There are differences between the two collaborations. Thomson's music is even more simple than before and draws more explicitly on American thematic patterns, and Miss Stein's book is at once more understandable and meaningful. No one has offered as yet a completely convincing explanation of Miss Stein's style, but if the manifest seriousness of her purpose in her first writings was replaced or covered over by her experiments with words during her middle period, there is no question that ever since *The Autobiography of Alice Toklas* she has allowed more and more of her preoccupation with fundamental human problems to show through her word-arrangements. Thus, although there are still plenty of passages that make only Stein-sense, there now shows through the surface comedy of witty, meaningful words a serious, even a moving and tragic story.

The book deals with the life of Susan B. Anthony, crusader for Votes for Women. Susan B. is surrounded by other type-forming Americans such as Daniel Webster, Ulysses S. Grant, John Adams, and a few fictitious characters, along with Gertrude S. and Virgil T. themselves. The dialogue, fast and funny, treats of the acute political and moral 'causes' of the 19th century, out of which the 'love interest' of the opera emerges. John Adams and Constance Fletcher love each other nobly and enduringly, but since he is an Adams, John cannot kneel and ask for her hand, and therefore they never marry. Indiana Elliott and Jo the Loiterer do manage to get married as the climax of the first act, but they also have a problem. Shall Indiana take Jo's name, or should she not? They finally settle matters by exchanging last names, chiefly because Indiana Loiterer is such a 'pretty name.' Gertrude Stein's main theme, of course, is what women think of men. Lillian Russell opens the subject by complaining that "It is very naughty for men to quarrel so." One of the high spots in the drama (and the chief soprano aria) occurs when Susan B. Anthony tells what she thinks of men: "They have kind hearts but they are afraid. They fear women, they fear each other, they fear their neighbor, they fear other countries, and then they hearten themselves in their fear by crowding together and following each other, and when they crowd together and follow each other, they are brutes, like animals who stampede, and so they have written in the name male into the United States constitution, because they are afraid of black men, because they are afraid of women, because they are afraid,—afraid." This may seem almost too lucid, too simple for Miss Stein, but although her hits are often direct, she is rarely simple. The real tragedy of the opera comes at the end, and there is a tear in every eye when on a darkening stage the statue of Susan B., newly unveiled in the Halls of Congress, reflects upon "My long life, my long, long life," which she now knows was a martyrdom, "Not to what was won but what was done." It is the tragedy of life-long devotion at hard labor to causes soon forgotten through being won, and which once won are found not to produce the hoped for, all-encompassing good they seemed to promise while the deeply serious struggle was on. The 'Amen' suggested by Thomson's plagal cadence is the more moving because much that Stein wrote of Susan B. in this piece, finished only a few weeks before she died, she might easily have written of herself.

No one should be misled into thinking that the extreme simplicity of musical means used in Virgil Thomson's setting is either commonplace or commonly found. The chordal simplicity is so radical that unadorned major triads form a large percentage of the chords. They are often arranged in unusual progressions, and occasionally there is an unprepared jump to a distant key, but the austerity of dominant triads, used more often than dominant 7th chords, is especially refreshing. The treatment fits the text with singular appropriateness, since Miss Stein on her side used the simplest sorts of words. She seems to have felt that basic, everyday words had more meaning, and she got her effects by placing these homely elements in odd rhythmic patterns or sentences with unusual syntax, not by using a large or strange vocabulary. Mr. Thomson follows her lead in choosing and arranging his musical materials. On the few occasions he introduces dissonance, it is used with equally radical simplicity. For example, in the middle of Act I, Scene 5, the extremely dissonant contrasting note of a minor 9th (or its inversion) is introduced, and accompanies every one of the otherwise severely concordant triads for 82 measures. Only after this enormous preparation are there twelve measures of the bare 9th minus the rest of the chord. For the prelude to Act I, Scene 4, biting lines of close major triads are set against each other in the simplest of 1st and 2nd species polychordal counterpoint, with the scheme sustained throughout the 32 measures of the prelude. Aside from these two passages, both introduced for special purposes, there is practically no dissonance. Instead, Thomson's style grows out of the period of the book; his "source" is the late 19th-century American hymn—sometimes quoted or imitated literally, sometimes with variations. His setting of the words realizes with admirable skill their natural rhythm and inflection of speech. Much of it seems close to recitative, although it is heightened emotionally on occasions, and there are sections in simple lyric melody.

While *The Mother of Us All* is more likely to run on other parts of Broadway than the corner of 39th Street, it will certainly remain in the standard repertory of college opera groups, whose audiences the country over and over are larger and more constant than any grand opera company can boast. I predict that a new American opera tradition will be established around it, a tradition founded on wit and clarity, conducive to widespread amateur performances, not on elaborate dullness and one hearing at the Met.

Maurice Grosser has succeeded well in constructing a convincing and understandable production for Gertrude Stein's unusual book, a summary of which is given in scenario form in this publication, and Music Press has achieved a distinguished edition for the whole, hard to match in printing and format. The two editions, incidentally, were printed from the same plates, but the special edition is on better paper, is bound, signed by the composer, and is accompanied by three, loose photographs, made and signed by Carl Van Vechten, of Stein, Thomson, and two singers from the original cast, Dorothy Dow and William Horne.

Harry Partch

43-Tone Minstrelsy

THIS IS A RECORD OF incredible zeal in pursuit of a monodic (single-melody line) music, a music whose aim is declared to be a disclosure of "a manner of impressing the intangible beauty of tone into the vital power of the spoken word, without impairing either." Mr. Partch wishes to re-establish the art of minstrelsy, music by a single voice with slight instrumental support. Profoundly impressed by D. H. Lawrence's attacks on modern man's loss of the "deep procreative awareness," the "instinctive, blood awareness" of which we all heard so much in the twenties, Mr. Partch hopes for a music which is "frankly and extremely corporeal."

His desire to establish "a rigid contract between tone and word" led him to work out what he considers the natural scale (as opposed to the tempered scale we ordinarily use, which he objects to, violently). Partch's scale has forty-three tones to the octave, arranged to produce forty-four unequal intervals (instead of the twelve equal intervals usual in our Western music); it is arrived at by computations based on the simplest ratios of the overtone series. He has built numerous instruments of different types which are capable of playing in this scale: a large kithara (a kind of harp); a viola and a guitar, both with frets; an adapted melodeon, and others. Mr. Partch is right in saying that the ear is capable of far more accuracy and complexity of response than has yet been demanded of it in our culture. However, the music to prove that a scale of forty-

Harry Partch (1901-1974) was a testy, self-educated composer who built his own instruments and then wrote for them, largely in microtones. This review of Genesis of a Music *by Harry Partch (Madison: University of Wisconsin Press, 1949. 362 p.) is one of HC's few discussions of new microtonal music. It appeared originally in* The Saturday Review *XXXII/48 (26 Nov. 1949) p. 65.*

three tones to the octave is as valuable as twelve has yet to be written. Mr. Partch is so far the only composer to use this scale, and as his attention has been directed almost exclusively to problems of pitch, rhythmic interest is at a minimum in his compositions and consequently give an oddly formless and wandering impression.

What Mr. Partch seems not to realize is that however accurate an instrument may be persuaded to be, the pitch of the voice is actually always a curve, not a fixed point. It is in the nature of voices to vibrate through several pitches; well-trained ones do it less coarsely than others but they all do it, and no singer is capable of holding a single tone so steadily that it does not waver through more than one of the forty-three intervals of Mr. Partch's scale. Why he persists in believing that his intervals are vocally possible and that he uses them, while at the same time he declares with some vehemence that our ordinary scale is never sung in tune and that it is quite impossible to sing the "arbitrary" and "arithmetical" interval of a quarter tone (which gives us only twenty-four intervals to the octave), is a mystery.

The author's vehemence, a rather special use of familiar terms, and frequent excursions into unexpected byways make really difficult reading.

Roger Sessions

IN JANUARY, 1927, Roger Sessions, then a Prix de Rome fellow living in Italy, finished his first symphony. Two years later the full score was published by the Cos Cob Press. Not until November, 1949, however, did this work, called simply "Symphony," have its New York performance, with the Juilliard Symphony Orchestra under the direction of Jean Morel. One wonders why it had to wait so long.

Sessions's music has never had the performances it deserves. He is universally admired by his fellow composers and his name is known to everybody who follows serious American music. Students all study his *Black Maskers* score, for example, but the work is never performed. No recording exists of this or of any other major work by Roger Sessions. This neglect is the less deserved because the earlier works, on which his reputation is based, are in general live and lean. A radical change in style has certainly been observable in his music during the past twenty years, and he seems now to have acquired a reputation for ponderousness. This is due as much to the rather Olympian philosophy expounded in his writing and teaching as to a certain lack of spontaneity, spareness, and rhythmic drive in his more recent works—the Duo for violin and piano, for example.

Cowell was never particularly close to Sessions (1896-1985) but this early symphony appeals to him. The work discussed here, which, pace HC, *is not really very Stravinskian except perhaps in the first movement, is now known as "Symphony No. 1 in E Minor," not just as "Symphony." Its world première was conducted by Serge Koussevitsky with the Boston Symphony in 1927. It had been scheduled for a 1949 performance by the New York Philharmonic, but was instead performed by Juilliard in the performance Cowell describes. During 1997, Sessions's centennial year, it finally received its belated New York Philharmonic première.* The Musical Quarterly XXXVI/1 (Jan. 1950) pp. 94-98.

In any case, the Symphony of 1927 is witty, gay, and flowing. That some aspects of its style are related to early Stravinsky in no sense detracts from the pleasure of hearing it. Stravinsky created a style that shook the whole Western world of music with excitement, but he himself never fulfilled his obligation to build an adequate repertory in this style. One can hardly expect his imitators to do this: it must be done expertly, and it may be imagined that expert composers will prefer to develop their own styles. This is not to say that Sessions is a mere imitator. While the last movement of his Symphony sounds so much like Stravinsky that one is amazed, the first movement combines Stravinskian elements with more formal symphonic development, including even some of the polyphonic devices of Schoenberg.

The Symphony is in three movements. There is a simple general plan for the work. Each movement is a consistent unit. The first is loud and fast, with formal development. The second movement is in entire contrast: soft and slow, with straightforward melodic writing. The last movement is again almost wholly loud and fast, differing from the first in that it has short contrasting sections informally juxtaposed. Many percussion instruments are used, at times over-balancing delicate strands in smaller-toned melodic instruments. Otherwise, the instrumentation is well handled, in a conventionally brilliant and dramatic fashion.

The opening theme (Ex. 1) is divided into two parts, which are developed sometimes separately, sometimes together. The first half is based on leaps of fifths and thirds, suggesting a minor plus an augmented triad; the last part introduces a passage in conjunct

Example 1. Roger Sessions. Symphony (1927) (= Symphony No. 1 in E Minor). Copyright 1929 by Edward B. Marks Music Company. Copyright Renewed. Used by permission.

movement. The development makes modern use of such devices of melodic extension as inversion (Ex. 2) and retrogression (Ex. 3), as well as the more familiar repetitions and sequences. The polyphonic implication of this type of development is brought to a head in the recapitulation of the second half of the theme in the form of a fugue. Up to this point the development is consistent

Ex. 2 and 3. Roger Sessions. Symphony (1927) (= Symphony No. 1 in E Minor). Copyright 1929 by Edward B. Marks Music Company. Copyright Renewed. Used by permission.

and effective. But then there occurs what seems a dramatic mistake. One expects the fugue to gather force, and to end the movement. Instead of this, after the exposition some of the voices drop out, leaving a very thin texture. Other voices enter briefly—many of them, one after another—and then disappear, leaving a series of what one can only call holes in the fabric of the music. Finally the whole idea of a fugue is given up in favor of a homophonic recapitulation of the second theme. Since homophony, in the writer's opinion, never drives forward as hard as polyphony does, the end of the movement lacks the dramatically inevitable climax promised by the fugal exposition that was so effective at first.

Ex. 4. Roger Sessions. *Symphony* (1927) *(= Symphony No. 1 in E Minor).* Copyright 1929 by Edward B. Marks Music Company. Copyright Renewed. Used by permission.

The unique thing about this movement, however, is that this sort of polyphonic development, associated in modern music with the Viennese school, should be employed in a style whose use of short diatonic snatches of melody, of polytonal chord relationships (Ex. 4), and especially of rhythm, is so closely related to the style represented by Stravinsky.

Sessions has indicated in his score that eighth notes are to be strictly equal in value. Ex. 5 shows a rhythmic development of the conjunct melodic section of the first theme, using first four, then three, then two eighths, irregularly accented across the bar line. He also marks some 8/8 measures to be grouped 3 + 2 + 3, a rhumba-like rhythm; a 7/8 measure grouped in 3 + 2 + 2 sounds

Ex. 5. Roger Sessions. *Symphony* (1927) *(= Symphony No. 1 in E Minor)*. Copyright 1929 by Edward B. Marks Music Company. Copyright Renewed. Used by permission.

like a variation of the 8/8 rhythm. Such rhythms are discoverable in Stravinsky, but Sessions uses them more as one finds them in American Negro music, particularly the Afro-Cuban. At about the time Sessions was writing his Symphony, Aaron Copland made a study of the relation of such irregular accentings to jazz, a study the result of which was published in *Modern Music*. Colin McPhee, in an article called "Eight to the Bar," published also in *Modern Music*, showed a relationship between this type of music and certain kinds of metric organization to be found in the music of India, China, Indonesia, and Arabia. These are the same rhythms that Roy Harris came to feel were in *his* music the mark of the spirit of the pioneer West.

The tempo indications of the gravely slow second movement of Sessions's piece are puzzling. It is in 2/4 meter, but the marking is ♪ = 52. At this speed a quarter-note beat is impossible. As a matter of fact Morel marked the score ♪ = 104 and beat it in 16ths. The melody is simple and open, not suited to the double-fugue treatment to which it is subjected and undeserving of being drowned out at times by a brass *ostinato* which turns up as a counter-subject.

Another puzzling tempo indication comes later, with a shift which is marked:

Ex. 6. Roger Sessions. *Symphony* (1927) *(= Symphony No. 1 in E Minor)*. Copyright 1929 by Edward B. Marks Music Company. Copyright Renewed. Used by permission.

Again the conductor rescued the situation by red penciling the clarifying suggestion: ♪ = ♩. .

The last movement resembles the first superficially, and contains newly developed inverted forms of the opening theme, with passing notes (Ex. 7); but this development is more choppy and more homophonic. There is a series of short episodes with sudden changes of mood and pace, all blocked in mosaically.

Ex. 7. Roger Sessions. *Symphony* (1927) (= *Symphony No. 1 in E Minor*). Copyright 1929 by
Edward B. Marks Music Company. Copyright Renewed. Used by permission.

There is much irregular meter change—for instance, at one
point (score numbers 80-82), it changes every measure: 6/8, 7/8,
2/4, 5/8, 2/4, 5/8, 2/4, 7/8, 3/4. During this passage there are
8th notes and rests in irregular thrusts on repeated and slightly
varied dissonant chords, with running 16th notes in tiny repeated
diatonic motifs in pseudo-polyphonic movement against the 8ths.
This is all very like early Stravinsky. As the Symphony approaches
the end, the sections become shorter, more contrasted, more caus-
tically humorous in scoring, and the work finally winds up with
delicious hurry and bang.

That often-discussed but still elusive element in our musical
life, the standard American orchestra repertory, should certainly
include this symphony. Its dissonant gaiety and polytonal melodiousness would make it really popular with modern-music lovers.
In the 'twenties a dash of Schoenberg with one's Stravinsky was
too much to be borne. But today this seems an added attraction,
an enhancement of formal values that give solidity to a work of
great clarity and charm.

II

"Does music actually communicate something it is capable of
defining clearly?"

"It seems to me quite clear that music, far from being in any

---

Roger Sessions' early works, such as his music for Leonid Andreyev's The Black
Maskers, *show mastery, which is less true of later works, such as the Second String
Quartet (1951), which follows twelve-tone construction in a curious and informal
way. But Sessions was an important teacher at Princeton University for many years.
Cowell here takes to task Sessions' most important theoretical writings as verbose,
pretentious and commonplace. This review of* The Musical Experience of Composer, Performer, Listener, *by Roger Sessions [Princeton, N.J.: Princeton University Press, 1950. (127 p., music)], which makes its criticism without rancor,
appeared in* Notes *VIII/1 (Dec. 1950) pp. 168-169.*

sense vague or imprecise, is within its own sphere the most precise possible language," says Roger Sessions, taking about 40,000 words to indicate that words are less satisfactory as a means of speaking about music than the material of music itself. He makes his point; for after reading the book, in spite of its clarifying discussion of countless points concerning musical philosophy, one still feels that Sessions' views about music are best exemplified in his own fine symphonies. The points of philosophy so warmly and tellingly set forth in the symphonies are, nevertheless, treated well enough with words by Sessions, who writes in as clear a style as is consistent with the need for precision. This need, however, does often drive him into a certain verbal ponderousness.

Next to a line of notation, in Japanese *shakuhachi* (vertical flute) music, are written down the thoughts one is to think as one plays the instrument. In Sessions' book one finds the thoughts one is to think and the philosophies one is to keep in mind as one composes, performs, or listens to music. That Sessions is more than a little inclined to believe his own ideas on music to be the only good ones, and that he would be very condescending toward any other views, is disguised by a friendly, disarming manner in presenting his thoughts—thoughts which always seem convincing, reasonable, and simple as they are stated. The author crystallizes in words a large number of rather vague feelings about music which are very commonly felt by those sensitive to it. These ideas or feelings are shared by so large a group, in fact, that one might say Sessions' views are often a formulization of a rather conventional philosophical approach to the functions of composer, performer, and listener. At the same time, this commonly-shared philosophy has not before been as clearly expressed in print.

Sessions often does not realize that he is expressing widely-held views. He feels quite daring, for example, in suggesting that music itself is a precise language. Yet I find that when I express the somewhat opposite view that Western music rarely has meaning, in the sense that words do, this statement meets almost universal opposition. Many of Sessions' statements, then, seem axiomatic, even when he introduces them as though they were quite controversial. Actually, if one tries out the plan of thinking, each time Sessions makes a point, what the reverse of it would be, one discovers a rather logical unconventional philosophy—a philosophy deeply disturbing to most people, as Sessions' is not; a philosophy indeed often put forth in some musically radical circles. One of these points, opposed to that of Sessions, is the belief that music is based on mathematical relationships and on the physical nature of sound.

There is interest in hearing a composer's own concept of how a composer should work: "It is characteristic...of the true composer that his music, while he is composing it, is constantly in his mind, always and everywhere, and that it is never a matter simply of a task accomplished during working hours, however regular these may be." Sessions further says: "While the relationship of the composer to music is a simple, direct, and primary one, that of the performer is already complex and even problematical." "If this role of the performer is a complex one, what shall we say of the listener?... By the listener I do not mean the person who simply hears music.... To listen implies...a real participation, a real response, a real sharing in the work of the composer and of the performer...." On the subject of musical materials, Sessions believes that "The basic ingredient of music is not so much sound as movement," and he later writes that "I envisage harmony as primarily a coordinative element, and not, like rhythm and melody, an impulsive one." From these points of departure, Sessions plunges fearlessly into discussions of some of the most difficult subjects in esthetic philosophy: the relations of feelings and thoughts, of the senses and of perception of musical art, of music to words or extra-musical "programs," and so on.

The author's presentation of his ideas is not always a model of consistency. One reads at one spot that musical notation is well-nigh perfect, capable of setting down the subtlest ideas, and at another that notation is inexact. Once it is said that composers set down all the musical symbols needed by performers; elsewhere it is noted with more truth that composers are often careless and inaccurate in the use of such symbols. These tiny inconsistencies, however, do not prevent the book from being the best presentation there is of the most familiar philosophies and feelings of the finest musicians of this period. No one interested in music will fail to gain a better understanding of musical esthetics through reading

Sessions' clear and feelingful statements, whether they simply express a familiar idea well ("'Structure' and 'passion' are not in any sense mutually exclusive—one may, when the occasion demands, be the very essence of the other") or whether they suggest something new in terminology ("'Atonality' implies the denial of tonality; but the facts, as I have tried to show, represent a tonal supersaturation. One could rather speak, then, of supersaturated tonality, and possibly speak of 'post-tonal' rather than 'a-tonal' music").

Altogether, many people will be interested in reading this book, even those who qualify neither as composer, performer, nor listener. There is little doubt, with the present differential between musical literacy and verbal literacy, that Sessions' book will sell more copies than the scores of his symphonies, even though the language of the latter may be a more precise one.

Lou Harrison

Sᴇᴠᴇʀᴀʟ ɴᴇᴡ ᴡᴏʀᴋs ʙʏ Lou Harrison have been performed during the past quarter. Of the many composers in their late twenties and early thirties who were presented this season by the Composers' Forum, he seems to have made the most profound impression. Harrison, in common with many men about his age in this country, incorporates elements of both diatonic and chromatic schools into his music. Instead of trying to integrate these elements into a single fabric, as is more usual at the moment, Harrison uses them as contrasting material for different movements. The first movement of his Suite No. 2 (Ex. 1) is diatonic and simple in out-line, with a few tonal dissonances in keeping with the quintal coun-terpoint. The second movement, on the other hand (Ex. 2), is atonal in nature. All twelve tones of the chromatic scale are to be found in the first sixteen tones of the opening melody. The third and last movement consists of a fairly conventional fugue.

Lou Harrison. Suite No. 2. © 1949 Merrymount Music Press. Used by permission.

Lou Harrison's Suite No. 2, Two Pastorales, and Solstice, *as reviewed in* The Musical Quarterly *XXXVI/1 (Jul. 1950) pp. 451-452. Cowell was an early admirer of Lou Harrison (1917-), not only of his percussion music but of his tonal music as well.*

There is a strong tendency in much of Harrison's recent music to employ elements drawn from styles other than those of Western European art music of the last four or five centuries. This tendency is shown for example in his *Two Pastorals,* where a drone tone is used and the diatonic melodies are tetrachordal in nature. Such elements are handled so smoothly that one is not particularly aware of them. In *Solstice,* a half-hour dance drama presented during the past quarter, the form is based on the successive use of five Oriental-sounding scales (Ex. 3).

Ex. 3. Chart of scales from Lou Harrison, Suite No. 2. © 1949 Merrymount Music Press. Used by permission.

The scales are used, however, not as exotic impressions but as necessary basic materials. The music is charming and varied, and the suggestion of Eastern materials is woven into a fabric related to the Occidental medieval as well as the Occidental modern styles...

II
"Drums Along the Pacific"

DURING THE LAST TWO YEARS an extraordinary interest in percussion music has developed on the Pacific coast. In Seattle, San Francisco, Oakland and Los Angeles, orchestras have been formed to play music for percussion instruments alone. They are directed chiefly by two young Western composers, John Cage and Lou Harrison, who have concocted innumerable creations for these instruments, and have induced others like Ray Green of San Francisco, Gerald Strang of Long Beach, and J. M. Beyer, formerly of New York, to write for them. In Cuba they found leading composers who had not only a vivid liking, but works already made for percussion—José Ardevol, Alejandro Caturla and Amadeo

This article appeared in Modern Music *XVIII/1 (Nov.-Dec. 1940) pp. 46-49. It presents Harrison and Cage as pioneers, exploring the frontiers of rhythm and percussive tone-qualities. See also Cowell's "The Joys of Noise" (1929), in Part Six.*

Roldan. Music by all these men has been rehearsed regularly in the various percussion orchestral groups, who thus acquire an ability to render intricate rhythms far beyond the capacity of professional symphony men, and to control countless gradations of tone-quality, many hitherto unsuspected. In 1939 the groups gave small demonstrations through the West, chiefly in the colleges. This year Seattle came down and joined San Francisco; and in July, Cage and Harrison combined with William Russell, a seasoned percussion performer apt to turn up anywhere from New York to China, to give a large concert at Mills College, Oakland. Seventeen "percussors" made up the orchestra. They used the following instruments: *drums*—one snare, two bass, five black Chinese tomtoms, five small painted Chinese tomtoms, one pair of bongos; *wood*: eight Chinese wood-blocks, six dragon's mouths (temple blocks), four pair of claves; *metal*: one mariembula, two pair of finger cymbals, one pair of crash cymbals, one Turkish cymbal, four Chinese cymbals, one pair of jazz cymbals, five gongs, one tamtam, one Chinese painted gong, three Japanese temple gongs, five Japanese cup gongs, thirteen oxen bells, one set of orchestra bells, twelve cow bells, one dinner bell, one trolling bell, one turkey bell, one small Chinese bell, three loose sleigh bells, four triangles, three brake drums, eight strap irons, one pipe, three discs, ten thunder sheets, one wash tub, one washboard set; *rattles*: one quijada (jawbone), four pair of maracas, one Indo-Chinese rattle, one Northwestern Indian rattle, one sistrum, one tambourine, one wind bell; *miscellaneous*: one tortoise shell, one guiro, four rice bowls, three Mexican clay bowls, four slide whistles, one conch shell, one lion's roar, one string drum, one slap-stick, one piano, one xylophone, and about eighty beaters of all sorts.

It is irrelevant, for the moment, to evaluate the compositions performed as good or bad, important or unimportant. Let it be sufficient to note that all were serious attempts showing considerable variety, and that musical form was present and recognizable.

Now percussion alone as music is of course no new idea. The pre-war Italian futurists gave the world what were then considered earsplitting demonstrations. They also issued manifestos on how important it all was. Few of us today have heard any of the results of that effort; it seems to have consisted more of talk than action.

From report the music was vague in form, unbalanced in sonority. Only one composer can be said to have carried these experiments forward. Edgar Varèse combined in his music an over-weight of percussion instruments with a few other orchestral ones, the latter used explosively rather than melodically. By gradual reduction of the non-percussive elements he came finally to *Ionization*, a work composed nearly ten years ago for forty-one percussion instruments and sirens. It was received with less disfavor by the public than any previous exclusively percussion music and it made a genuine impression among musicians. Earlier percussion efforts had met grim resistance and adverse criticism. Today, Percy Grainger's *In a Nutshell* suite is generally well-liked, its unusual percussion section in the orchestra calls for no special comment. But on December 19, 1916, the critic of the *San Francisco Chronicle*, wrote: "Much of the Pastoral in Grainger's *In a Nutshell* suite filled this hearer with a wild longing to flee the place. I could not relate the din to anything within the realm of the art of music. The discordant shriekings were punctuated by rhythmical whacks on many kinds of drums and other instruments beaten with a stick, and a wail, a caterwaul, a helpless moaning howl was the way it sounded to these ears. It was as though anarchy were clamoring for musical expression or hideous madness shrieking for a transcription of its frenzies."

Percussion music is not all alike, nor is it all related to one school of music. The approach of the Italian futurists was in essence artificial, the basic idea being to create, ready-made and without gradual development, or experience with the instruments, a highly complex and sophisticated art-form. Varèse's music was the culmination of this tendency. Grainger used percussion as an incident, to enhance and punctuate his orchestration. The Cuban composers create from direct experience; they are in close contact with the native Afro-Cuban music which is largely based on enticing primitive percussion rhythms. Our newest Pacific coast group—Cage, Green, Harrison and Strang—have also developed their interest naturally, as composers for the modern concert dance. In that field percussion instruments are essential as aids in defining rhythmic change. All dance is of course dependent on a well-defined beat; when the beat shifts constantly, as in much of modern dancing, it is vitalizing to have the changes sharply indicated on percussion instruments. Composers who work with dancers come to know percussion instruments and their possibilities; daily association with the problem of rhythm forms their background. Having mastered the gamut of the instruments used in the studios, they very naturally proceed to compose for them works in larger forms, with enough tone-qualities and rhythms to achieve independent musical compositions.

Potentially rhythm and tone-quality are as important as melody and harmony, but the former are underdeveloped in our music. The full possibilities of percussion, whose accepted role is to provide unimportant splashes of color, have hardly been tapped in our symphonic literature. The work of a young, talented and well-trained group experimenting with rhythm and percussive tone-qualities, may lead to their development as genuine structural materials to create differentiated outlines and combinations. It is encouraging too that the interest of these men is not the result of an abstract theory, but has grown quite naturally out of their own working musical environment. Some of their efforts already prove exciting to audiences, some seem boring. The question is raised why the group should deliberately exclude melodic instruments. To which the answer is simply that these have never been present. As a matter of judgment why is it more reprehensible to write for four percussion instruments than for two violins, viola and 'cello? The string quartet may at times be quite boring as a combination of instruments. Percussion alone may prove monotonous, but it is less apt to, because it is still in a state of experiment. New tones and rhythms are constantly being discovered. When the young experimenters have succeeded in fully exploring the field, there will remain the untried possibilities of combining these results with the better-known resources of the full orchestra.

John Cage

WHEN I FIRST MET John Cage about 1932 he was writing strange little piano pieces with an unusual sense of the sound-interest created by odd tonal combinations. Then as now the music showed little desire to move about actively; it rather depended on very slight and subtle changes for its elaboration. Influences to which he subjected himself in the mid-thirties enlarged and enriched without changing this orientation. He studied dissonant counterpoint and composition with me for a season in California, and when he went to New York to prepare with Adolph Weiss for lessons with Schoenberg, he continued intensive explorations of his own into rhythmic form and percussion music, and the musical systems of other peoples, particularly in the Orient, in my classes at the New School. Later he studied with Schoenberg, who felt that Cage was more interested in his philosophy than in acquiring his techniques. Since then Cage has written a great deal for the dance, and he has organized percussion orchestras to play music especially composed by himself and other people. Some of his more recent music uses conventional instrumentation for string quartet and for small orchestra. Concerts of his music are a regular feature of the season in New York and, for the past several years, in Paris also, where his music has been extravagantly admired.

This review of "John Cage and his circle" appeared in The Musical Quarterly *XXXVIII/1 (Jan. 1952) pp. 123-134. It is the earliest account we know of the aleatoric compositions (music using chance) of John Cage (1912-1992), a fine overview at a time when most critics were dismissing Cage as a charlatan. The mention of "events" is interesting, and though he attributes the concept to Cage, Cowell used the term frequently in his classes. As Cage was one of his students, it wound not be unreasonable to speculate that Cowell was the source of this term.*

To John Cage, a brief series of sounds, or even a single combination of them, has come to seem complete in itself, and to constitute an audible "event." But he does not use the conventional organization of music, in which such events are related through planned rhythmic, melodic, and harmonic succession to produce what we are accustomed to consider an organic musical development. Instead, since Cage conceives each musical "event" to be an entity in itself that does not require completion, he simply places them one after another and sees them as being related through their co-existence in space, where they are set in a planned order of time. Each "event" is an aggregate of materials of sound that cohere, making a tiny world of their own, much as physical elements find themselves joined together in a meteorite. A work of Cage's, therefore, might well be likened to a shower of meteors of sound.

Cage's pieces for what he calls the "prepared piano" offer an array of tightly organized little sounds of many colors. They are played on an ordinary grand piano whose strings have been muted at various specified points with bits of wood, rubber, metal, or glass. These mutes produce a variety of timbres whose pitch and tone quality are entirely altered from those of the unmuted strings. Each piece may have its own recipe for the arrangement of the altered sounds, a kind of tone-row of timbres. They suggest the sound of the gamelan or the jalatarang, with some delicate buzzes, clacks, hums, and sometimes an unaltered tone as well. The player is guided by a piano score that is read and played entirely conventionally but produces, of course, sounds entirely different from those suggested to the eye, in accordance with the mechanical preparation for the particular piece.

In spite of his idea of the separateness of musical "events," Cage has always had an intense interest in rhythmic structure, in absolute time-values, and in the dynamics of sound and silence. His wide palette of minuscule timbres, used in what may be thought of as melodic succession, is made rhythmical by the recurrence of such successions. This is the most noticeable aspect of Cage's music on first hearing. What is less obvious is that for many years his works' larger rhythmical forms have been based on one or another set division of absolute time, such as a unit of sixty seconds. For example, a five-minute work may be divided into five sections of one minute each, and each of these one-minute sections may then be divided into five phrases of twelve seconds each. The tempo may be varied by the performer in accordance with any scheme of his own, just so the large units of the work take exactly the specified number of seconds, no more and no less. This basis for establishing form can be found in Cage's prepared piano music, in the piece for twelve radios, and in much of his other music as well.

Enough amused curiosity to overflow McMillin Theater at Columbia University was aroused when the first performance of John Cage's *Imaginary Landscape,* a composition for twelve radios, took place last spring. This was not a broadcast of Cage's music played at and transmitted from one, or from twelve, radio stations. Twelve radios were, instead, to be treated like musical instruments and played in concert. How does one turn a radio into a musical instrument? This was not entirely clear in advance, so *avant-garde* New York appeared in person to find out.

On the stage were the twelve radios, with two players at each, and the composer-conductor—twenty-five people in all. The score calls for one performer to manipulate the dial that selects the various stations desired by the composer to be heard in the course of the work, and another performer for the dial that regulates the dynamics. The composer's directions for tuning the various stations in and out use notes and rests; the wavelength for each station is indicated in kilocycles. Therefore if the piece is played in New York City, one set of stations will be drawn upon; if in Denver, another set of stations, the ones using the same wave-lengths in that locality, will be heard. The player who regulates the dynamics follows indications in the score that correspond to numbers along the dial from zero up, producing a dynamic range from barest whisper to a full *fortissimo*. Like a choice of wave-lengths, the dynamics have definite rhythmic indications.

This is a music in which some elements customarily imprecise, such as dynamics and rubato, and everything on which form depends, are indicated with the greatest exactness. Melodic lines, harmonies, and instrumentation, which we have come to expect the composer to interest himself in controlling precisely, are on the other hand entirely determined by the accident of radio station programming.

At the actual performance of *Imaginary Landscape* the hour was later than anticipated before the work's turn came on the program, so that the "instruments" were unable to capture programs diversified enough to present a really interesting specific result. Members of the performing group said that some of the rehearsals captured much more exciting ingredients for the montage, and expressed regret that a recording of one or two of the practice sessions was not played at the concert instead. Cage's own attitude about this was one of comparative indifference, since he believes the concept to be more interesting than the result of any single performance. One aspect of the work's failure to communicate must be laid frankly at the composer's door: his ever-present interest in the most delicately minute distinctions and gradations led him to admit too many low amplitude dynamics, through setting their range too low to begin with, so that many parts could not be heard at all as far away as the audience.

The dynamics of silence, a relativity of silence as well as of sound, expressed by rests and extreme *pianissimi,* is a major concern in most of Cage's music. This feeling for the rhythmical pregnancy of silence seems an ultimate sophistication. In primitive music, beats must always be actually sounded; as music becomes more elaborately cultivated there are more and more places in which the beat, once established, may be taken for granted. Sometimes in the improvisatory jam sessions of jazz players, there will be, by agreement, at fixed intervals in the music, a sudden two-measure silence, after which everyone comes in full tilt with gusto. Obviously the exact duration of two measures and their division into beats must be forcefully present in the minds of the performers during that silence. Cage enjoys presenting longer and more complex silences in the course of his works. Sometimes he leads one toward absolute silence by increasingly greater degrees of softness until one can hardly tell whether one is really hearing anything or not.

As this article was being written, George Antheil called my attention to the score of his *Ballet mécanique,* which has a section in which silent measures of 8/8 appear periodically. This was written in 1924, and its generative ideas derived from long sessions spent with George Herzog in Berlin, listening to recordings of the music of India, China, and more primitive cultures. Around this time Antheil developed an interest in the time-space concept and music in absolute time; Ezra Pound's book on Antheil gives an account of these theories.[1]

In Cage's recent (fall 1951) *Music of Changes,* for piano solo, uses this instrument without special "preparation" for the first time in many years. He does not abandon his predilection for extraordinary sound, for at almost no point does the piano sound as one expects. Rather he seems now to be interested in discovering how nearly like a prepared piano he can make an unprepared piano sound, by means of special tone combinations, timbres, and dynamics. An original feature is that highly controlled changes of tempo are used to establish the rhythmic structure. One starts at a given metronome mark (quarter note = 69), then accelerates for 3 measures to quarter = 176, then retards for 5 measures to quarter= 100 for 13½ measures, then retards 5 measures to quarter = 58, and so on. The form is thus presented in terms of a sliding scale of tempos rather than by an arrangement of fixed numbers of measures to constitute phrases, sentences, and sections. Note durations, often complex, are measured horizontally with 2½ centimeters to equal a dotted quarter note. Measurements are made from one note-stem to another. Precisely noted dynamic extremes (*pppp* and *ffff* are sometimes next to each other in eighth notes) help to make *Music of Changes* an unprecedented experience in sound.

If these pieces by a single composer were the only ones of the sort to appear now, interest in them might be more casual. They are, however, examples of a new approach to composition that has drawn a number of adherents, all of them younger men who are friends or students of Cage; several of them have had works performed in New York recently. The compositions of Christian Wolff, Morton Feldman, Pierre Boulez, and John Cage vary widely in style, but a common philosophy unites them: a concentration upon unfamiliar relationships of space and time, and sound and silence, rather than on new melodies and chords, and a conviction that all musical relationships, whether arrived at by chance or by design, have potential value and are worth examination. They all believe there should be more room in music for improvisatory factors, for the elements of casual choice and chance.

In their hands, however, chance is called upon to operate systematically. Cage has often used the *I Ching*, an old Chinese method

Ex. 1. John Cage. *Imaginary Landscape.* © 1960.
Used by permission of C. F. Peters Corporation on behalf of Henmar Press Inc.

of throwing coins or marked sticks for chance numbers, like our use of dice.[2] Cage's method of employing the *I Ching* to ensure that his compositions are "free of individual taste and memory in their order of events" is based on a complicated system of charts. These govern "superpositions" (the number of events happening at once during a given structural space), tempos, durations, sounds, and dynamics; and all the charts are derived from tosses of the coins.

The concrete operation to produce the *Imaginary Landscape* for twelve radios proceeded more or less as follows: "The first tossing related to superposition and tempo of a certain tuning and the second tossing related to structure; the third tossing to duration (whether sound or silence) and finally dynamics." The actual tossings brought a form represented by 8 plus 4 plus 15, repeated 25 times. Dynamics ranging from *ppppp* to *sffff* are selected by further tossings, and applied to the station-selecting (wave-length tuning) dial of the radio (upper numbers in Ex. 1) and the dial controlling dynamic amplitudes (lower numbers in Ex. 1). Because the figures obtained in this way do not always correspond to the center of the band for any given station, the station might happen to be heard rather vaguely, from the peripheral point along the dial that was established by the tossing. Similarly the amplitude numbers are sometimes too low for audibility. Cage however insists on consistency in allowing the operation of chance, and sticks faithfully to its decisions. Thus chance determines whether things remain static or change, what type of change is to occur, whether there is an event or a silence, whether a given radio will play or not, whether the dynamics will vary or remain constant; and if they change, which of the dynamics will apply. And chance, operating in another way, is also responsible, of course, for what will be heard on the twelve radios. No one can say in advance what tunes, rhythms, chords, timbres, or other simultaneous elements of the heterophony will be contributed to any given performance. All one can be sure of is that they will never be twice alike.

The station selection and dynamic structure, once tossed for, are of course retained; and this constitutes the composition, if composition it be.

Various combinations of chance and choice, pre-established or improvised, are not without respectable musical precedent, in the tala and raga systems of India, and possibly, on a less serious plane, in the music of Mozart. Mozart is said to have composed a set of contra-dances in which dice are to be thrown to determine the order in which the measures are to appear. Ex. 2a shows Mozart's chart, and Ex. 2b the directions for using it.[3] However, Mozart eliminated many of the hazards accepted by Cage, for he composed and set down all the measures that might be called for by the dice; a typical collection of opening measures for the first

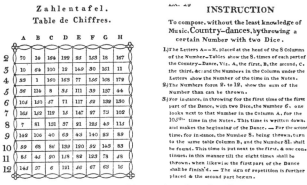

Ex. 2a and 2b. Mozart's chart and instructions for using dice to compose waltzes.

measures for the first cast, a typical set of second measures for the second cast, and so on. Otto Luening has an early work in which there is a plan for partly controlled improvisation; Charles Ives wants performers to feel free to make certain kinds of changes in his music, under some circumstances.

Ex. 3 shows the opening of Morton Feldman's *Intersection #3*, for strings, woodwinds, and solo 'cello. It is written on coordinate paper, the squares taken horizontally representing a time-unit of M.M.=72.

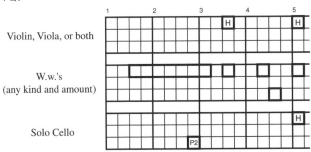

Ex. 3. Morton Feldman. *Intersection #3.* © 1962. Used by permission of C. F. Peters Corp.

Vertically, each of the three squares represents a general pitch level: low, medium, and high. Each instrument comes in when its part has a blocked-in square; it may enter at any time during the period represented by the square, but once it has entered, the tone or tones must remain until the blocked-in square ends. Sometimes the composer indicates by an H that he wishes harmony, or by Pz that a pizzicato tone would be appreciated. But the actual pitches and their duration are entirely left to the players in all other respects. So a conservative group will employ familiar types of sound, and some "modernists" might employ the less familiar. This is a plan for the control of improvisation and the music will of course never sound twice alike. Its success depends upon what the players contribute.

I should like to follow the above strictly lay account with Mr. Feldman's own statement about his set of pieces:[4]

> My Projections and Intersections is a weight either reminiscent or discovered. Weight for me does not have its source in the realm of dynamics or tensions, but rather resulting from a visual-aural response to sound as an image gone inward creating a general synthesis. Weight involves the finding of a pulse which allows for a natural fluidity. Discovered weight implies discovered balance. Discovered balance implies discovered movement from this pulse. The notation is presented graphically where each box is a clock time duration. What is desired in the execution is a pure non-vibrating tone.

Ex. 4 shows the first four measures of a trio for flute, clarinet, and violin by Christian Wolff. Only three different tones are used.

Ex. 4. Christian Wolff. *Serenade.* © 1963. Used by permission of C. F. Peters Corporation.

No two measures are alike; the changes are rung on the possible combinations of three tones on three instruments, in various rhythms. Listening becomes a reaction to the intricacies of these variations. An interest in exploring all the possibilities of certain musical materials handled within strict limits is characteristic of the thinking of this entire group of composers.

It will be observed that Wolff's concept of variability in the order of measures is especially close to that of the coin tossers.

Pierre Boulez, a young Frenchman whose Second [Piano] Sonata was played in New York at a League of Composers concert not long ago, and John Cage met in Paris, exchanged ideas, and have since spent much time together. Cage says: "Boulez influenced me with his concept of mobility; my influence on him is that he accepts my idea of aggregates." An aggregate in Cage's sense is the relationship of miscellaneous and apparently disparate objects established by their juxtaposition in space, as furniture and other objects in a room are related by their simultaneous presence there. Similarly, different sorts of musical media may be conceived as constituting an aggregate, and so used as a unit of building material for the creation of musical forms.

Boulez deals with what he calls the drama of the contrast between the thematic (tone relations derived in a rather distant fashion from the twelve-tone row) and the athematic (rhythmic essence). A basic rhythmic unit he calls a cellule; this consists of some related time values (a quarter-note plus an eighth-note, for instance). Each of these time elements may be "developed" by subdivision, the quarter-note then becoming two-eighths, or a triplet, or four-sixteenths, and so on. Boulez's rhythmic process has been described by a nonbeliever as "dividing two rhythmic units into as many small notes as possible, tossing the notes into the air, then taking them the way they light and calling it a composition." On the other hand, recent Paris performances of music by Boulez have had sufficient impact to generate comment circulated in this country by the big press services.

Boulez's main investigations have been into extensions of the twelve-tone row idea. By changing the row numbers according to his plan, he may obtain a complete transposition (Ex. 5); and for formal unity he applies his row to dynamics (Ex. 6), stresses (Ex. 7), duration (Ex. 8), and rhythmic figures (cellules) (Ex. 9).[5]

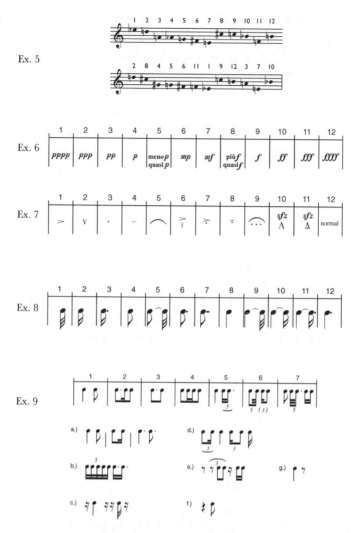

Ex. 5

Ex. 6

Ex. 7

Ex. 8

Ex. 9

John Cage speaks for all these young men when he voices enthusiasm over freeing musical continuity from "individual taste and
memory," and from "the literature and traditions of the art." It is
in the accomplishment of perfection along these severely logical if
hitherto uncharted, unaccustomed paths that Cage and his friends
employ their creative fervor, even in the case of the more subjective Feldman. Shocking as it may seem to their elders, it is certainly true that for these young men no fact or set of factual aggregates is incapable of giving esthetic pleasure under some circumstances.

However, it is evident that much more remains to be done in this direction, for in spite of his best efforts to the contrary, Cage has not succeeded in eliminating his highly refined and individual taste from the music derived from the *I Ching*. Unfortunately, from the point of view of this group of composers, no order of tossings can give anything more than a variety of arrangements of elements subjectively chosen to operate upon.

Since it can be shown that Cage and his friends have come together at one time in one room, the group may be considered an aggregate. So we may toss to decide whether the group is to change or to remain the same, and toss again to decide whether the esthetic pleasure to be derived from the work of its members is to play the role of silence or of an event in sound.

And if one must decide whether genuine value is, or is not, to be found in this music, a last throw of the coins of *I Ching* will have to determine that for us too.

1. *George Antheil and the Theory of Harmony,* Paris, 1925. See also Antheil's discussions of time-space and absolute time in music in *De Stijl* (Rotterdam, 1924-25), *Transition* (Paris, 1925), and the *Little Review* (1925).

2. See *I Ching, Book of Changes,* translated from the Chinese by Richard Wilhelm and from the German by Cary Baynes. "Bollingen Series XIX," [New York:] Pantheon Books, 1950. [The discussion of Cage which follows is based on Cage's discussion in *trans/formation: a world review* I/3 (1952) pp. 171-172.—DH].

3. Mozart's account was all but unknown at the time Cowell wrote this (1952) although today (1996) on the internet there are at least two different web sites which cover it. Also, Mozart's proposal was far from new: Haydn frequently composed started his melodies with a flip of coins, and there is an account of composition with dice in a standard lutenist's work of the early seventeenth century by Pedro (or Pietro) Cerone of Naples, *El Melopeo y Maestro: Tractado de Musica Theorica y Pratica...* (2 v. "Biblioteca Musica Bononiensis" 25. 1613: Bologna: Forni Editore, 1969" vol. 2 p. 1124).—DH.

4. A very similar but slightly longer statement by Feldman appeared at about this time on page 168 of the issue of *trans/formation* 3 mentioned in footnote 2. There too Feldman links his *Projections* and *Intersections* series together. Perhaps Cowell picked up on the statement from *trans/formation* and asked for an abbreviated version. Neither is in the collected essays of Morton Feldman, *Morton Feldman Essays* (Cologne: Beginner Press, 1985). Also, Cowell calls the piece which follows, by Christian Wolff, "Trio," but, per a letter to myself from Christian Wolff dated August 31, 1996, it is actually "Serenade," now published by C. F. Peters.—DH.

5. Cowell's charts of Boulez materials are based on Boulez's notes in *trans/formation* 2 pp. 168-171. These appear to have been edited for publication by John Cage.—DH.

6. That is, in this instance, music in which the characteristic rhythmic combinations of second, third and fourth species counterpoint are used simultaneously.—DH.

Ferruccio Busoni

F ERRUCCIO BUSONI WAS A PERSON of extraordinary impact,
better known in the United States for his high rank among the
world's great pianists than for the music he wrote. His philosophy
and training were major factors in the development of Dimitri
Mitropoulos, and so it is appropriate that Mitropoulos should give
us the first performance of one of Busoni's principal works—his
comic opera *Arlecchino*.

Busoni has never established for himself a major position as a
composer, although his work is idolized by a group of special ad-
mirers that includes many famous people. He was unexpectedly
receptive to new influences in music, and it was very shortly after
Schoenberg wrote Opus 11 that Busoni undertook to call attention to the then unpopular music by making a piano version of his
own—a heartwarming enterprise in spite of the fact that a piano
arrangement of a work originally written for piano seems a very
strange idea.

Arlecchino is surprising in that the music sometimes goes beyond
Richard Strauss in the direction of Berg, and surprising again in
that it so often falls back on commonplace ideas. The style, sometimes heavy, dissonant, and rather bombastic, and at other times
possessed of a rather obviously derived Mozartean clarity, is a kind
of missing link between *Rosenkavalier* and *Lulu*. Written between
1912 and 1916, it is the only opera to betray knowledge of
Schoenberg's early style before *Wozzeck*—a knowledge that in
Arlecchino is however displayed sparingly and rather humorously.
The music is subject to chameleon-like change: atonal chromatic

*Ferruccio Busoni (1866-1924) was, among other things, Varèse's teacher. Cowell
knew him in Berlin. This review was appended to the piece on Cage in* The Musical Quarterly *XXXVIII/1 (Jan. 1952).*

dissonance is neighbor to polytonal melody; there is speech, *Sprechstimme,* and song (but no conventional recitative). When some lush post-Wagnerianism and some crisp eighteenth-century music are added, the general effect is eclectic rather than integrated, and no sense of an overall style plan emerges. The melodies are vocal and understandable, and the work is far from dull. But the mixture of several styles, with a large orchestra and a small cast, makes it rather unwieldy and awkward.

The staging was original and amusing. The orchestra was deliberately kept on stage as part of the *mise-en-scène,* and the singers, in costume, entered from all four sides: from backstage, from either wing, and from the aisles or the auditorium among the audience. Lines for their movement penetrated the orchestra in all directions, with enough space in the center near Mitropoulos so that the ladies could act coquettish and the men could draw swords. The staid New York Philharmonic-Symphony Orchestra even put up with a (fake) donkey marching about among its members. The action was carried much farther than in Mitropoulos's previous operatic ventures, such as *Wozzeck* last season, and was correspondingly enlivening. I, for one, did not in the least miss the customary stage trappings, so artificial and so expensive.

For an opera in which music is the primary consideration, this sort of concert presentation, to which costumes and some movement are added, is perfectly adequate, and certainly an attractive change. Obviously a piece like [Menotti's] *The Consul,* which relies primarily on the play and its staging, and in which music plays a role secondary to the drama and the characterization, would be less satisfactory done in this manner.

Arlecchino has vitality, and because of its prophetic position it is a work of some historical significance, without being anything one is anxious to hear often. It is important to hear such music from time to time, and we are grateful and indebted to the conductor and the musicians.

Igor Stravinsky

IGOR STRAVINSKY's *Cantata* for soprano, tenor, female chorus, and a small instrumental ensemble has just been given its first performance anywhere. This is a setting of anonymous 16th-century English words, and it is a serene, dignified, simply wrought work, immediately under standable in form. It is also an excellent example of what one may expect to find in Stravinsky's recent music.

Stravinsky is a composer whose personal way of doing things is always a powerful factor in any composition. This is true of many composers—Chopin, for example, developed a very personal style, in which the same musical mannerisms recur and are easily identified. Stravinsky, however, has written in many different styles; certainly each of his early major works has a character of its own, deliberately different from that of any other, and at the same time unmistakably the work of Stravinsky's hand. This went on into what has been called his "neo-Classical" period. Here again he concerned himself not with one style alone, but with many—this time virtually every European style, in fact, writing now like this individual, now like that one: Perotin, Des Prez, Lasso, Handel, Weber, Tchaikovsky, Mussorgsky, Debussy—one can even find some neo-early Stravinsky.

Later, however, Stravinsky arrived at a single style that he marked for his own and that, with minor differences, remains identifiably the same. It is a style rooted, in the main, in a feeling for late 15th- and early 16th-century practices. Traces of his earlier explorations may be detected here and there, in elements drawn

While Cowell despised neoclassicism in general, he admired the strong style of Igor Stravinsky (1882-1971), as evidenced by this review of his Cantata (1952). Incidentally, the cantata is based on fifteenth-century texts, not sixteenth-century ones, as Cowell asserts. Musical Quarterly *XXXIX/2 (Apr. 1953) pp. 251-255.*

from several other periods, but they are not of major significance; such combinations might easily seem in painfully bad taste, but Stravinsky manages to make them sound perfectly natural, for they are always exquisitely integrated.

The new *Cantata* is a fine example of this comparatively recent style. It is quite simple in outline. It follows the plan of a rondo, although, in keeping with the old practices, the material is more polyphonic than that of the rondos to which we are accustomed. The first section—an instrumental introduction followed by an accompanied chorus—appears four times without change (*Versus I, II, III, IV*). A Ricercar for soprano appears between *Versus I* and *Versus II;* a second Ricercar, for tenor, is interpolated between *Versus II* and *Versus III* This employs a carefully marked "cantus cancrizans" (Ex. 1). The retrograde is rhythmically free, and the material is modal, in 16th-century fashion, not at all chromatic, as in Schoenberg. After *Versus III* in the Stravinsky Cantata, pages 12-21 of the vocal score are devoted to tiny sections alternately marked "canon" and "ritornello." It is not clear why the "canons" are so labeled: they are not recognizably in canon form; the ritornellos really return. They lead to a final recapitulation, without variation, of the *Versus*.

Cantus cancrizans (page 10)

To - - - mor - row___ shall be, shall be___ my danc-ing day

Example 1. Igor Stravinsky, *Cantata*. Copyright © 1952 by Boosey & Hawkes, Inc. Copyright Renewed. Reprinted by permission.

The new Stravinsky style may be either polyphonic, with some harmonic implications, as in the *Cantata*, whose style is related to church music despite the secular Words; or Stravinsky may write, as in *The Rake's Progress*, in a style that is primarily harmonic, with polyphonic implications. In either case the foundation is largely modal, though one may at times detect hints of more modern key relationships.

The opening measures of the *Cantata* are typical (Ex. 2). Each part plays an independent fragment of melody in the polyphonic fabric. Plain triads are placed together so as to imply polychords. The first two measures hint at Phrygian harmony. The next two might be thought of as being in C major with a tonic chord suggested in the bass and tenor, while the upper parts move from tonic to subdominant to dominant at the same time that the tonic is being outlined below. In the counterpoint no diatonic intervals are treated as dissonant. There are chords built on fourths and seconds as well as on thirds. In the example shown it is noteworthy that the tenor and alto lines are consistently separated by more than an octave, despite the severe rules to the contrary. The frequent consecutive fifths are used as in organum, the consecutive sevenths and ninths as in the Notre Dame school. Independent voice lines and retrograde as in Renaissance music, diatonic poly-

Example 2. Igor Stravinsky, *Cantata.* Copyright © 1952 by Boosey & Hawkes, Inc. Copyright Renewed. Reprinted by permission.

chords as in Debussy and early Stravinsky, secundal chords as in early Cowell, and many other kaleidoscopic bits and pieces are woven firmly into this music. Tones are lowered or raised one at a time in gingerly fashion, following the sequence of sharps and flats in the circle of fifths. After the seven natural tones have been thoroughly established, an F-sharp comes in according to the laws of *musica ficta* (rather than as an introduction to a modulation). This soon revels to F-natural, but it has been established and it wanders in again later. Meanwhile C-sharp is sounded; after its disappearance G-sharp appears independently. B-flat and then E-flat are introduced in the same way in a later movement; eventually A-flat is heard. The smaller enharmonic cycle of fifth relations from G-sharp to A-fla*t* is thus completed.

The rhythm is usually very simple indeed. The 'syncopated and accented off-beats for which Stravinsky used to be famous are not characteristic of the new style. They are not, however, totally absent. At the end of the first measure (Ex. 1) the word "morrow" shows such syncopation, and later in the same line on the word "dancing" there is the form of syncopation known as the "Scotch snap"—a frequent figure in the *Cantata*. The third and rough measures in Ex. 2 shows a cross-rhythm of two against three across the bar line. Ex. 3 shows a relationship between the words and the metrical beat, a relationship common in early English song, where the least important words are often on the strong first beat.

Ricercar I, measures 14-15

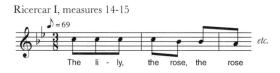

Example 3. Igor Stravinsky, *Cantata.* Copyright © 1952 by Boosey & Hawkes, Inc.
Copyright Renewed. Reprinted by permission.

Melodically the lines usually are in accordance with 16th-century modal writing, with two unobtrusive differences: there are occasional wide dissonant leaps (see the tenor part in Ex. 2) and sometimes the lines run along chords (measures 3 and 4 in Ex. 2). This last they would not have done before the Baroque period.

No one would call the *Cantata* tuneful, but it would be considered melodious and pleasant to listen to by most music lovers. It is an impressive work, if only for Stravinsky's masterful ability to combine so much from many periods, and individuals, into music that sounds so integrated, so natural, so easily, even casually, done.

George Antheil

A NEW OPERA TO ACHIEVE a summer's run was George Antheil's *Volpone,* produced by Punch Opera at the Cherry Lane Theatre, with two pianos taking the instrumental parts. This is Antheil's third opera, and it had been given only twice previously—in Los Angeles. Ben Jonson's story is ideally suited for opera, and the librettist, Alfred Perry, is exceptionally good. The words are singable and understandable, the dramatic action secure and constant. The amusing situations are easily perceived, and not pounded in until boring. *Volpone*'s success as a play is retained. Antheil's music is in general tuneful, but the tunes are composed through, so that they do not come to cadences that might attract attention away from the drama. The rhythm gives the action great urgency and an impelling drive that also adds to the dramatic force, and the fact that the rhythm is usually quite simple does not detract from its value. There are many sections of um pah, and others of um pah pah. They do not last long enough to be tiring, however, and one must agree that such rhythms serve to propel the stage movement without being obtrusive. Sometimes the um pahs and the um pah pahs are laid next to each other in a meter of five, and sometimes they are placed across the regular meter (Ex. 1). There are um pah pah pah pahs starting on weak as well as strong beats. If the chords are at times tonic and dominant, this continues a very short time before there is a change, and for the most part, the chords are irregular without being unpleasantly dissonant.

The whole opera is built on the use of some standard concords and some mild dissonances that appear unusual because of con-

Although Cowell was usually very critical of George Antheil's music, in this review he defends Antheil's opera Volpone. *Cowell's article appeared originally in* The Musical Quarterly *XXXIX/4 (Oct. 1953) pp. 600-604.*

stant shifts of key. At no time is there anything that calls special attention to the music, but there is a feeling that it is well done and right for the purpose, with nice things happening at any and all times, if one focuses attention on it. In the New York production, the two-piano version seemed quite enough for the tiny theater, but on listening to a recorded version with complete instrumentation one must admit that the ingenious scoring makes the whole musical picture far more interesting. The instruments are used with unusual clarity, and unusual diversification. The singers succeeded in making every word heard, yet the general range is higher than is usually thought to be good for the understanding of words; and there is lots more *forte* than *piano,* which is not good for the sense of musical climax. There are too many small climaxes to make the more important ones sound effective.

The style includes eclectic elements drawn from repertory operas, mostly French and Italian nineteenth-century models. There are, for instance, several quotations from *Depuis le jour,* from *Louise,* which last long enough to be fully recognizable, and then move along rapidly to something different and remote. The original aria is for soprano, but the quotations are for low men's voices. Antheil obviously feels that this adds to the amusement; he is right—the displaced musical suggestions are laugh-getters. The quoted snatches are always short, and they are balanced by the composer's own melodic lines, which are often partly in recitative manner, but with definite tune outlines. Ex. 2 shows such a passage, taken from Pepita's song to Volpone in Act II. Note that while there is a cadence on G flat, it comes where there is a comma in the text, and the melody undergoes a sudden key change before ending the word sentence, at which time the melody does not come to a cadence! By following such a criss-cross plan in the words-music relationship, there is always something that drives onward; and this is one

Dear-est my own Vol - po-na I'd glad - ly part with, I glad - ly part with all that I
(Um-pa-pa-pa-pa in eighth notes, starting on second beat)

own, If it would on - ly re - vive you, dar - ling. If it would on - ly give you new life.

Ex. 2. George Antheil. *Volpone*. Copyright © 1991 by Weintraub Music, a division of Music Sales Corp. (ASCAP) International Copyright Secured. All Rights Reserved. By Permission.

of Antheil's main methods of through-composition. It may be noted also that in the first phrase the words and the musical rhythm and melody line all fit together naturally, but toward the ends of the example the two climactic notes in the melody, F ♯ and G ♯, come respectively on the unimportant word "it" and the difficult-to-sing-on-a-high-note word "new." This is sufficiently unbalancing vocally to force even the most serious-minded singer (who may be thinking of her voice so much that she forgets she is singing a funny song) to sound comical. The words do not fit the tune, and since Antheil proves fully that he is capable of relating them, these many exceptions would appear to be for the sake of fun; and, like the little melodic bits from well-known operas and the introduction of airs with one too many um pah pahs in the accompaniment, it aids merriment. In a measure, this is musical buffoonery, yet it is the piling up of these things that caused the audience to have a very good time, as we observed them at the performance.

When the music runs along without dramatic interruption, it is apt to have several polyphonic lines (as in Ex. 3) spaced rather

Ex. 3. George Antheil. *Volpone*. Copyright © 1991 by Weintraub Music, a division of Music Sales Corp. (ASCAP) International Copyright Secured. All Rights Reserved. By Permission.

far apart for the sake of clarity in scoring, and independent in rhythm. In the example one notes the high piccolo part widely separated from the alto line, which is sustained enough to glue the texture together, and is again two or more octaves from the bass tune. The return to the note C in the bass suggests a sustained organ point on this note without the heaviness of its actually being held. While the bass and alto are definitely in C minor, the piccolo is slightly free, with its independent A natural and E natural, to say nothing of the C♯ and F♯ in passing. All this serves to decorate the fundamental C minor.

Volpone's New York daily press was lukewarm, which we found surprising and displeasing; and it was reassuring, therefore, when several well-known operatic composers expressed to us their own disagreement with the reviews, and the feeling that an injustice had been done to Antheil. The public apparently took Antheil's side too, since the little Cherry Lane Theatre continued to be filled night after night.

The truth is that *Volpone* stands up very well in comparison with other American operas. Some recent operas are awkward dramatically when music takes over to too great an extent, while on the other hand many of the newer through-composed operas have almost completely vague and meaningless music (one thinks of *The Barrier*). It is hardly necessary to point out the number of failures due to words that are not suited for singing, and in which the plot, if any, is almost completely buried.

Volpone is an ideal plot, Perry's libretto is clear, singable and dramatic. The music is written to serve the story, and for this purpose it is effective at all times. Musicians are perhaps disappointed that there is no spot of great musical significance, in which the attention shifts to the music; but stage people are delighted that the flow of the play is never so impeded.

Antheil gets around the difficulty of making through-composed music meaningful by his tongue-in-the-check quotations in both rhythm and tune, so that although everything ends in a different key from the beginning, one feels that there is something to grasp. The relation of the music to the staging, influenced no doubt by his experience in writing music for pictures, is largely that of incidental music for a play (one is reminded at times of Alex North's music for *Death of a Salesman)* except that the music is continuous and, since it is sung, plays a somewhat more important part. It would be hard to say, therefore, that the music is in itself important, but it contributes to an evening of delicious enjoyment.

Béla Bartók

THE MUSIC OF Béla Bartók, as we all know, has attained tremendous respect during the years since his death. Many who do not react with entire pleasure to twelve-tone chromaticism or to neoclassic stylization find in Bartók something quite sympathetic.

It is particularly fitting that Bartók's son Peter should issue an impressive list of recordings of his father's works, making available many of the lesser-known compositions as well as better-known ones. Peter Bartók's record company was founded with this idea especially in mind. It may be observed here that the younger Bartók is an excellent sound engineer; the recorded sound is not thin and scrawny, but on the other hand it does not employ so much amplification of extreme ranges that the result is artificial, a frequent fault of high-fidelity fans among engineers. Bartók's product sounds as music should in a concert hall. The performances are all expert, and the difficult music has evidently been rehearsed more carefully than is the case with some orchestral recordings. Rehearsal time is tragically expensive; but in these records the musicians seem to know this music as well as they do standard classics. As conductor, Tibor Serly makes a live experience of the performances. His

Béla Bartók's son Peter, a recording engineer, founded a record company devoted to his father's music; musical aspects were musically directed by Béla Bartók's friend, the composer, conductor and trombone virtuoso Tibor Serly. The result was a brilliant series of twelve recordings reviewed here by Cowell in The Musical Quarterly XXXIX (Oct. 1953) pp. 641-645. [Recording review of Béla Bartók: 44 Violin Duets. Victor Aitay, Michael Kutmer. BRS 907. Concerto for Viola and Orchestra. William Primrose, New Symphony Orch., cond. Serly. BRS 309. Dance Suite; Two Portraits. New Symph. Orch., cond. Autori. BRS 304. Suite from The Miraculous Mandarin. New Symph. Orch., cond. Serly. BRS 301. Two Rhapsodies for Violin and Orchestra. Emanuel Vardi, New Symph. Orch., cond. Autori, Serly. BRS 306. Deux Images. New Symph. Orch., cond. Serly. BRS 305. Divertimnento for Strings. String orch., cond. Serly. BRS 005. All 12" LP's. Bartók Record Company.]

own personal acquaintance with Bartók, and his long experience as a composer and orchestra man aid him in achieving exceptional vitality and contrast. Conductor Autori, in guiding the Dance Suite and *Two Portraits*, is not a whit less satisfactory.

The fact that Bartók's style is related to Hungarian folk music has been made too much of, and gives rather a false impression of the nature of his most important works. At an early age, Bartók collected music of both Hungary and Rumania, and later worked with music of other Balkan countries and Turkey, as well as the Arabs. The influences are therefore not Hungarian alone, but embrace the whole East European musical culture also, with special reference to those elements that stem from Turkey and from Greece. The several invasions of the Southeast in medieval times by Turkish armies left musical traces, particularly recognizable in the folk music of the Magyars (as opposed to the better-known gypsy Hungarian music). But while Bartók collected much music, and arranged some of it for concert performance, its influence on his own style is only a starting-point. He built for himself a highly sophisticated new musical world, grounded in the folk practices of Hungary and its neighboring countries, but no more an imitation of them than Beethoven's music is an imitation of German folk tunes.

Bartók's style is a unified one, and was, with minor differences, the same during most of his career as a composer. He found in folk music the use of modes derived from tetrachords as one studies them in Greek history. Most frequent, of course, are the three diatonic tetrachords—major, minor, and Phrygian, representing the three possible forms of one minor and two major seconds, and the Lydian (whole tone) form. In addition, Bartók uses all three forms of the chromatic tetrachords, based on two half-steps and an augmented second. The Hijaz form, with the augmented second in the middle, is very well known; but the other two forms, with the half-steps together and the augmented second respectively at either end, is found very rarely in folk music outside the Southeastern part of Europe. Bartók delights in them, and uses them, along with the other forms, in all possible orders one over the other to form complete modes. All the more familiar modal outlines are present, but many more are also formed, even when he has the more customary whole tone between the tetrachords; but Bartók also uses the interlocking form with the high note of one tetrachord as the beginning of the next, so that the total mode has a span of a seventh. When this happens it is natural to use chords built in fourths in the harmonization, and Bartók often does so. This means that chords in fourths have a real relation to the melodic material, and are not dragged in artificially. Secundal chords are also used, and these are treated (usually) as a tetrachord filled in—all the tones sounding at once, sometimes, instead of being used successively. So there is some genuine musical purpose in employing both the secundal and quartal harmonic systems, which he uses as well as the familiar chords in thirds. Secundal chords are often used to give special drive and emphasis to off-beats and irregular meters in the passages related to dance. Especially characteristic are scales formed by using tetrachords over each other a half-step apart. For example, one finds such a succession as C, D, E, F, and then the major tetrachord again starting on F♯ so the total is C, D, E, F, F♯, G♯, A♯, B. Another favorite is the major plus the Lydian, a whole step apart: C, D, E, F, G, A, B, C♯.

Bartók studied the elements of folk music with care, and added to them his own new modes and scales. He uses chromatic passing tones between diatonic tetrachordal tones, and employs chords related to the melodic lines (having no fear of either dissonance or consonance). He creates a new world of sound, related to that of Stravinsky in modal background, related to that of Schoenberg in free use of chromatic elements in the tetrachords and in passing chromaticism, and in more minute organization of materials than Stravinsky's music usually possesses. These things he pours into Classic form, not trying to change the nature of the form for each idea, but rather sticking to the general principles of the sonata-allegro. In longer movements of all of the orchestra works there is a majestic first idea, usually featuring winds, and a lyric second theme in which flowing strings enter. Episodes are clearly defined, as are development sections; and once one listens with understanding to the new sounds, which at first may tend to throw one off, the form is easier to follow than that of almost any other composer since the eighteenth century.

Such is the unification of Bartók's style that the musical elements we have discussed are present in all the Bartók Records re-

leases, from *The Miraculous Mandarin,* written in 1919, to the Viola
Concerto, finished in sketch in 1945. These two works are in many
ways the most interesting of the orchestra records. *The Miraculous
Mandarin* was written as a ballet, but is known to us in this country
only as an orchestral suite. The music, barbaric in spirit and furi-
ously colorful, seems related to the *Sacre du Printemps;* and indeed it
is interesting that at a time when Stravinsky had turned away from
the style of the *Sacre,* Bartók should have carried it forward so
impellingly. Using a much smaller *orchestra,* the *Mandarin* attains an
even greater intensity than the *Sacre,* piling up rhythm upon rhythm
with a whiplash of deliberate discord which is like Stravinsky in-
tensified, mixed with a more decisive off-beat thrust suggestive of
bebop. In the contrasting lyric sections there are some pre-
Hindemith uses of consecutive perfect fourths in the melodies, and
in the development section a long series of melodic thirds outlining
a chord that does not stop at being a 13th chord—it goes on the
15th and 17th and 19th, with the notes in the latter three chromat-
ically altered so that they are not the same as the 1st, 3rd, and 5th.

The Viola Concerto was completed in rough sketch just before Bartók's death. Much of it was in his peculiar musical shorthand, and the designations of instruments were only clear to those
who understood the refinements of his ways of scoring. Tibor Serly
took several years to complete the arduous task of reconstructing
the work in full score. It is wonderfully done, and there is no hint
that any mistakes were made—it sounds completely as Bartók
would have wished. Bartók was one of the greatest masters of string
writing, and all this mastery is observable in the fine viola solo
part, as well as in the relation between this and the orchestral strings.
He does not avoid having orchestral strings when the viola is playing, but often places them together in duets and trios; and there
are times when the viola is buried deliberately, and then emerges
effectively. Some of the utterances are rhapsodic in the expected
Hungarian style, some of them are quiet and neat, with some
Western European influence, and some are quite Turkish. It is not
surprising that Serly, who worked with the score so long, gives an
especially stirring performance, and William Primrose is at his famous best. Altogether this seems to us the best music and the best
played of any viola works that we have ever heard.

The *Divertimento for Strings* starts with immediate life. Is it amazing that in his sublimation of dance rhythm into sonata form Bartók never repeats himself—it is always new and fresh. The second theme is a vibrant, sustained, throbbing lyrical passage in a combination of dissonant counterpoint and secundal chord progressions. The second movement contains an unusual sort of recitative in which the chords that punctuate the melodies shift from one part to another. The last movc mcnt is in fugal manner, containing a stretto, and such melodic devices as inversion and retrograde. Classical forms are used very clearly in thin work, although they are applied to materials so thoroughly twentieth-century in nature that recognition is made difficult.

The Dance Suite consists of six short movements, with a ritornello that returns between some of them. Although there is some rather remote relationship between the movements and folk dances, the music as a whole is highly sophisticated and is far removed from folk feeling. The notes on the jacket would lead one to expect a series of folk dances transcribed by Bartók. Actually, this is a highly original work. The third movement is surely one of the world's most exciting scherzos; and nowhere else is Bartók's ability to deal with diverse and rather overwhelming elements more strikingly illustrated.

The 44 Violin Duets, although engaging chamber works and well presented by Aitay and Kuttner, are not nearly as exciting as the string quartets. The Two Rhapsodies are well known, and hardly need comment here. The performance by [Emanuel] Vardi is respectable, but not equal to the [Josef] Szigeti performances. *Deux Images* are charming and effective bits in Impressionistic style, leaning more toward the French than is Bartók's custom. The recording is excellent.

Altogether, the collection of works made available through his son's good engineering and Serly's fine musicianship constitutes a magnificent monument to the memory of Bartók—the sort of monument every composer would want. Through these records everyone may become acquainted with some of the most stirring, provocative, and extraordinary music of this century.

PART THREE

Music of the World's Peoples

The Scientific Approach to Non-European Music

WHAT CONSTITUTES THE scientific approach to music systems with which we are unfamiliar? The first impression—one that for some people is not overcome for a long time—usually is that the music is "unmusical," "out of tune," "unmelodious," "monotonous," etc. Obviously it represents aesthetic criteria so different from those conventionally accepted by us that impressions of this sort must entirely be ruled out. Furthermore, the material forms are usually so unlike those of our conventional styles that any comprehension of their content or judgment of their value is completely out of the question.

It is clear that a certain limited aesthetic experience of exotic music is possible for some of us; but anything comparable to the experience of our own music can be reached only upon the basis of a more extensive and profound knowledge firstly, of the technical processes and critical standards involved, and secondly, of the role of music in the social system from which it has sprung.[1] Here I shall speak chiefly of the former.

Music Vanguard *lasted for only two issues in 1935, but in its brief existence it published Bertolt Brecht, Cowell and several other figures of importance. Charles Seeger served on its editorial board and contributed his "Preface to All Linguistic Treatment of Music." In* Music Vanguard *I/2 (Summer 1935) pp. 62-67, Cowell took up the refrain in this article, "The Scientific Approach to Non-European Music," an important statement of his approach to world music as this concept was taking form. However, at about this time the Communist party line shifted its emphasis from the cultural vanguard to popular culture, discrediting anything that smacked of elitism, and thereby isolating any point of view such as Seeger's or Cowell's from a large part of their presumed public. Be that as it may, Cowell does a fine job here of describing the early methodologies of the first comparative musicologists and of pointing to some of the issues which still invite serious discussion today.*

Just what is the scientific approach to non-European music still remains a question of much controversy. In the nineteenth century, musicians believed that the rules of harmony which were then (and unfortunately are still) studied in schoolbooks, constituted the foundation of music. The method, there laid out, of constructing scales and chords was felt to be the only proper one—thoroughly scientific. For this reason, there was, at that time, very little interest in the music of non-European peoples. Western musicians, confronted with an unfamiliar music, merely felt it to be "wrong," "out of tune," etc. Certain musical explorers, however, went so far as to write articles, even books, on the music of China, India, and other regions. In these early writings, the attitude adopted, was that since some of the notes of their scales were nearly the same as ours, the music showed some signs of being musical! All musical values were measured by whether or not they were the same, in some respect, as those conventionally accepted by us in our music. In a great majority of cases, the musicians who wrote these papers deluded themselves with regard to the pitches of Oriental tones, They heard them in terms of the nearest equivalents in our own scale and notated them as such. In their discussions, they stated that the music had been written in our scale, but that it was actually a bit out of tune. In the same way, rhythm was misunderstood. Rhythms of great subtlety and complexity were heard as simple 4/4 thumps, and so notated. Elements in non-European music which do not officially exist in ours were rarely mentioned.

This procedure was changed by an Englishman, Professor A. J. Ellis, who is considered the father of the study now known as Comparative Musicology. He took the thoroughly scientific attitude that we must not measure the music of different peoples by our own—that we must find out facts concerning their music by more reliable methods than by simply trusting to our musical ears, trained as they are in a different musical system from the one to be studied. In the course of his work, he devised a way of measuring exact pitches in music. His method was to divide the half step, or minor second (equal temperament) into one hundred degrees. He soon discovered that the scale tones of the non-European Oriental peoples were not at all as they had been depicted by earlier musicians.

Professor Karl Stumpf and Professor Erich von Hornbostel of Berlin have continued Ellis' work, and have made many brilliant scientific investigations of primitive and Oriental music. Professor Curt Sachs and Dr. Robert Lachman may also be added to the list of important research workers in this field. Each man, however, emphasizes a different element of the study. Hornbostel thinks that music has not been completely investigated unless its pitch has been measured in "cents," or hundredths of a half-step. He gives the impression that once this is done, the most important aspect of the work has been treated. Lachman is of the opinion that the most important factor lies in the melodic line of the songs collected, and that the understanding of them depends largely upon a knowledge of the texts. He finds little value in measurements of pitch alone. Sachs on the other hand has made extensive studies of the instruments. To him the scientific approach is to discover the instruments of a specified locality, to measure them carefully, and to find out the exact materials of which they are made. The measurement of the pitch of the individual constituents of the tonal system of any music, he believes, can be made more easily from the playing of the instruments.

In addition, the history of the music of a non-European region is an indispensable approach to the music itself; but at present this approach is very difficult, because the records, monuments and sources of information are so faulty and so misleading. Lachman, especially, has set himself the task of finding, studying, and having translated, original historical treatises on music from Arabia, China, Persia and India.

Other possible approaches to the study of these musics are lacking. The differences in tone-quality between various instruments, which at present remains unmeasured, are undoubtedly of more purely musical value than the measurements of length, breadth, and thickness upon which Sachs is so insistent. And instead of placing so much stress on the texts of particular songs (since all songs are sung in accordance with prescribed musical convention, irrespective of text) would it, perhaps, not be more fruitful to attempt to discover more of what the musicians themselves think of the music and its relation to their lives and what they are trying to convey by means of it? This would undoubtedly help to achieve a more well-rounded view of non-European music. From the same standpoint, the writings of Oriental scholars concerning their music should not be so greatly discredited. They may contain serious inaccuracies as to dates, but in them is to be found the real spirit and approach of the Oriental peoples to their musical art.

From my point of view, there is at present no satisfactory synthesis of methods used in the examination of non-European music. Each of the methods commonly used has a certain value, but they should all be employed together instead of separately. To study a given work, one should measure its pitches in cents, should know its text (if a vocal work), the history of its musical system, and as much as possible about the conditions of life of the people from which it springs. One should measure its rhythm with suitable instruments, find the scale in which it is written, if there is one, and analyze its musical form. But when this is done (and usually only a part of it is), one should not make the mistake of thinking that the study is finished. More accurate types of measurement must be found, and certain factors not measured at present must be included.

The measurement of the pitch in cents seems subtle enough to satisfy any scientist, and musical scientists pride themselves greatly on this measurement. When one reads that the pitches of tones have been measured to within one-hundredth part of a half-step, one shivers at the precision of scientific achievement, and even the most exacting are led to believe that the pitch has actually been measured. Yet the fact remains that the pitch has not been accurately, not in many cases even approximately measured, despite the measurement in cents! The reason for this is that in most non-European music, such phenomena as slides of pitch, or controlled glissandi, constitute an essential part of the pitch scheme. It is true of all vocal music, and of all instrumental music in which the voice is imitated. The old description of music according to scale does not apply here at all, because the basic total units used in the music are not steady, level pitches, which can always be grouped into scales (no matter how these may differ from ours) but rather, small *curves of pitch*, which in turn are parts of the larger curve of the melodic line. Although these units may not remain for an instant at the same level of pitch, their execution is, nevertheless, in many cases, standardized. A study of such curves and their differences is essential to the understanding of all non-European musics, except those played on tuned percussion instruments. Yet I am informed by both Hornbostel and Lachman that no thorough study of these basic tonal units exists. The subject is usually dismissed briefly with the statement that the units are "intoned" differently. Each unit, therefore, is considered as if it were a single tone with a steady pitch, despite the fact that its pitch is continually changing, and only a certain point of it can be measured at any one time.[2] A point somewhere along the pitch-curve is first measured in cents. The pitch of this point is wrongly considered as the pitch of the whole curve of the basic unit, and the "scale" is then notated. At times there are great discrepancies in the findings of different scientists who have measured the tones of the same work—and with good reason—having happened on different parts of the pitch-curve. These differences often lead to accusations of inaccuracy back and forth! The curves of some of these basic units extend over as much as a major third between their beginning and end—in which case, the scientist runs the risk of measuring the tone anywhere within 400 cents.

In the measurement of tone-lengths (i.e., in the field of rhythmic study) there is again a lack of accuracy. The general tempo, which is often steady, can and has been measured. The lengths of tones within this tempo, however, are notated by ear, and often have no relation to the actual phenomena. Our system of notation cannot disclose the finely organized rhythmical schemes which are an integral part of so much non-European music. Hornbostel has invented a method by means of which he has measured several tone-lengths. His findings have differed widely from measurements made by ear. He has definitely proven that our rhythmic notation up to the present has been incorrect. But his system of measurement is so complex that to measure the rhythms of several pieces by means of it, would probably constitute a life work.

We still often make the mistake, in measuring non-European musics, of presupposing that the most important elements to be measured are those which are important in our own music. Secondary elements in our music, such as measured shades of dynamics, and nuances of pitch on a single tone, often constitute the most important parts of such musics. So much so, that among some tribes (the ancient Hilo Islanders, for example)[3] the actual pitch-changes may differ each time a song is sung, but should the singer alter the tone-quality or dynamics, he may be condemned to death. It may also be pointed out that although European musicologists have erected complex systems of chord construction and chord connection in their own music, they have left almost entirely unsystematized equally important rhythmic conventions. Most primitive[4] music does not employ tonal harmony in our sense (except sometimes in embryo) but often uses rhythmical combinations which are so altered and varied that they may be considered a veritable harmony of rhythm. These combinations are the subject of lifelong study by the musicians of non-European peoples. Up to the present time no study has been made of the laws which govern the practice of such rhythm-harmony. Perhaps our investigators, hypnotized by the conventions of our music, do not regard the study of such practices as of importance; or perhaps they are technically not equipped for the task.

To make a scientific investigation of a non-European musical work, all sciences related to music must be brought into play: firstly, those sciences which deal with the musical materials themselves, and then those which have to do with other elements which may influence the music. In the application of each science, care must be exercised to avoid the prejudices of our own approach to things; the start must be made from as neutral a standpoint as possible. Thus in the application of acoustics, measurements should be made not only of one point of a moving, sliding pitch, but of the whole tone-curve. Not only the pitch, but also the tone-quality should be measured. This can be done by finding the single-tone-overtone complex. Not only the pitch of clearly distinguishable tone-curves should be measured, but the percussion-noises of drums and other percussion instruments should be classified and their tone-qualities measured. Such noises play a very important part in primitive music.

The tonal and rhythmical systems as well as the sense of form of Oriental and primitive peoples should be studied more accurately, not only from the standpoint of musical science but from the point of view of the peoples themselves. An attempt should be made to discover which element of music is most emphasized by the particular tribe in question, and what the native conventions are with regard to it. Psychology plays an important role in estimating the mental attitude of the native musician toward his own music and the responses he expects to produce with it. It is equally important in the matter of self-questioning on the part of the investigator. He must make every effort to keep his subjective bias in favor of the familiar music of his own people from interfering with his objective study of the unfamiliar music of a strange people. Physiology plays, in many ways, a large part, not yet nearly enough considered. Several important facts in this connection are the construction of the hearing apparatus of non-European peoples, whether they differ and how; also the exact type of response to sound-stimuli both expected and unexpected.

One need hardly point out the necessity of knowing more about the relation of religion to music; of social conditions to music; of climate, vegetation and animal life to the types of musical instruments used in various regions; and a thousand other such factors, different in each case.

Comparative Musicology is still a young science. Its branches are still, many of them, undeveloped. We must work for their ultimate coordination in the form of a mature study that will give us not only a correct understanding of the musics of other peoples, but also a proper perspective in which to understand our own music, and its role in relation to the other musics of the world.

1. This latter approach has been discussed in "Preface to All Linguistic Treatment of Music" by Charles Seeger in *Music Vanguard*, March-April, 1935.—EDS.

2. With the phono-photographical method of Metfessel, it is possible to measure accurately these melodic curves. But this has not yet been widely done because of the laboriousness of the process.

3. In Hawaii. Cowell once mentioned in class that he had been looking unsuccessfully for years for traditional Hawaiian music, presumably of this sort.—DH.

4. In this article, the word is used in its popular sense. For a discussion of its several uses, see Charles Seeger, op. cit., p. 20 et seq.

Folk Music

H OW WILL YOU TAKE your folk music: longhair, Broadway or straight? The first two are easy to find on records, and the last, the real mountain music, was fairly well represented during the days when the talking-machine companies wanted to build up their market in rural America. But such music is the rarest of collectors' items today. For a good many years the record companies have been playing it safe, assuming that city people are too frail to stand the shock of hearing the real thing in the old mountain style. So we have been carefully spoon-fed on diluted versions, mixed with as many elements of familiar popular or symphonic music as possible, so that folk music won't prove too hard on our nerves. It is hard for those of us who are familiar with American music outside of the big cities to understand why such careful translation into urbanese has so long been considered necessary. The wonderful things in the old Bluebird and Brunswick catalogs, for example, have all been allowed to go out of print. Yet the few that turned up in the drives to gather old records during the war were grabbed up instantly by city collectors, and dealers' lives were made miserable by demands for more of them.

The result is that today you can get Roy Harris' "Folksong Symphony" and Aaron Copland's "Lincoln Portrait," both of which use American tunes in serious symphonic composition, without any pretense that the result has anything to do with the folk

Listen *was a middlebrow music magazine, popular in the suburbs of the 1940s, given to publishing articles on subjects which would uplift their readers in some way. This article was published as the third part of a survey of American music, "The American Scene," and HC and Sidney Robertson Cowell (who co-authored this text) discuss certain elements of what was then called the "Folk Song Revival," describing its impact on American art music. First appearance:* Listen *VIII/1 (May 1946), pp. 8-12.*

tradition, except rather indirectly and incidentally. You can also get a lot of pieces which use titles implying some connection with folk music, although that connection is usually so remote as to be more hopeful than real.

But can you buy a commercial recording, by a real country singer, of "Springfield Mountain," the tune Copland used in his "Lincoln Portrait?" No indeed. Yet, with "Young Charlotte" and "Barbara Allen," "Springfield Mountain" is certainly known to more country people, in more different parts of the United States, than any other traditional tune of Anglo-Celtic origin.

Fully as longhair as the Copland and Harris pieces, but not equally legitimate, because they are being sold to the helpless city public as something they are not, are the easily available recordings by people like John Jacob Niles and Richard Dyer Bennett. Niles came from a Kentucky community where folk singing was common; he makes instruments which are elaborations of the simple 3-string dulcimer he must have heard as a boy, and he accompanies himself with these instruments very musically and attractively. Unfortunately, the seventh and ninth chords, the key changes and chromatic tones which he uses, are entirely foreign to the country versions of the songs he sings. He has also developed a singing style which is far removed from anything a folk singer is likely to do; it is much nearer to Italian operatic singing of the nineteenth century, overdramatizing the ballad plots and sentimentalizing the music with *portamenti* and *fermati* as unlike any traditional folk use of these devices as it is possible to conceive.

Niles has no objection to the alteration of folk tunes when he feels they can be improved. There would be no harm in this if they were then frankly presented as art songs. Instead, Niles argues that he is justified because many folk singers do the same thing. This is true in a way; but Niles' changes are aimed at something dictated by a sophisticated musical taste, and are not kept within the scope of the folk tradition. A folk singer's changes are usually quite unconscious, made to fit variant words; or they may represent an unconscious process of selection, as when a tune in a 7-tone scale is altered to fit the pentatonic or hexatonic scale with which the singer is more at home. Or a singer may transpose his song from one mode to another. This means a change of no more than a note or two in the whole song, rarely occurs on rhythmically accented tones, and does not change the general melodic outline radically. It is only after many small changes by successive singers that widely different versions are produced.

Fine folk singing is on the whole rather severe and impersonal, almost ritualistic; its lyricism is classical rather than personal and romantic like Niles' performances. Moreover, a true folk singer depends on understatement in his "projection" of a song. This understatement characterizes the traditional texts, too, and is very deeply ingrained in the character of both songs and people of British ancestry. By keeping his performance and aesthetic whole in this way, the folk singer proves himself a more sensitive artist than his commercial imitators. The recent recording of Gladys Swarthout singing "I Wonder as I Wander" is very lovely, but it is quite unrecognizable as folk music. Artistically it would have been much better if Niles had left Miss Swarthout alone with her orchestra (which plays the introduction) without trying to interject his dulcimer accompaniment while she is singing. No one could object to a frank "translation" into art music of such a song.

Richard Dyer Bennett's records are not so misleading, because he is simply described as a ballad singer; he does not claim to be an authentic folk singer. He wants to sing the old ballads in night clubs and in formal concerts, and that is just what he does. His diction is English, his voice is trained but unpretentious, and most of the songs come from published English versions, not the American oral tradition at all.

Among the people whose singing is approved by country people and city people alike are Burl Ives, Arthur Rowan Sommers, and Tom Glazer; all three have several times been cited to the writers[1] as "the only city fellers who get the music right." They all sing in a modified country style, of course; their music is not so exotic as that of the older singers in the mountains. Peter Seeger of the Almanac Singers is a rare example of a "furriner" who is able to play the 5-string banjo in the very fine old style—as well, in fact, as many of the best old-timers in the mountains. Seeger spent the better part of two years in the mountains with his banjo, thinking of practically nothing else 18 hours a day.

Twenty years ago or more, Broadway began to pick up a sort

of second-growth mountain music, widely known as hillbilly music, along with its cousin, the cowboy song. Recordings of this music were made by Broadway crooners and blues singers, accompanied by the wrong kind of banjo and electric guitars; the rhythms were syncopated a bit and the result was fed back to the mountains via the country stores and, later, the juke boxes. Some country singers were influenced by what they heard on these discs, and have supposed that this was what was expected of them. So now you can hear, as a matter of course, a syncopated version of the 16th century ballad, "Barbara Allen," sung in an insinuating Broadway fashion on small local radio stations. The Broadway cowboys have taken the long, loping swing out of cowboy songs, too; the ones they write now sound just like fox trots.

So the record collector, or the teacher, or the student, who wants the real thing in Americana is having all sorts of translations and imitations palmed off on him, and usually he has no way of knowing this. However, the record sets issued by the Library of Congress are all real country music sung by real folk singers, although it is true that the Library has not yet dared to issue some of its most unusual-sounding, yet most characteristic, American music. The fantastic number of orders for these albums of the real thing which swamped the Archive of American Folk Song at the Library of Congress following a recent Readers' Digest article would seem to indicate that the big commercial companies have been missing a bet. Interest in early blues and the older types of jazz, and the best contemporary swing music, has accustomed large numbers of people to all sorts of strange new sounds. Someday soon, somebody is going to discover that records chosen frankly for their novelty, without slicking up their accompaniments for the trade, and without selecting merely pretty voices, will sell like wildfire.

With the current boom in historic examples of jazz, for instance, it is perfectly absurd that it should be impossible to buy any examples of the wonderful wild blues singing and the still more primitive "field hollers," from which stem the familiar Negro blues, and which are the rhapsodic counterpart in song of the best solos in swing music. Country fiddlers have a fine bite to their tone and amazing rhythmic vitality, and it is a shame that the thousands of people interested in square dancing in America cannot buy authentic recordings of "Leather Breeches," "Hell Among the Year-lings," and "Cacklin' Hen or the Devil's Dream." There should also be a few unaccompanied ballads, from the northern states as well as from the south, with the beautiful curves and catches in the voice which belong to the strong old ecstatic style of singing. A few such records made easily available to the general public might prevent some prevalent absurdities in the discussion of folk music. Recently a well-known critic in one of the better weeklies betrayed an incredible ignorance of folk music when he patronizingly informed Leadbelly that his measures were too short by a half-beat. The fact is that such irregularities are characteristic of true folk performers in many countries, not only in America; they are not a "mistake," but are part of the style, and are so common in rural music here that one of the easiest signs of Broadway influence to detect is the reduction of a song to consistent squareness of a 4-beat measure and a 4-measure phrase. In lumber camps of the northern United States, where clogging is a popular after-supper stunt, fiddlers try to trip the dancers by shortening a phrase occasionally, sometimes by half a beat, sometimes by a whole beat. A good dancer can follow accurately. This is the old Irish slip jig, and, in fact, such solo dancing in this country is called jigging or clogging, indiscriminately. The tunes are Irish bagpipe melodies. (Tap dancing is a more recent form of the same thing.) Instrumental interludes between verses of a folk song are very commonly expanded or contracted by a half-beat or a beat, as well.

There is a practically untouched market for albums of authentic regional music, chosen by people who can distinguish the commercialized imitations from the authentic in traditional music, for use with the social studies programs in schools, which are organized on a regional basis nowadays. Elementary school youngsters study the history of various occupations like mining, the lumber industry, and so on. Where are the albums of mining songs, loggers' songs, sea songs and river songs, sung by the people for whom these songs are a living tradition? The Library of Congress has some fine examples of this sort of thing and is issuing them gradually; but they cannot begin to meet the demand.

It really seems that even the general public may be "hearty" enough now to bear the sound of American folk music in its origi-

nal state, without any musical bowdlerizing. To the increasing number of people who know what folk music is like in this country, the
careful concealment of native musical styles that has gone on is a
sort of silly anachronism, comparable to putting Greek statues into
pants to protect sensitive folk from the shock of reality. We often
play an extraordinary version of "Pretty Polly" and other early
Brunswick releases long out of print, in a general lecture on the
music of the world's peoples. The style is so different from that of
familiar popular or cultivated music that it seems to come from a
quite different world. City audiences never suspect that these songs
are American, and the guesses range from Africa to China. When
they discover that they are hearing music from Kentucky or Mis-
souri, we have to tie the records down.

1. The Cowells. A few lines later, note that "Pete" Seeger, Charles Seeger's son and
not yet the celebrity he has since become, was still "Peter Seeger."—DH

Music of the World's Peoples

INTRODUCTION

EVERY PEOPLE IN THE WORLD has music, and music is a strong part of the life of most peoples. In a vast majority of cases, this music is not read from notes, but played or sung "by ear." Such is the music of which this series deals [see note below]. Some of it, as in the case of many oriental musics, belongs to a highly cultivated, old, and carefully-wrought system, and its tradition is meticulously preserved by precise aural training. In other cases, the tradition is maintained in a more carefree manner; but there is a well-recognized tradition and style in all of it. Whether there is specific training or not, folk singers and players pick up the elements of such tradition and style by ear. In most cases these musicians perform music which is already well-known to their people — they learn particular songs and dances from their parents as children, or from good older performers in their locality. Old songs are sometimes changed a bit, so that variants often may be found

Cowell's preferred method of approaching world music was a composer's one: play the music, then comment. His pattern—hear, remember, relate, and synthesize—has vast implications: what would Cowell say about the entry of copyright law into this process? The following three texts were written for Folkways Records, run by Cowell's old friend Moses Asch. Taken from HC's private notes, there are many typographic errors and inconsistencies (is the instrument "kanun" or "kanoon"?) which Folkways chose not to correct; I have done so where I could, in the interest of fluency. These notes provide a very rich harvest. Most of the albums are still available in one or another form, and the reader who wants to know more should contact Smithsonian/ Folkways. These album notes are excerpted from Music of the World's Peoples, Volume 1 *(Ethnic Folkways Library Albums P 504, P 505, P 506). As for the title, "Music of the World's Peoples," it became a radio show with a loyal following, which even after Cowell's death was rebroadcast for many years.*

in the case of folk music, less often in tradition cultivated musics of the Oriental peoples. Completely new tunes are seldom born—a "new" tune will have elements of known older ones in it as a rule, snatches of melody, rhythm, and in some cases chords unconsciously remembered from general musical experience.

There is much more interplay between cultivated music and folk music than is usually realized. Just as "classical" music frequently strengthens itself by drawing on folk sources, folk musicians utilize musical materials heard in surrounding written-down music. Chords have been discovered from hearing European cultivated music and are used in many parts of the world; the scales and modes of the Byzantine culture are used in folk music wherever these scales and modes are preserved in nearby churches, and so forth.

Styles of performance differ widely among different peoples. Ways of singing that please one people may disturb others (the average Chinese has as much trouble understanding our singing as we do his), but there is often much resemblance in actual musical material. One of the oldest known tunes in the world—"Peach Blossom" from China—is fundamentally the same as "Nobody Knows the Trouble I've Seen," a Negro song; but the styles of singing are so different that this is more noticeable than the tune resemblances.

Subtleties of pitch and rhythm are often impossible to notate, so that written-down versions, although they may remind one of the original, do not do more than to suggest the living reality. It is necessary to hear people sing and play their own music to gain its real feeling.

The world's music is a lateral history, for music in every stage of development exists somewhere today. There are still primitive tribes whose culture has not gone beyond that of peoples of ten thousand years ago; their music is very like that which must have existed then, as far as this can be reconstructed. There are other tribes, sometimes called primitive, whose culture is extraordinary and diversified. This shows in their music. Tribes of Central Africa, for example, use a great variety of scales and tonal patterns, and their control of simultaneous rhythms is not exceeded by any other people. Many oriental musical cultures are highly complex and sophisticated. Some of them exceed Western practice in certain respects; for example, the ragas of India form the world's most highly organized melodic and scale system, and the same people's tala system is an orderly study of countless rhythmic forms. The earliest writing on music in ancient China recommended a simplification from 56 tones to an octave to a mere 24 (quarter-tones). This was later (about 300 B.C.) changed, in China, to the 12 tones which form the basis of the Western scale. The earlier microtones exist now in the form of sliding tones in Chinese opera-dramas. Large orchestras—from 500 to 900 players—existed in China in the T'ang Dynasty (about 700 to 900 A.D.). Large choruses—up to 50,000 strong—were known in ancient Hebrew culture. The sort of instruments used in the T'ang Dynasty orchestras, exquisitely constructed, are used all over the Orient today. The kind of melody sung by ancient choruses (such as the Hebrew) is sung today throughout the Near East.

Chords and harmony have been the special point of development of Western musical culture; and while folktunes, as sung by farmers and mountaineers the world over, used to be sung as melodies alone, today the use of chords to accompany tunes has spread widely. Guitars, banjos, lutes, harmonicas, accordions, etc., or their equivalents are found nearly everywhere. In places where earlier traditions are undisturbed, these instruments play a "ground" tone —a steady underlying tone like the drone of a bagpipe. Later there may be two or more such ground tones (as in Scottish warpipes) and still later, major and minor chords will be picked up by ear and played, at first with no changes, later with only one change, and still later with a growing number of chord shifts. Where folkplayers come into contact with commercial popular music—as over the radio—the more modern seventh, ninth and chromatic chords may creep in; but so far, this is quite rare among non-notereaders.

The music of some peoples of the world will sound extremely strange on first hearing. Yet all of this music contains richly rewarding values. That which may seem raucous at first may come to sound beautiful on further hearing; and at the very least, it will be found to be full of meaning and feeling. There is no better way to know a people than to enter with them into their musical life...

SELECTED NOTES FROM VOLUME I [P504]

3. GEORGIA (CAUCASIAN): Greek Orthodox Church choir. Intense choral music which preserves the "organum" style of medieval Christian music, combined with modes preserved from Byzantine culture. The part singing, very prevalent in this region, is spontaneous.

4. GREECE: Shepherd clarinet-like pipes, kanun accompaniment. The shepherd who plays on this record made his own clarinet-like pipes so that they could play a chromatic scale, and are flexible in both extremes of range. He makes highly virtuosic variations on a tune which is said to have come into Greece at the time of the Persian wars. The accompaniment is on the kanun, strings played on directly by hammers held in the hands of the performer.

5. JAPAN (GAGAKU): IMPERIAL SHO KOTO CHANT. Male singers accompanied by the koto and sho. Music for traditional dances of the imperial court, intoned in low men's voices in dignified measure, with rhythmical punctuation of the koto, a harp-like instrument, and the ancient sho, a mouth organ with tiny pipes arranged like those of a pipe organ, playing the melody four octaves higher than the singers. The octaves are deliberately played slightly out of tune to give a rubbing, dissonant sound.

6. NIGERIA (YORUBA TRIBE): Choral "singing" conversation with signal drums. Wild singing conversation interspersed with choral strains from a "singing band" is transmitted by drum signals which are not only understood as a language, but which also must fit rhythmically with the music...

13. TIBET: LAMENT FOR THE DEAD. Lamas chanting in unison with percussion and bells accompaniment. Chanting of the lament for the dead by Lamas has been steadily practiced for many ages. The chorus of deep bass voices is impressive to a point of seeming almost sinister.

14. UNITED STATES: PRETTY POLLY. A Tennessee mountaineer singing, accompanying himself with banjo. Mountain singers in Tennessee delight in preserving old English-style ballads, served in American style, sung straight out with no prettifying of the voice, but with lots of verses. The present ballad singer knows a thing or two about picking a banjo, with which he accompanies himself.

15. ICELAND: SONG OF GREETING—HLIDARENDAKOTI (RYMUR). Nearly every Icelander is a folk singer. The older people often sing in two parts in open fifths, in preservation of medieval European religious forms; "rymur" are improvised songs of greetings to guests. The present unaccompanied song is a typical simple, serious folk tune...

SELECTED NOTES FROM VOLUME 2 [P505]

17. CUBA: A "son" is a Cuban development of a Spanish-type folk song. This recording is of a son performed as a rhumba in Afro-Cuban multiplicity of incisive rhythms. It was made long before the rhumba hit Broadway and became watered down. The chorus sings in chords picked up by ear; and in the percussion section African-type instruments are used to produce from 5 to 7 simultaneous rhythms...

22. SERBIA: The vocal rhythm of ecstasy without beats is preserved from medieval times on this expansive tenor solo. A bass tamboritz (mandolin-like instrument) plucks repeatedly on a ground tone which is also sustained by bass voices. The voices finally move on a counterpoint against the tenor in twelfth or thirteenth-century style, using [the] Dorian Mode. Later the minor third is exchanged for a major third, giving the Mixolydian Mode. The style seems Oriental, but is actually an adaptation of early Christian modes as used in the Serbian Orthodox Church, into a secular love song. A violin plays [an] ornamented modal melody in the interlude...

SELECTED NOTES FROM VOLUME 3 [P506]

43. HUNGARIAN GYPSY: The Magyars of Hungary have their own musical styles, scales and modes, a great many of which were made known to the world by Béla Bartók.

Gypsies throughout the world have a very characteristic way of playing, and they apply this to the folk music with which they find themselves surrounded. There are a great many Gypsies in Hungary, and they have developed a music there made up of a combination of their own style of playing with Hungarian (Magyar) melodies.

This record is of a group of Gypsies playing a typical czardas. The soloist plays violin with a dashing, strongly-accented virtuosity, accompanied on the cembulam, a predecessor of the piano on which the performer plays with a hammer held in each hand. The music is in minor; and tonic, dominant, subdominant and submediant chords have been picked up by ear from Western European music...

The World's Vocal Arts

INTRODUCTION

V OCAL ART IS NOT the same the world over. Vocal styles are
affected by language and tradition, and by different ways of
cultivation. The tastes and wishes of different peoples are widely
divergent as to what sort of tone they prefer. The greatest separation is between the Orient and the Occident; Eastern peoples prefer open, uncovered, nasal tone, and Western peoples prefer covered tone of various sorts. All cultivated training, however, includes
breath control and bodily support, as far as I am aware.

When a singer in the Western world takes a vocal lesson, the
teacher will try to "place" the voice. This means the establishment
of a tone quality according to the experience and taste of the
teacher, and will be according to his background and tradition. In
the case of a fine teacher, there will be also consideration of bringing out some of the native quality of the singer's voice; but if the
voice is by nature too far removed from the teacher's tradition, he
will just consider it a "bad" voice; and even in cases where the
teacher tries faithfully to bring out the native quality, he is often
hardly aware of the extent to which he channels the production
towards his own concept of tonal excellence. There are months
and years of lessons during which the teacher will yell "good" or

*Cowell's specialties in folk music, to the extent that he allowed himself to have any,
were vocal music and Indonesian music, especially Javanese. Vocal styles fascinated
him (see his "Vocal Innovators" text in the "Music and Other Arts" section). For
Folkways in 1955 he edited* The World's Vocal Arts *(Ethnic Folkways Library
Album #FE 4510), a cross-cultural selection of vocal recordings ranging from American Negro blues to crooners, to Russian and Thai and North Chinese operas, to
Korean classical and Ethiopian singing, Swiss yodeling, North Indian classical singing, and so on. Here is Cowell's introduction to the recording.*

"bad" about the tones, and the "good" tones are spread throughout the vocal range. The teacher's value therefore lies in his being able to exercise fine judgment in tonal selection. He will try to give the student one reliable, fundamental type of tone, spread and balanced throughout the singer's entire range. This tone will usually contain a mixture of "head" and "chest" qualities, with a different blend owing to the background of the teacher and the range of the student's voice. The student may have developed for himself a consistent style, so that the teacher changes it very little; in this event the singer picks up his idea of style by ear through hearing others. In most cases, however, the teacher creates the style; and the final product — voice, tone and style, — might have been surprisingly different if the teacher had been from a different background and tradition.

By and large our Western vocal tradition came from Italy. "Bel canto," or beautiful singing, was perfected for the singing of Italian songs and opera, and a church style of singing of Gregorian chants was closely related. The Latin and Italian languages both have clear vowels, and so the vocal style is based on a clear, ringing tone, covered to produce a maximum of head resonance and brilliance. The vibrato is rapid, and of small range, so the effect is that of the steadiest of cultivated Western tones. The consonants are produced cleanly and quickly, so as to interrupt the flow of sound as little as possible, and the sound is continued through the consonants whenever physically possible. The sliding tones (portamenti) are reduced to a minimum; in legato, the pitch is sustained until the last moment, and the slide to the next tone is so rapid as to be almost indistinguishable. There are some exceptions in practice in opera, in which there may be a big scoop[1] into a climactic tone, but this is not part of the theory of vocal style in bel canto.

The Italian style spread, and was taught increasingly all over the Western world. At first, the Italian language was always associated with this style of vocal music, but gradually, in the seventeenth and eighteenth centuries, attempts were made to apply it to other European tongues.

Little by little it became evident that there should be some changes in tone production and style to suit other languages and tastes. By the late nineteenth century there had arisen a French style in which there is a somewhat less covered tone than in bel canto, and more nasal sounds; a German style, in which a darker and richer quality is admired (much of it would be called "throaty" by Italian teachers); and a Russian style based on Slavic language considerations, but as an art combining the French and German, having less to do with the original Italian base. In England there was much singing in the sixteenth and seventeenth centuries, but we have no way of knowing just what the cultivated singing style was like; later, England adopted Italian vocal training as a standard, and operas sung there in the seventeenth and eighteenth centuries were in Italian. The German style branches into a lieder-singing style, with controlled phrasing and sustained rich tone; and a dramatic opera style, in which vocal perfection is abandoned for the sake of fervent expression, and the voice competes with a large orchestra. In France there is also a song style and an operatic style, and in addition a popular music hall style which has become an ingredient in popular songs all over Europe, and in "torch" and "croon" styles in the United States.

Turning to the Eastern vocal styles, we find that they have in common a preference for open rather than covered tone, for nasal quality, obvious in the Near East, and continuing in greater intensity as one approaches the Far East. In case the listener has trouble in digesting and enjoying these styles, he should recall that singers do not sing the way they do because they can't sing in Western style; they do it because they like it, and because it is, in each case, a carefully taught tradition, often many centuries old. My own experience is that one comes to prize and like it greatly.

Outside of Europe there are five main vocal worlds and their mixtures. The Near Eastern includes Jewish music and the music of Arabic-speaking peoples (embracing some from North and East Africa). The Middle Eastern contains some Islamic influence from the Near Eastern culture, but is based mainly on ancient Indian and Persian vocal art; Malayan style embraces Burma, Thailand, South Eastern Asia and Indonesia; Far Eastern style includes China, Korea and Japan. In addition, there is the culture of West, Central and South Africa. There the singing is only slightly nasal, with development of a rather straightforward folk singing tone, and much emphasis on speech syllables and rhythm. It should not be confused with American Negro vocal style, which is different, as represented in "blues," etc.

It is impossible to describe tonal distinctions in words so that a deaf man could gain a clear [picture] of them. It is recommended, therefore, that to acquaint yourself with differences in Eastern styles, listening to the music several times is the best method. However, there are some elements which may be especially listened for. 1) Sliding tones, highly cultivated and perfected in all Eastern vocal cultures, each in a very different manner. (2) Trills, shakes, mordants and other vocal ornaments, which also include a sort of artistic bleating, or moving the same tone forward and back, and glottal trills, in which the tone is interrupted in the middle of the trill. Some of these ornaments are based on microtones (those less than 1/2 step apart); some are slow, others fast. (3) The influence of language and highly individual modes or scales. Italian church music is affected by ecclesiastical modes; Italian song and opera are affected by major and minor scales. Oriental style is affected by the many Oriental modes which differ from major and minor, and also from the early ecclesiastical modes of the Roman church. It should be noted that in their training, classic singers of the Far East learn seven different vocal styles, one for each of seven emotional situations, instead of one voice placement as in the West…

1. Does Cowell mean "swoop"?—DH

Music of Indonesia

THE MUSIC OF INDONESIA is a whole world of music, different yet alike, running the gamut from primitive to highly culti-vated. Most cultivated music uses an orchestra, usually consisting of tuned percussion instruments, called a gamelan. Sometimes, especially for women's music, there will be a small flute with a wisp of a tone on top, and perhaps a bowed string rebab, taken from Persia. Otherwise the gamelan consists of tuned gongs, metal and wooden bars, and drums. The five-tone scales are two in number—Slendero, in which there are five almost equal intervals between A and A a bit over an octave distant; it sounds to us like A, B, C ♯, E, F ♯, A; and Pelok, which is like G ♯, A, C ♯, D, E, G ♯. Pelok is somewhat more elegant, Slendero is more popular. A gamelan has to be tuned to one or the other of these scales; both cannot be played on the same gamelan.

The gamelan is usually in three octaves, one player to the five tones of each octave (thus there are nine fundamental players—three each on the three octaves of gongs, metal bars and wooden bars), the low octave in longer tones (we usually write these as half-notes), the middle octave in slightly faster counterpoint, the top octave in high variations. The form is four-square; everything is in 4/4 meter, and the form in groups of four, eight, sixteen, thirty-two, etc., measures. On the first beats of longer form sections there is apt to be a lower large gong, often slightly displaced in pitch with the rest of the scale. The deepest gong in the gamelan will be

Though he never visited Indonesia, Cowell studied Indonesian music in depth in Berlin. (See the review of McPhee's Tabu Tabuhan *in Part Two). Here, in his introduction to* Music of Indonesia *(recorded by Phil and Florence Walker, edited by Henry Cowell: Folkways FE 4537 A/B and C/D), he discusses the Indonesian mythological theory of music and the gamelan orchestra.*

sounded only at the junction of very large form sections. The main tone here will be the end of the past section and the beginning of the new.

In the quasi-mythological theory of music, music goes on all the time about us, but is inaudible unless brought into reality by a gamelan. The time-sequence is controlled by musical priests, who calculate where the continuous music has arrived at any given moment. The great cycle is seven years long, and once in every seven years the end of the old cycle and the beginning of the new is marked by the sounding of the great gong—said to be the world's largest—the Sultan's temple.[1] The tone lasts for slightly over an hour, and when it is sounded, pilgrims from all over the East come to hear it. Once started, the music runs continuously (though inaudibly) for the next seven years, and some of the main smaller cycles are marked by the sounding of other large gongs in various temples. When a gamelan actually plays, it is thought that it merely makes audible that which is already going on in the musical cosmos. One hears by way of introduction therefore, a few tones leading the gamelan to a main point, for it to get in tune with the infinite, so to speak.

While orchestra (gamelan) music is commoner in Indonesia than with any other peoples of the world, there is, of course, some vocal music. The cultivated voice is thin-lined, nasal, and steady —no vibrato. The Rama legend of India is often used for the opera-dramas, which may last several days. The shadow plays also have their own music. In recent times, boys of Bali have developed an astonishing rhythmical group-singing style which seems to have grown out of whole cloth—its fulsome titillating rhythms have no historical basis, and while this manner was apparently developed for tourists, it is certainly a fine new beginning point. Westerners are not the only ones who are inventing new musical [forms]…

1. Presumably in Jogjakarta.—HC

Music of the Orient

I PRESENT MYSELF TO YOU as a person who realized from his own experience that the music of Japan, as well as that of China and other oriental countries, is part of American music.

I was raised in San Francisco. We lived between the Japanese and Chinese districts and I had many Japanese and Chinese playmates between the ages of five and nine. I sang their folk songs in their native language, just as many children on the eastern seaboard sing those songs in German and French learned from their playmates. By the time I was nine years old, the music of these oriental people was just as natural to me as any music.

My father was born in Ireland and sang old Irish songs; my mother was born in southern Illinois, but came from a family that knew the songs of the Ozarks and of the Kentucky mountains and she sang these songs for me.

When I was five years old I was pronounced musical and, therefore, I took violin lessons from a teacher who was 75 when I was five. A New England man, he wouldn't let me hear any modern music such as Beethoven, Schumann and Schubert.

Most people who live in the middle and eastern parts of this country don't realize that Japanese and Chinese music is part of American music. As an American composer I would like to point out that oriental music has influenced me a great deal. I feel that we have laid too much emphasis on the music that comes from continental Europe. We also need to be able to draw on the great music of the Orient. Each one of the oriental countries is as differ-

This text is Cowell's penultimate statement concerning world music, in this case Asian music. Presenting Cowell's idea of polymusicality without using the term, it appeared in Music Journal *21 n. 6 (Sept. '63) 24-6, 74-6 and* Peabody Notes *XXVII/2 (Winter 1964) pp. 2-5, from which it is reprinted.*

ent from every other in musical traditions, certainly, as the European countries, and perhaps more so.

Most of us don't know anything about this music or else the music has been presented to us as something not very musical. Certainly all that we have ever done in the past has been to take it as oriental color and mix it in as a seasoning ingredient in some of our western music. But this isn't enough today because there are old, classical, well-honored traditions and rather rigid traditions that we need to know about. They are complicated. It is hard to study them. You have to take lots of time. But the composer who is influenced by oriental music in the western world today, and there are increasing numbers of these, finds that it is quite necessary to go into these traditions extensively.

We are glad to be able to draw on the traditional music of Germany, France and Italy, let us say, or of England or Ireland, or of China, Japan, Indonesia, Persia—any of the great oriental musical cultures, as you wish. But we have to know something about them. You can't get by with studying two or three courses for Japanese color and then study counterpoint for eight years as it is taught in European conservatories. You have to realize that there is a great tradition, which is being explored to a certain extent by increasingly informed composers in America. Sometimes these are specialists, sometimes they are more than specialists.

Howard Hanson lived for seven years in Indonesia and writes music strongly influenced by the Indonesian; he probably knows more about the music of this land than any other living person (including anybody in Indonesia itself).

If you want to study harmony or chords, this is the specialty of the western world of music. If you want to study melody and rhythm, you go to India, because they know a great deal more about these as a study than we do in the western world.

I would like to point out that if you look at the theoretical studies in western colleges, there is always the study of harmony, usually several semesters. There is usually no study of melody and no semesters of rhythm and, when you are finished, it is not nearly so complete as it would be if you had studied in India.

Here, we have two principal scales. First of all, a child must study major scales. Then, hopefully, minor scales. If he is thought to be very bright, he may study the church modes. These, for the most part, died out in the late sixteenth century, but were revived again in modern years by composers such as Debussy. There are usually about four of these modes to add to the major and minor scales, but only if you are quite bright.

A child in India learns the fundamental scales. There are 72 fundamental ones, so he learns those first before allowing variations.

I was shown, with a certain amount of pride, in the Madras Academy of Music, a volume which looked like our encyclopedia in which there are 32,000 varieties of scales. I looked a bit alarmed about this and was hastily told that no one musician could do more than 600, just as we don't know every word in our dictionary or encyclopedia.

Japan doesn't have quite such a number of different scales in its traditional music. The traditional music, so-called, corresponds with our serious music and includes several schools of thought which have grown up in just about the same period as our music has. Some is serious, some is classical, some is romantic, some is modern. In Japan, most of the music on which these traditions are founded was brought in from Korea and China. This started in about the sixth century and ended in about the tenth century at the time of the T'ang dynasty. The musical manuscripts of the Emperor's court in China were brought for safekeeping to the court of Japan. Only in recent years have they been unraveled.

One of the world's great harpsichord players, a Viennese woman, was interned in Japan during the war and was sufficiently famous so that she became the teacher of the children of the Emperor. She therefore had access to the manuscripts which were in the palace and which no one, for the most part, had ever seen. She found there the music manuscripts which came from the T'ang dynasty in China.

This was a period of wonderful achievement in China. They had great orchestras there from 908-910 [C.E.]. The small orchestra would be about 500 [musicians] but they went up to 900 in a regular orchestra. Following this [period there] was a collapse, so that no orchestras appeared in the Orient after this that were anything like it at all.

In Japan, the instruments once played by 200 musicians are

now played by one. There is now a finer line. But this fine line has become very Japanese through these many years. It did have its initial idea coming from elsewhere. Now, it is a fine art of music and it is drawn from the continental countries, namely Korea and China, both with ancient musical cultures.

As an example, take the Japanese *sho*. It was called a *sheng* when it was used about 1300 B.C. in China and resembles our first pipe organs. When it was brought to Japan, it was called a *sho*. It is the same sort of instrument. It is held to the mouth and has little reed pipes just like a pipe organ. This is one of the oldest instruments. Other old instruments are still preserved in the *gagaku* or court music of Japan which was built on the music of the Chinese and Korean courts.

The *koto*, a harp-like instrument, with 13 silk strings tuned over moveable bridges is played mostly on the ground. It can be played with great virtuosity and we have in this country, at present, Mr. Kimio Eto who is called the greatest *koto* player alive. I have written a concerto for him, incidentally, and three symphony orchestras are bidding for the premiere. Another instrument is the *shamisen*, a banjo-like instrument coming from the Loochu Islands originally about 200 years ago. This is a Chinese-type instrument, played often with the *koto*.

About 175 years ago, the *shakuhachi* was played by gentlemen in almost any capacity. It had previously been played by the samurai. Occasionally, you will find the *shakuhachi* played with a basket over the head. This is a tradition which arose when a samurai became impoverished and played the *shakuhachi* for money. The basket concealed the identity of the samurai. And you can still give a *shakuhachi* player, with a basket on his head, money—even though he probably will not be a samurai.

Japan is a large and diversified country and, as in the case of all such countries, there is music of many different kinds. There is, for example, popular music which you hear a great deal of on the radio at the present time and this is a combination of the music of the geisha girls and Broadway hits—something that I am sure would be successful if introduced in this country.

On the other hand, Japan is a country which has a number of different peoples. The Ainu, who were probably in Japan before the present Japanese were there, live in the extreme north. They worship the bear. They have music in this far northern region which is far more primitive than the music of our own Indians.

As in practically every country that has a cultivated music, the Japanese have folk music. Folk music doesn't mean that this music is made up as it goes along by the person who sings or plays it. It does mean that these tunes are traditionally handed down from mouth to mouth, from father to son and from neighbor to neighbor and that nobody can name the composer, although it was probably the most musical person in the small district who actually put the tune together at some point in history. This becomes a tradition of its own.

The singing is not exactly the same as in western styles but in folk music it is not nearly so different from our own standards of singing as the music of the highly traditional and artificially cultivated music, which is the artistic singing of Japan.

Learning more about western music is popular among Japanese musicians at the present time. The musicians have had, for many generations, western-type orchestras playing the classics. I was rather astonished, when first going to Japan in 1957, to find eight full-fledged symphony orchestras playing western-style symphonic music in Tokyo alone. This doesn't mean some sort of little pick-up orchestra. These were musicians in orchestras which played extremely well, which had good conductors, some Japanese, others imported from Germany, France and even the United States. Some of our conductors out of New York were there with orchestras. On the other hand, Mr. Watanabe conducts one of the orchestras. He is an excellent conductor from Japan, whose orchestra is made up entirely of Japanese people playing western music.

The orchestras tend to specialize—not wholly—but in part, so that one orchestra will specialize in the classics and will be more apt to play Beethoven, Brahms and Mozart and others will be built for performance of the works of Tchaikovsky and Wagner.

A third orchestra—for instance, the Japanese Philharmonic Orchestra—will specialize mostly in twentieth century music. All these orchestras are really first class. When I say this, I don't mean they are the equal of our first half-dozen orchestras. They come in the very next category, which is really quite remarkable.

There are some very interesting things happening in the field of western music in Tokyo. There are little teahouses seating from twelve to twenty-five people, where you can drink tea as long as you like and even order other things too with the tea if you must. Each of these teahouses is dedicated to a certain composer. In the outlying district where I lived, having been fortunately invited by former students of mine from Columbia University, there were two such teahouses. One was a Bach Teahouse where only Bach's music was played and another played only Bruckner. I must say I know a great deal more about Bruckner than I knew before.

Another thing that is provocative in this respect is what is happening in public schools in Japan at the present time. A friend of mine is the supervisor of schools in a heavily populated district of Tokyo. He called together twenty-four music supervisors from all the districts of Tokyo and he translated while I spoke to them. They presented me with the eight books used in the primary school grades. There wasn't one Japanese tune in any of the books.

Children, 10 or 11 years of age, played for me and they were really astonishing. At this age they play three- and four-part counterpoint works by Corelli and so on, in the most amazing fashion—almost all on harmonicas.

Every child can afford to have a harmonica and after they have graduated into the secondary schools, they are given additional parts on the accordion. These reed instruments are very nice for older music of this sort and everything sounded delightful except that there was nothing Japanese about anything that happened at the hall.

Presently, I said to these twenty-four supervisors, "You really ought to know something about the traditions of Japanese music. If you will come to Columbia University, I have a class there." They all agreed that this was their fault. I think they have revised the primary grade books so that they include Japanese music. But at present the Japanese child living in Tokyo does not hear traditional music. He has to go to a Japanese music school!

PART FOUR

HC on Works
by HC

Persian Set

THIS IS A SIMPLE RECORD of musical contagion, written at the end of a three-months' stay in Iran, during which I listened for several hours nearly every day to the traditional classic music and the folk music of the country—at concerts, at private parties, at the National Conservatory for Traditional Iranian Music (where the instructors gave wonderful demonstrations of virtuosity for my benefit), and at Radio Teheran. Tape recordings at the Department of Fine Arts were especially helpful in displaying the rich variety of music in regions too difficult to visit in midwinter.

Of course I made no attempt to shed my years of Western symphonic experience; nor have I used actual Iranian melodies or rhythms, nor have I imitated them exactly. Instead I have tried to develop some of the kinds of musical behavior that the two cultures have in common.

The musical cultures of Asia have remained monodic in theory, but they are often polyphonic in actual performing practice. Attempts to combine the old classic melodic styles of the East with eighteenth and nineteenth century European harmony do not seem to me to be successful. But where a need is felt for the tonal variety of the Western orchestra, I think polyphony (based on the actual structure of the melodies used) is a natural direction for musical development to take in the East.

The tonal coincidences in *Persian Set* were suggested by the

Most of Cowell's notes and indeed most of his comments on his own music are fairly schematic and unexceptional. He seems to have had more trouble analyzing his own works than those of others, a fairly common situation among composers. In some cases Cowell's notes consist only of a chart which shows special characters employed in a piece. But there are exceptions. One is this note, written from Tokyo in May 1957, to Antal Dorati, the conductor, to accompany the score of Cowell's Persian Set *(1956-57).*

polyphony actually heard from Iran's three-to-five man ensembles. In one of the most commonly heard musical styles the instruments (with or without a vocalist) and the drum take turns leading the melodic improvisation on one of the many inherited formal structures. A second melody instrument then follows the leader more or less in canon, at intervals varying according to his ability to keep up. Sometimes he will even take off in a parallel but different phrase of his own.

At Radio Tehran, European and Iranian instruments are sometimes combined. *Persian Set* adds the *tar* to a small Western orchestral ensemble. This is a beautifully shaped, double-bellied, three-stringed Persian instrument of very elaborate technique, for which the mandolin is an approximate substitute.

Persian music is modal (usually tetrachordal) and its modes rather persistently take either the note G or the note D for their tonic, as I have done here. There are five tetrachords in customary use which Iranian musicians combine in a number of ways. Four of these are used in *Persian Set*. They correspond quite accurately to our tunings for (descending): C-B-A-G; C-B♭-A-G; C-B-A♭-G. The fifth tetrachordal form has the famous quarter-tone interval at one point, and it is used just as much as the others, but one hears many pieces without it. It corresponds to the Western C-B♭-Ahalf-flat-G (not used in this composition).

This quarter-tone is blamed by Iranian musicians for the difficulties in "modernizing" Iranian music by "harmonizing" it, but an even more basic trouble derives from the fact that it is not yet generally understood in Iran—what we in America have discovered only recently ourselves—that classic European harmony fits scales but not modes, whether the modes be those chosen for development in the Orient or in the Occident.

One of the traditional musical styles heard in Iran today is a quiet, improvisatory one, arhythmical, like a prose invocation. Traditional Persian music was a great classic art which is said to have spread westward into many parts of the Arab-speaking world, reaching Greece about 600 B.C. In the seventh century A.D. the Arabs returned it to Persia in somewhat altered form as Islamic music. Moslem distaste for music had much less effect on the peoples of Iran than it did upon the Arabs, so that the practice of the art of music was never quenched in Persia after the Moslem Conquest. A few melodies surviving today are believed by Iranian students to be pre-Islamic, and certain types of mordents, and particularly the trill across a tone and a half, widespread today over the whole Middle East, are commonly called "Persian" by musicians of other countries. The elaborate Persian drumming techniques have been admired for generations, and even today in Cairo, Beirut and Istanbul most drummers will claim to be Persian—and sometimes are.

Quartet Romantic
and Quartet Euphometric

PREFACE

THE TWO QUARTETS that I called "rhythm-harmony" pieces at the time were composed between 1915 and 1919, when I was stimulated by the relationship between harmonic and rhythmic ratios.

The possibility of a demonstrable physical identity between rhythm and harmony occurred to me when I entered the University of California in the fall of 1914 and was faced for the first time with an actual textbook in music theory—the famous *Foote &* *Spalding.* I was already exploring the possibilities inherent in counter-rhythms—2 against 3, 3 against 4, and others much more complex—and on first opening *Foote & Spalding,* I was struck with the fact that the lower reaches of the overtone series were expressed by the same ratios I had been using to describe counter-rhythms. Could they be somehow the same?

HC's notes on the Quartet Romantic *(1915-17) and* Quartet Euphometric *(1916-19) are more extensive than those on most of his other pieces. The theory underlying these two quartets—they are not string quartets—is described most fully in Cowell's book* New Musical Resources *(1930, see Bibliography), some notes for which were written as early as 1918. The disks described by Cowell and certain examples written by Schillinger and Schillinger's students are now in the Rodgers and Hammerstein Archive of Recorded Sound at the New York Public Library in Lincoln Center. The second Rhythmicon was eventually given by Mrs. Joseph Schillinger to the Smithsonian Institution in Washington, DC. For these notes we are indebted to Don Gillespie of the C. F. Peters Corporation, New York. A version also appears with a CRI long-playing recording,* Homage to Iran *and* Three String Quartets. Beaux Arts String Quartet *(Composers Recordings, Inc., CRI-173). While here a more detailed discussion of the* Quartet Romantic *follows the more general one, there is no comparable HC note for the* Quartet Euphometric, *though Peters's published score includes a brief analytical note by Stephen Fisher and Don Gillespie.*

A little later a graduate student in the physics department at Stanford, with whom I discussed the matter, mentioned that he had access to a pair of sirens. Our experiments with two simultaneous sirens showed that if they are tuned in the relationship 3:2, they will sound the *interval* of a perfect fifth; if they are both slowed down, keeping the same 3:2 relationship, they arrive at a *rhythm* of 3 against 2, heard as gentle bumps but also visible in tiny puffs of air through the holes in the sirens, and so easily confirmed. Tuned to any other harmonic ratio, of course, the same thing happens, proving that these ratios express a single physical relationship which is heard as rhythm when slow and as pitch when fast.

I made innumerable written examples showing those relationships in duration of tones, in counter-rhythms and in accents in counter-meter, some of which were later used in the book *New Musical Resources.* But I also used these ideas more freely, in actual polyphonic compositions, whose flowing melodic lines were conceived with utmost precision rhythmically. The two rhythm-harmony quartets that appear here seem to be all of this sort of music that has survived from this first period of concern with such ideas, and they may be all I completed at the time. In any case, the meters for the most part were necessarily so complex that they were obviously unperformable by any known human agency, and I thought of them as purely fanciful.

However, I always hoped that an instrument could be devised that would put under human control even more complex rhythms by means of comparatively simple performance on a keyboard. A letter from Russell Varian, who was one of my boyhood friends, sketches such an instrument in 1916, but none of us had any money for such enterprises in those days. Later it occurred to me that the principle of the "electronic eye" might be applied to such a device and, about 1929, I presented this idea to Leon Theremin in New York City, and he built for me a keyboard which produces one to sixteen rhythms—either any number together, or all of them at once, or one after the other. There is also a seventeenth key to produce syncopation, one eighth-note off. The instrument, which I christened the Rhythmicon, is tuned to match the overtone series, so that all the ratios in rhythm and pitch, up to the sixteenth, may be given; and it may be pitched high or low. But since there was no way of giving melodic freedom by varying the note-lengths in a single part, and no method of accenting, these early quartets still could not be played on it. Therefore I composed other sorts of rhythm-harmony pieces for it: a Concerto for Rhythmicon and Orchestra and a number of solo pieces which I used in lectures with the instrument for several years.

The first Rhythmicon built for me by Leon Theremin did not work too well and, when Nicolas Slonimsky asked my permission to order one for himself, Theremin was glad of the chance to make some improvements. I had taken the first one to California on a lecture tour, and I left it in the psychology department at Stanford University, where it was used for some tests, among other things. About 1938 it was discarded as past repair. The second instrument was eventually bought from Slonimsky by Joseph Schillinger, who wanted to use it in his teaching. Schillinger recorded illustrations from some of my solo compositions for the instrument on aluminum disks.

Both quartets are polyphonic, and each melodic strand has its own rhythm. Even the canon in the first movement of the *Romantic* has different note-lengths for each voice. The second movement relaxes into more conventional rhythm (hence the name "Romantic") but continues with dissonant counterpoint. The *Quartet Euphometric* ("euphonious meters") has a similar spare polyphonic structure, but there are accents which give a different rhythmic grouping to each part.

In both quartets the tonal material is not based on modes or scales. Since I used all twelve tones freely, the pieces are atonal. But unlike the atonal styles then developing abroad (with which I only became acquainted later), the melodic lines are more often conjunct than not, and the vertical combinations use consonance as well as dissonance in varying degrees, not, of course, conventionally resolved.

In both quartets the musical intention was flowing and lyrical, not severe or harsh, or ejaculatory. If the day should come when the first movement of the *Romantic*, with all its rhythmic complications, is actually playable, I should like to point out that it was conceived as something human that would sound warm and rich and somewhat *rubato*. Whatever the electronic or other means used for it, its composer hopes that it need not sound icy in tone nor rigid in rhythm.

COMPOSER'S WORKING NOTES ON
THE QUARTET ROMANTIC[1]

In the first movement of the *Quartet Romantic*, the relative note-lengths are based exactly upon the ratios of pitch vibrations according to the overtone series. The numbers assigned to successive overtones are the source of these ratios. The same ratios determine the note-lengths.

Thus, if we take low C (below the bass staff) as our fundamental, it becomes, in Example 1, No. 1:

Ex. 1. Henry Cowell. *Quartet Romantic.* © 1974. Used by permission of C. F. Peters Corp.

The first overtone, an octave higher, becomes No. 2; the second overtone, the G an octave and a fifth above the fundamental, will be No. 3; the third overtone, No. 4, is two octaves above the fundamental; the fourth overtone, No. 5, is two octaves and a major third above our low C; the fifth overtone will be given the number 6, and is two octaves and a fifth above the fundamental; the sixth overtone, No. 7, is a minor third above No. 6 (two octaves and a minor seventh above the fundamental). And so on, each successive overtone closer to the preceding one as the distance from the fundamental expands upward.

When taken in relation either to the fundamental or to each other, these numbers represent vibration ratios (expressed as a fraction), no matter what the actual number of vibrations per second may be. Thus the relationship between the fundamental and the octave above (which has twice the number of vibrations per second that the fundamental has) is expressible as 2/1; the fraction (or ratio) 3/2 describes the second overtone, (No. 3), which is an octave and a fifth above our fundamental low C, having 1 ½ times the number of vibrations that No. 2 has. Or if you wish to describe this G in relation to the fundamental C, you can write the fraction 3/1 which accurately defines the relationship of the number of vibrations per second between the two tones.

In the *Quartet Romantic* the relationships between note-lengths follow the same pattern. Having demonstrated to my own satisfaction that note-length ratios may be derived from the overtone ratios [in the experiment with two sirens already described], I composed a very simple four-part theme (Example 2), assigning to the low C (as fundamental) the length of a whole note. The harmonic theme was then translated into rhythms as in Example 3.

Ex. 2. Henry Cowell. *Quartet Romantic.* © 1974. Used by permission of C. F. Peters Corp.

Ex. 3. Henry Cowell. *Quartet Romantic.* © 1974. Used by permission of C. F. Peters Corp.

In Example 3, and throughout the first movement, the time scale is multiplied by four, so that a quarter note of the basic four-part piece supplies rhythms for a 4/4 bar of the quartet.

The fractions set down for the first two measures in Example 2 illustrate the process. It will be seen that the note-length that corresponds to the first overtone (No. 2) above low C (its octave) is a half-note; that the third overtone (No. 4, two octaves above the fundamental whole-note C) turns into a quarter note. The fourth overtone (No. 5, two octaves and a major third above the fundamental whole-note C) will correspond to a meter of five, and the fifth overtone (No. 6) will give us six notes in the time of a whole note.

In the second measure of Example 2 (written out metrically in full beginning with measure 5 of Example 3), the pattern of note-lengths for each voice is that produced by the vibration ratios of the tones of a chord of F, in relation to the same low C considered as the fundamental. The F an octave and a fourth above the fundamental (not shown in Example 1) is expressed by the fraction $8/3$: It produces six third-notes plus two third-notes, or a total of $2\frac{1}{2}$ beats per measure (bass voice, measure 5 of Example 3). The tenor C still maintains the time of four to a measure; the alto F two octaves and a fourth above the fundamental requires $5\frac{1}{3}$ beats, and the soprano A is found to be the equivalent of $6\frac{2}{3}$ beats per measure.

In the seventh measure of Example 3, the metric ratios are derived from the overtone ratios of the first G above the fundamental low C; this G is related to the C as three is to two (or $1\frac{1}{2}$ per measure). Thus the alto part contains six beats per measure, the bass maintains $2\frac{2}{3}$ beats per measure, the tenor has $4\frac{1}{2}$, and the soprano $7\frac{1}{2}$ beats per measure.

All the note-lengths of Example 3 are derived precisely from the harmonic sequence in Example 2: the ratios in the harmonic series that define each note of the harmonic "theme" in Example 2 are translated exactly into the metric values of Example 3. These metric values are followed exactly throughout the first movement of the quartet (through measure 56), although the pitches vary.

For various note-lengths not provided for in our traditional system of writing music, I had to work out my own ways of setting them down, and this delayed the writing-out of these two quartets for some years after they were more or less complete in my head. At times, throughout the first movement, triangular notes are used for divisions of a whole note, or its fractions, into thirds (as in Example 3, measure 5). Square notes are used (as in measure 29 of the score) for divisions of a whole note, or its fractions, into five parts. Square notes with a stroke through the heads were required (as in measures 27-28 of the score) for notes dividing a whole note, or its fractions, into fifteen parts.

1. Cowell's four-part theme (Example 2) provides the rhythmic framework for only the first fifty-six measures of the first movement. A second short piece..., using G as fundamental, is the underlying basis for measures 57-129. A harmonic sketch for the remainder of the first movement has apparently not survived.—STEPHEN FISHER AND DON GILLESPIE

United Quartet

"THE UNITED QUARTET is an attempt toward a more universal musical style," the composer begins. "Although it is unique in form, style and content, it is easy to understand because of its use of fundamental elements as a basis, because of repetitions which enable the auditor to become accustomed to these elements, because of the clarity and simplicity of its form, and because of the unity of form, rhythm and melody... There are in it elements suggested from many places and periods. For example, the *Classical* feeling is represented not by the employment of a familiar classic form, but by building up a new form, carefully planned... *Primitive* music is represented, not by imitating it, nor by taking a specific melody or rhythm from some tribe, but by using a three-tone scale, and exhausting all the different ways the three tones can appear, which is a procedure of some primitive music... The *Oriental* is represented by modes which are constructed as Oriental modes are constructed, without being actual modes used in particular cultures... The *Modern* is represented by the use of unresolved discords, by free intervals in two-part counterpoint, and," concludes the composer with triumphant logic, "by the fact that the whole result is something new, and all that is new is modern!"

There are many other very short notes by Cowell on his pieces comparable to this one on the United Quartet, *including the liner notes on Joseph Szigeti's recording of the Violin Sonata No.1 for Violin and Piano (Columbia Records, "Modern American Music Series" 1953 ML 4841) or in the liner notes for the recordings of the various* Hymn and Fuguing Tune *works. The* United Quartet *dates from 1936 and was written at Redwood, California. Some of Cowell's avant garde colleagues were critical of Cowell's use of a more popular style than in the earlier works, though the general public still found Cowell's music difficult. This note attempts to place the work for both kinds of listener. In left wing politics this was the time of the "united front." Perhaps this work, ending with a march, had a progressive ring to it at the time.*

PART FIVE

Music and Other Arts

Vocal Innovators
of Central Europe

A N EXTENSION OF VOCAL possibilities, particularly in the use
of voice alone, is the keynote of a new musical development
now growing rapidly in central Europe. There may be a hint of
neo-classicism in the idea of returning to the voice; but it is not the
purpose of the young composers to revive the old vocal style. They
are finding new sorts of vocalization, sometimes quite foreign to
anything formerly considered singing, yet always strictly within the
easy capacity of the voice without undue strain.

Outstanding innovators are three young men, E. F. Burian,
Hanns Eisler, and Kurt Schwitters. Their music is not alike nor
does it belong to the same general "school," although probably all
of them are a bit influenced by Schoenberg's half-spoken songs.
They live far apart, and have not influenced each other; the idea
of investigating new vocal possibilities seems to have struck several
talented men quite independently.

Burian, the Czech, has a vivid personality, cleverness, jazzi-
ness, and a liking for publicity. By profession a drummer, he is generally considered the best trap-artist in his country. As a member
of one of Central Europe's first jazz bands, he invented numerous
new percussion noises on his own group of instruments and wrote
a Sonata for piano and trap instruments, using the latter so that
they spice the piano tone to quite an uncanny degree.

He first began to employ the voice in an unusual way when he
discovered that some desired qualities of noise could not be pro-

This is the earliest American account I know of of what we today call "sound
poetry." Hanns Eisler (1898-1962) was German, not Dutch. E. F. Burian became
an important Czech theater director, active into the 1960s. Kurt Schwitters (1887-
1948) was one of the most important visual artists of his generation, but his
Ursonate, which Cowell calls simply "Sonata," is a landmark of sound poetry.
This article appeared in Modern Music VII/2 (Feb.-Mar. 1930) pp. 34-38.

duced by any of the instruments in his jazz band but were easily within the range of the human voice. What he wanted was a sort of vocal noise to be sounded in some particularly pat position in the rhythm of a piece of jazz. Finding that these "vocalisms" added greatly to the popularity and hilarity of his band, Burian experimented with a wider gamut of entertaining sounds. Finally he segregated his vocalists into what he calls a "Voice-Band," which then practiced, a capella, more serious compositions, some of which were based on noises and distinctly jazzy rhythms, while others were quieter and built up on the recital of poems.

Two or three years ago, when this Voice-Band was still in its infancy, it rather over-hastily courted world interest at the International Festival of Contemporary Music at Sienna. Critics from every country vied with each other in downing it, either with sarcastic humor, or deadly digs. A few grudgingly conceded originality, but none saw that here was the germ of a new way to treat the human voice, always the most powerfully gripping of instruments. The Band has now rehearsed together for a number of years and has been brought to a degree of perfection; original crudities have been weeded out. It gives many performances in Czechoslovakia, but opportunities to hear it elsewhere are few.

The music which Burian writes for this band is polyphonic at base. Every singer has his own melody or line of vocalism. In order to help the auditor follow the voices separately, different languages are often employed simultaneously, a language to each vocalist. It is hopelessly puzzling to try to follow the words and according to Burian, they are not meant to be followed. The music makes no attempt to express their meaning; they are merely a convenience, an ordered succession of vowels and consonants on which to hang the vocalics of the performers. The languages, used for their different sets of sounds are treated as if created for the express purpose of use in a Burian composition. Sometimes a purely musical tone is employed; sometimes a tone which has pitch but is partly noise; sometimes sounds which are almost pure noise. Sometimes the vocalist takes a vowel sound high, with a shriek, dropping down in stages and with each change to lower pitch, emitting an altogether different sort of howl or moan. This music often causes an instantaneous reaction of hearty laughter, and Burian is by no means unaware of the effect; much of it is deliberately calculated; for, a thoroughly modern young man, he values publicity at any cost. But whether or not he himself will develop solider and more conscientious ways of using his materials, his innovations may eventually be employed by musicians of more earnestness.

Hanns Eisler, a Dutch Jew who makes his home in Berlin, has studied with Schoenberg but has reacted away from his influence. His music is based on singing in the ordinary sense of the term, and on harmonies familiar in music, but not vocally employed. Modern music has built up certain sorts of harmonies, accepted today as pleasing, which have been developed instrumentally. Partly because of the difficulty of training any body of singers to render them, very little application of these has been made vocally. If they were used in choral just as they are in instrumental music the result would be unsingable. Eisler has evidently made a thorough search through a wearying amount of material, and picked out those which could be used to accentuate certain choral passages and are at the same time practicable to sing. By very simple leading of each individual part, he builds up a counterpoint in which there are an amazing number of modern harmonies never heard before in chorus, which thus take on a new character; the fabric created is decidedly original.

This material Eisler uses not as an end but only as a means to further his primitive desire to give vent to the feelings by shouting, howling, and otherwise making vocal sounds. A vital joy permeates his composition and carries his audience with it. They forget the flaws in the vivid sweep of tone, which lashes to enthusiasm. It is the sort of music that singers whole-heartedly like to sing. I heard his *Arbeiter's Chor* in Berlin at a concert of modern music, with the audience cheering lustily at the end, forgetting all about the far greater formal perfection of Hindemith's *Trio,* played the same evening. The *Chor* is made up of a number of short choruses, the words of each dealing realistically with some aspect of workaday life. It is lively and gripping. The fullness of sound, the primitive rhythms, the refreshing relief of hearing unaccompanied voices singing new harmonies, all create a state of pleasurable excitement. The rhythm of the otherwise purely musical choruses is sometimes punctuated with hearty shouts and cries, quite pitchless, startlingly right in the rhythmic inevitability of their positions.

Kurt Schwitters, one of the leaders of modern art in Hanover, has experimented in building compositions of words to be spoken aloud. The words are invented to suit the vocalization he wishes; or letters of the alphabet are spoken in different tones and pitches. To such compositions, Schwitters applies musical form, sometimes quite precise and classical. He has written a Sonata with all the movements. No musician need be told where the first theme ends and the episode begins, or where the episode ends and the second theme begins, for he almost exaggerates the clarity of outline. The idea of his new art which is curiously effective when heard, although hard to explain, is to reveal an abstract beauty in the spoken voice, dissociated from the meaning of words, but preserving all the subtle innuendoes of which speech is capable. This has already been attempted in poetry, but Schwitters contends that as soon as the interest in words is entirely disconnected from their meaning and exclusively centered on the sound, it becomes musical rather than literary; poetic attempts in this direction have therefore failed because of a lack of musical form. However this may be, he proves that the technic of musical variation can produce thrills when applied to the shades of tonal distinction with which words may be pronounced.

Schwitters himself renders his word-compositions to perfection. He uses a wide gamut of pitch and a wide range of dynamics from a slight whisper to a tremendous yell. He makes a sparing but precise use of wheezes, bleats, and unusual noises. Unfortunately, like Burian, he has not unraveled the problem of notation. No one who had not heard him could conceivably take the words and make what he does of them. If he would even use present musical notation to indicate the rhythm, tempo, dynamics and approximate pitch of his performances, it would be an aid.

Of these three talents, Burian, Eisler and Schwitters, Schwitters' is the most finished. Burian is developing an art and is continuing to enlarge its possibilities. He lacks entire seriousness but not persistence, and he has cleverness enough to see new ways ahead. Eisler has poured primitive and vigorous feeling into a new choral harmonic scheme. But his music is technically crude and he makes no attempt to improve it. Schwitters has taken one original idea of expression, and kept it within such limits that he has developed an exquisite perfection of form and technique.

The League's Evening of Films

T HERE APPEARS TO BE a great attraction in music-with-films, much more, one gathers, than in music-minus-the-films. Unfortunately few American composers of the first rank have written such scores and usually only for short documentary films. If one wishes to see and hear the result, it is necessary to find out where these documentaries are being performed—and they are hard to trace. Sometimes they are buried among "coming attraction" trailers at the big theatres; sometimes they run semi-privately in preview showings, and one needs to belong to the charmed inner circle even to know of such invitation performances. The League of Composers is to be especially congratulated for its recent Evening of Music with Films at the Museum of Modern Art, where a representative musical public heard and saw excerpts from a half dozen movies with music by nearly all the important Americans who have tried their hands at documentaries.

Aaron Copland, in the pointed remarks of introduction to his own music, frankly admitted the hope of all his colleagues that documentaries will help them to break into Hollywood. The problems, however, are different. Documentaries are filmed silently; both music and unctuous comment are added afterwards. In Hollywood the musical performance and the screening are far more closely joined in common plan and execution.

This is straight journalism, with Cowell describing an evening at New York City's Museum of Modern Art when a half dozen or so film scores were presented with comments by the composers. Cowell is disturbed that music is composed after a film is shot; he proposes that music be composed first, with the film coming afterward. Hanns Eisler had now become a refugee from Hitler and was teaching under Cowell at New York's New School for Social Research. This article appeared in Modern Music *XVIII/3 (Mar.-Apr. 1941) pp. 176-178.*

Few of the films presented by the League appeared to be exceptions to this rule. The lack of planning showed at its worst in *Roots in the Soil*, music by Paul Bowles. Bowles, speaking in advance of the showing, said that he himself had not yet heard the synchronized result; he simply handed his score to the film people and hurriedly left the country. (He didn't say whether that was the reason.) From what little one could hear of it, the music seemed both good and fairly apt; but it was drowned out by a bullying commentator whose purpose seemed to be to distract attention not only from the music but from the film itself.

The fleeting scene of cornfields from Roy Harris' *One Tenth of a Nation* is hardly a fair sample for judgment of the whole work. As it was, the music seemed delightful and beautifully wrought. The sophisticated tonal weaving and the tone-quality of city-union string section were, however, very much out of place in the cornfields. I had the same feeling about the music for Douglas Moore's *Power and the Land*. As music it was appealing and well-written, in a style neither very simple nor very complex, but nicely between the two. The parts for whistling alone were perhaps the most fitting sounds of the entire evening. Yet as a whole the familiar tones of symphonic instruments gave an unavoidable impression of city-concert-hall rather than of the bucolic atmosphere of farm life. Why should not the farmers sing their own tunes to the strumming of banjos and guitars?

Marc Blitzstein was not present but Copland introduced his *Valley Town*, which was fitting, since the music for Blitzstein's film and for Copland's *City* are curiously alike; not that they in any way imitate each other, but the approach is similar. When things get too tough in his picture Blitzstein characteristically breaks into song—a wailing semi-popular style social-content song. Skillfully scored dissonant passages contrast with naive, simple tunes which seem to fit the film in mood. Copland's music in *The City* is gripping. There is much phrase-repeating, used with humorous effect. It is a relief to find a composer detecting humor in a picture and acting upon it. In Hollywood that seldom happens; musical effects are ludicrous rather than funny. Copland's was the deftest score of the evening and is musically so self-sufficient that it can stand up as a suite in a concert.

The surprise performance of the evening was Virgil Thomson singing the tune he had used for his celebrated *River* film. The tune, called "Mississippi," he found in one of those very old music books. His singing, wonderfully in the character of the Southern uncultivated tunesters, did prove what he wanted to show, that it was simple and American. Coming from Paris-loving Virgil this provided an unusual amusement; the audience enjoyed it hugely. The music benefited by this introduction. In the film it sounds far from naive; there it seems rather attenuated and dissonant. However it does roll along with the waters in a way that sound quite proper, one doesn't know quite why. The score is suited to the film in a measure lacking in all the others: it does not try to be complete in itself. Music and film together form an integrated documentary; the music alone would not be complete and the film needs the music to enhance its interest.

All in all, an evening like this is historic for the record it makes. It showed music and film combinations in the experimental stage; nevertheless what was seen on January twelfth is the best America has done up to now, and it justifies optimism.

The evening had an anticlimax, and so this review will have one too. The audience was thrown into wild guffaws by a Disney short showing his animals going through rhythmic contortions to the tune of Rossini's *William Tell Overture*. The success of synchronization in this bit is all too clearly due to the fact that the picture is set to the music, and not the other way around. Let us see a fantastic film similarly constructed to music by some of America's best composers—music which is complete *before* the picture is started.

How Relate Music and Dance?

Aᴿɢᴜᴍᴇɴᴛs ᴏᴄᴄᴜᴘʏɪɴɢ ʜᴀʟꜰ ᴛʜᴇ ɴɪɢʜᴛ and getting nowhere, fights lasting half the rehearsal time and still getting nowhere, comments from all sides in the dance press: these frequent happenings are but symptoms of the puzzling problems presented today in the relation of music to the dance.

Each dance leader will have some sort of solution to offer. Yet none of the experimental solutions seem to be very satisfactory, and there is a notable vagueness in the ensuing results.

Let us take the time-honored historical method and examine what some of the relationships of the past have been. The most important and fundamental of these is the practice which is universal among primitive peoples. Irrespective of geographical location, almost every primitive tribe in the world performs ceremonials which utilize dance and sound together. It would be impossible to say which came first and I find it a numbskull angling after intel-

---

Cowell's three articles for Louis Horst's magazine Dance Observer *(1934-1964), on music and the dance, are among his most important theoretical contributions, because in them he presents, among other things, the concept of "elastic form" (which he had used compositionally almost twenty years before in* Quartet Euphometric*). Louis Horst (1884-1964) was a composer friend of Cowell's and also was the sometime mentor and lover of Martha Graham (1894-1991), a key figure in modern American dance.* Dance Observer *was the most important intellectual periodical for the modern dance. HC had worked with Martha Graham since 1931 and the best account of elastic form we know is in Janet Mansfield Soares'* Louis Horst *(1992) p. 135. HC's first article, "How Relate Music and Dance?" appeared in* Dance Observer *I/5 (June-July 1934) pp. 52-53, while the second, "Relating Music and Concert Dance," was in* Dance Observer *IV/1 (January, 1937) pp. 1, 7-9. The third and last, "New Sounds in Music for the Dance," deals not with structure or philosophical issues of composition, but with sound. Reflecting HC's interest in the new percussion music, it appeared in* Dance Observer *VIII/5 (May 1941) pp. 64, 70.*

lectual swank to try to opine which did come first. It seems apparent that they grew up together. The sound is, of course, not "interpreted" by the dancers. Yet it would seem that the sound is the first step toward inducing the proper rhythmical urge which finally bursts into bodily expression. For in all ceremonials the drums begin beating first. The dancers begin after the atmosphere has been surcharged with rhythmical impulse by the drums, and often also after singing has begun. In the most primitive places the dancers apparently burst into movement as the surrounding waves of rhythm beat in on them irresistibly. In higher primitive civilization there is more order and the dancers are ready to begin, and do so, after a certain number of beats on the drums have given the pulse. In some cases there are additional tribe members who sing rhythmically either with or against the drum beats. In some cases, the dancers sing. In others, the dancers also perform on percussion instruments. In some South Sea Islands the dancers produce their entire percussion sound by the clapping of hands as they dance. Here also, however, they begin clapping first and gradually work themselves into the bodily rhythm.

The drummer or drummers in the primitive dance, therefore, occupy the position of conductors, in a sense. They set and keep the rhythmical flow, sometimes playing a simple succession of beats, sometimes playing a succession of different and varying beats, and sometimes playing counter-rhythms against each other as, for example, in the case of Central African tribes.

The position of conductor is one that the chief percussion player still holds in the cultivated music of the Orient. The woodblock and gong player conducts the movement of a Chinese orchestra in operatic performances today. In the ninth century, when the Imperial orchestra contained over six hundred players, the conductor stood on a platform and played a percussion set of bells which were suspended on a drooping stem before him much like the blossoms of a canterbury bell along their stem. As the conductor's beat went from one to another of these bells, those who could not hear the sound of them could see his beat. The same type of beats are still preserved by our symphonic conductors, and the Chinese orchestra is where they originated.

Now, no one in his right senses would claim that a symphony

orchestra playing a Beethoven symphony is interpreting the conductor's movements. The orchestra is playing Beethoven, but is guided rhythmically and dynamically by the leader, or rather, still more important, by the leader's beat.

I see no reason why a dancer should be afraid that he or she will be accused of being "interpretive" (this now being in great disrepute) if he bases the dance on some definite rhythmical flow, and this flow is given forth through the sound of instruments or other sonal means. If he does so he is in step with the practice of primitives whose art of the dance is the most strongly ingrained of any which exists in the world.

If this is accepted, there are many ways in which the relationship can progress. Merely to imitate primitives would lead nowhere. But to rest the fundamentals of relationship on the solid foundation of primitive practice, and progress from that point of departure, gives some interesting results. Before we discuss them, suppose we examine the flaws in some of the past practices.

"Interpretive" dancing came under bad repute not only because under it the dance was assumed to have no meaning in itself but also partly because in almost no instance, was the music really interpreted. The interpretive dances in the schools now so much laughed at were usually just about alike, no matter what the music. All that was taken from the music was the beat. The interpretation usually consisted in bouncing about the floor in a wide circle, flapping the arms and occasionally kicking up a foot while doing so. The form, melodic line, and harmonic structure of the music was not considered. The dances usually had no outline. A few years ago, one or two groups developed a really complete presentation of the music, in which the whole music structure was apparent in the dance. Doris Humphrey's dance based on the Grieg Concerto is a notable example. This was a splendid advance on the other interpretations, but still retained the unfortunate difficulty that the dance was a parasite on the musical form, and it was music that was being danced, not the dance! The same is true of some dances on Bach fugues which have been offered.

The Russian formal ballet solved the problem by taking very obvious dance music built in eight measure cadences and constructing the dance on the same stereotyped forms. As long as one is satisfied with the trivial conventionality of this scheme, it works well; and from the dancer's standpoint it is perfect, since the music never distracts the audience from interest in the dance. The music is so uninteresting that one can never be distracted by it!

Isadora Duncan performed the greatest classical masterpieces of music for her dances, which went with the music in general outline and dynamic sweep, but not in particulars. There were several difficulties. The music was so interesting that it tended to distract the auditor from the dance. One missed the primitive relationship of the movements to the actual beat of the music. Not that this should always be identical, but one feels there should be some relationship, either with or against. A total lack of such relationship leads to vagueness.

The Stravinsky music, written for the Ballet Russe, is too interesting and detailed. If one watches the dance, one loses interesting musical values. If one listens to the music, the dance is not duly appreciated.

Some dancers solved the problem by eliminating music altogether. This was a natural reaction against the subservient position of the dance, which was not given its proper standing in some former relationship with music. Yet, while a certain number of such dance compositions are possible, the general tendency is for them to seem dry. Sound is a primary part of the dance ceremonial the world over.

Some groups use percussion only with the dance. This at least is a fundamental and normal relationship. But the trouble is that those who use percussion usually have simply gone back to the primitive, adding little or nothing to the connection between the dancer and the beats, usually less rather than more interesting and varied than among primitive peoples. It would seem that the only excuse for going back to the primitive would be to add something to the ceremony in relationship.

Martha Graham and I made a new experiment in establishing a contrapuntal relation between the high points of interest. We worked out all details together, ending with a complete dance and musical composition in which the music rises to its point of interest when the dance is quiescent, and then the music dies down in interest while the dance rises. In this way, neither one of the arts relied on the other, and neither is a servant of the other, but each is given its time for shining and holding the attention of the audience.

A relationship based on the primitive, but which I feel is capable of great expansion, is one which is peculiarly omitted by dancers. It is somewhat suggested in Lehman Engel's dance written for Martha Graham in which there is an instrumental part of the voice, but other more definite developments are very possible. This little used relationship is that of the voice with the percussion instruments for the dance. In nearly all primitive ceremonials there is percussion, dance, and group singing.

Would it not be possible to develop these three elements into a harmonic whole, in which there is an inextricable blend, as in primitive ceremonials, but in which cultivated rhythms, dance movements, and singing would be employed?

Relating Music and Concert Dance

THE RELATION OF MUSIC AND the dance is one of the most discussed subjects by concert dance artists. There has been much written about it. Some composers of music, unfortunately only a few, have interested themselves in this problem. Yet in spite of the agitation on the subject, all concerned must admit that it has never led to a really satisfactory solution. And even now, the ideas advocated by the leading concert dancers and their associate musicians, and which are practiced by them, lead to a frustrated relationship between the music and dance in most instances.

Let us examine briefly some features, historical and contemporary, in the relating of musician and the dance which are often discussed in order to clarify the situation.

Among ancient peoples, without doubt, as is today the case among primitives, music and the dance were not separated. By drawing conclusions from primitive practices, we can surmise that all music was never unaccompanied by bodily movements of some sort; while such bodily movements as would constitute a dance, namely those which are rhythmically organized, were never without a background of sound—either percussion, singing, or melodic instruments, or combinations of the three.

Then music and the dance separated. Music began to develop independently, in the Christian world, largely because the Christian church adopted music as part of its method of worship, and fostered its study and development; while, except for the comparatively slight dance interest in the early ritual, it abandoned the dance as a means of worship, relegating it to paganism, except in a few isolated instances. The dance continued, of course, among the people, as a secular means of having fun; and the folk dance developed. But being disassociated with religion, it was not cultivated as a fine art and made into a composition, in the sense of a concert dance, nor in the sense of a ritual. The art-dance almost died out in the Western world.[1]

When the art-dance was revived, it was in the form of a stiffly organized technical display, concocted for the amusement of monarchs and nobles. The music was light. The relation between the music and dance movements was childishly simple. Each note or beat of the music was represented by a dance motion. The ballet of almost recent times still possessed a great deal of the same sort of juvenility.

Since then, many phases have been gone through. Concert dance has come into being, and grown apace. At first, it was practically all composed after the music, and rested on the form and emotional content of the music, because music has advanced to such a great independent height. Some dancers "interpreted" great music, often with movements that had nothing to do with the rhythm of the music. Some "interpreted" cheap music, with the idea of bringing the dance instead of the music to the fore, and hiding the fact that music was more developed than the dance. Usually such dancers, however, fell back paradoxically on making motions to the music's rhythm.

Then came various "modern" ideas. Nearly all of these, as far as music is concerned, have arisen from the natural and correct desire of the dance to be independent and not reliant on the music for its form and content. There have been dances without any music or sound. There have been dances to percussion sound only. There have been attempts to write the music in the studio at the same moment that the dance is being invented. There have been many dances composed first, after which music was written for them. This reverses the older idea that the dance should be made to the music.

All of these methods may lead to some excellent results, and there is no reason why any of them should necessarily be abandoned. There is no need to feel that one solution, and one only, must be found to cover all cases.

There have been, and will continue to be, some dances which are very effective with no accompaniment of sound. But a number of these becomes tiresome. The need of the sympathetic-vibration response of human beings to rhythm and sound becomes felt.

The naturalness of the association can be shown by the universality of use of music and the dance together.

Some of the best modern dances have a percussion accompaniment, and there is a recent tendency to expand and cultivate the percussion music idea to a point where it will express civilized subtleties. But the danger of use of percussion, suited as it is by nature to go with the dance, is that the whole thing will degenerate into a going back to the primitive, and that the dance and its percussion will be merely an inexpert attempt to revive a primitive ceremonial, usually with a bit of sophisticated tinsel mixed in. No cultivated person can hope really to achieve a genuine throwback to the primitive, even if this were desirable.

When the attempt is to create the dance and music together, there is a practical difficulty. This would be a good idea, but the result is in practice that both dance and music are improvised rather than composed. Usually the dancer improvises a movement, and the musician sits at the piano and improvises something that he feels goes with the movement. Then there is another movement, and the same thing happens. The final result is often apt to be a mere string of movements which the dancer has found interesting enough to retain, and the music improvised to them, with little in the way of form or logical sequence, or definite conclusion.

Perhaps the most recent method is for the dancer to work out his dance in its entirety and then call in a composer to write music for it. Now, there is no reason why a composer should not take a dance-form already created and be able to write freely and well in it. Our classic masters of music vied with each other in composing minuets, gigues, alamands, etc., which are all dance forms. If a modern dancer presents them with a suitable form, composers should not object. However, there are two major dangers with this method. The first is that the dancer rarely presents the composer with a genuine form. The common factor in the form is found in rhythm and dynamic line (or climax content). The classic dances have a set form; so many measures with certain kinds of distinctive beats, and certain set places for changes in types of movement, in both music and dance.

I have had occasion to observe the work of composing in many of the major dance studios throughout America of those who fol-

low the modern dance, and have written for many modern dancers. But I have never yet observed a really perfectly worked out
rhythmical form which was presented by the dancer to the composer. Anyone who has worked in a dance studio knows that the
dances are always being subjected to alteration through repeated
trials, in semi-improvised fashion. In a very few cases, the dancer
will give the composer a definite plan, worked out in so and so
many measures of certain rhythms, and giving the climax points.
But when the music is written to this, the dancer will inevitably
wish to change something. The form had not really been perfected.
Then the music must be altered to suit. In a majority of cases, the
rhythmical form as given by the dancer is not correctly expressed
so that it can be deciphered by a musician. After much difficulty
and struggle, I found that the trouble usually is that dancers make
a beginning of a musical measure from the beginning of a dance
movement; while the beginning of a movement usually corresponds
to the beginning of a phrase in music, and is more apt than not to
begin in the middle of a measure somewhere. If the composer
follows the dancer's plan, then, the music will be rhythmically un-
suited from beginning to end! The answer to that, of course, is for
the composer to watch the dance being enacted in rehearsal until
he gets familiar with it, and knows its rhythm and climax without
recourse to a written down form presented to him by the dancer.
But this brings us the danger number two. If the composer does
this, then he will inevitably "interpret" the dance, thus reversing
the old mis-relation when the dance "interpreted" the music. It is
no more ideal for the music to follow a certain particular dance
than the reverse.

The relationship between the two allied arts is in the form;
either artist may create a composition based on a certain agreed-
upon form, and it matters little which has composed the form.
There need be no stigma attached to the process of a dancer's
taking a form given her by a musician, and composing a dance to
it. She will not be interpreting the music; she will not know the music. And of course, reversely, a composer may take a form presented
to him by a dancer, and write in it without fear that he is following
the dance to the loss of the independence of his own art. The main
thing is that the form really must be perfected. If a dancer gives a

composer a certain form, and he creates a composition on it, he will have created an entity in which each part is related to each other part. If the form is altered through a whim, a malformation results.

This trouble of the composer in trying to cope with constant change in the working out of the dance can be met, I believe, in a way which I will propose later. But one of the things which the dance can legitimately learn from music, which through its uninterrupted centuries has developed greater understanding of its form than dance, is the difference between improvisation and composition. The dance would be improved if its creators worked toward so perfected an architecture that its balance would be destroyed by any changes that would not serve to enhance the structure. Dancers need not be afraid to take such general principals from music. They may do well to recall, and composers also, that music has grown too top-lofty through its independence from the dance. Only by association with the dance will modern music be prevented from decay. So the need of the arts for each other is mutual.

While the dance errs on the side of too great a tendency to possess vague structure, and to be improvised in creation, music today undoubtedly errs in the opposite direction of being too rigid. The classic dance forms found surprising diversity in the manners in which they were adapted to concert music by the old masters who first made use of them, but later they were crystallized by lesser composers, perhaps in order to teach them more easily in textbooks on musical form! These textbooks have made things easy for themselves by assuming that all musical form is based on a subject and its answer, and that these will always be the same length. The lengths which are permitted are all in even divisions—two measures, four measures, eight measures, and sixteen measures. Larger sections are almost equally rigid in their textbook construction.

The development of musical notation also was a determining factor in making music more set. In ancient art music, during the time when notation was just being experimented with, a composition was the kernel of an idea, and its actual production was expected to vary, each performer being expected to add his own touches to it. In this way, pieces developed in such a fashion that by the time they became somewhat crystallized in tradition, numbers of different people had aided in creating each of them. There is much evidence that the troubadours and minnesingers never sang their products twice exactly alike. Granted an underlying theme that was apt to be known and looked forward to, it was the differences in each performance that interested the auditors, rather than the mere repetition of something already familiar. Folk-music develops in the same way. A player or singer, in performing a traditional piece feels free to make changes, and may alter the history of the piece in doing so. Today there is a mixture of tradition. As a class, performers of music wish to "interpret" the works they play, which means they wish to make alterations of their own; but these alterations must be very slight if they are to be considered in good taste. The rhythm, dynamics and rate of speed are subject to certain slight fluctuations; but even here, the higher grade the player, the more apt he is not to vary from the composer's markings in these respects. It would be unthinkable that a performer would add new notes or subtract others, or add new entire sections, in playing Beethoven or Chopin. He would be considered a lunatic. And he would, of course, be wrong; Beethoven and Chopin constructed their works to be performed in a certain way, which is indicated in their notation. I mention Chopin in particular, because he was noted for his "rubato" or freedom in playing certain passages of his own music, and many of them are written down with more freedom than one finds in the works of most famous composers; yet his rubato was really a certain style of playing, which is expected to be followed as a tradition. It is, really, no less exact than the others.

Modern composers take for granted that they must compose an absolutely set piece, with each minute detail carefully planned, and that the performer must always play it as near as physically possible the same way. He prides himself on the rigidity to the smallest detail. The freedom of form, as compared to the older classics, consists of more irregular sections and diversity of lengths in the phrases. But once decided upon, these are rigidly set in the composition.

There is no complaint against the composer creating all the details of his own work. If he trusts performers to alter his work, he will usually be the one to suffer. There are not many performers who can improve upon Bach, although I seem to remember a number who have tried!

There is, however, no reason to believe that all music should be alike, and that there is any stigma attached to music that is free-flowering instead of already set. Perhaps the feeling that such music cannot be very important is because there has been nothing to offer by way of evidence which occupies a middle ground between music definitely set by its composer and music so freely improvised as to be vague and purposeless, wandering formlessly.

One of the elements that have disturbed the modern concert-dancer the most in trying to adjust his dance to already composed music has been its setness of form, which is incompatible with the greater natural freedom of the dance. And it is very hard for him to realize that when he has given a composer his dance-form to work with, he has taken it as a set form and constructed music to it that cannot be altered without the gravest difficulty. That is because the composer knows no other way of working. Either he creates music in a certain form—which may be very new, irregular and made to suit the particular dance, but which once made is set—or his work is formless.

In order to establish a meeting ground for musical and dance composition, in which the dance will be more definite than usual in form, although just as free to make changes, and the music will be less rigid than usual, although no less containing structure, I would propose the establishment of what might be called elastic form. This type of form would be used as a foundation for both dance and music, and either the dancer or the musician could take the first step in making a creation in it. Its relation to older form would be much the same as the relation between the ancient and modern concepts of the Universe. The ancients regarded positions as being fixed, and while they recognized the stellar movements, these were thought to be set according to an unvarying plan. Now, we regard the galaxies of Universes according to relativity of motion; and while we may still regard the motions as belonging to a greater general plan, the plan makes provision for constant changes in speeds and orbits, and new relations between speeds are found at any given moment.

The practical method of creating elastic form is something which must be studied, and since the subject is in its infancy, anyone who works at it has the opportunity to make new discoveries.

One must begin a little at a time. Possibilities of infinite elasticity are remote as a practical measure. But a beginning has been made if there are even as many as two possible avenues of expanding a certain form, where there would have been only one before.

Following are some ideas which I feel are practical to incorporate at once into certain musical structures, specially written to be adapted to the dance. Since my province is music, I cannot opine what the dancer would wish to invent toward such a form, in case the dance is created first.

1. Each melodic phrase should be so constructed that it may be expanded or contracted in length, by the shortening or lengthening of certain key tones. In writing down, the composer should give the different versions.

2. Each sentence, as well as being capable of varying length, should be so constructed that it may be used as a block-unit in the general structure. This means it may be used and then another sentence may follow, or it may be repeated, either in the same form or in a varied form (which the composer may indicate) if it is desired to expand this portion of the dance.

3. Each section should be so constructed that it may be used in the same way as suggested for sentences; that is, as well as being capable of being long or short, owing to how many repeats are employed in the sentences, it must be able to be repeated or not repeated, owing to circumstances.

4. Both sentences and sections may be so arranged, in final cadences, so that they may be shuffled about, and not always appear in the same order. For example, let us suppose that three different sections are used. They might appear the first time in the order 1, 2, 3, 1; and follow afterward in the order 2, 3, 2, 1. In case not all possible orders of sequence are practical, the composer may indicate which ones may be employed.

5. If percussion instruments are used, they should be scored in such a manner that the rhythms may be played on different sets of instruments—that is, one part which may be played on either dragon's mouths or wood-blocks, another which may be played on either Chinese or Indian tom-toms, etc. Also, there should be a full set of parts for use in case of a large performance; but a certain few of these parts should outline the essential rhythms, and be

so marked, so that it is possible to cut down the number of instruments used, and still preserve the outline. The parts which may be played on alternate instruments enables a dance studio to rehearse the work, irrespective of what type of drums and percussion instruments it happens to possess (provided it has any at all!).

6. The melodic and harmonic part of the work should be arranged so that all of it may be played on a piano, as that is the instrument usually at hand to rehearse with; in many cases, it is also desirable to have other melodic instruments used in a performance, since the piano is more colorless from backstage; therefore, optional parts for instruments should be included. These should be so arranged that either one orchestral instrument may be used, in case of a smaller performance, giving the main melody; or several may be used, in case of a larger performance. The scoring should be so arranged that each part may be given to any of several different instruments, owing to what is available. Thus, the high part might be constructed in such a fashion as to be played on either a flute or a violin, the middle part on either a viola or a clarinet, the lower part on either a 'cello or a bassoon, etc. This means that the work may be performed with the players at hand, instead of having to go to the expense of engaging additional players to suit exact instrumental requirements for each number, and which may be merely a whim on the part of the composer.

7. The whole work may, then, be short—the minimum length being determined by performing each sentence and section once only—or as long as is desired, by adding the repeats ad libitum. It may be performed with percussion alone, with piano alone, with orchestral instruments, or with one orchestral instrument, or with any combination of these. In this way, the individual rhythm, the phrases, the sentences, the sections, the whole work, the rhythmical and the tonal orchestration are elastic. The whole work will, in any of its ways of presentation, have form; but it may be easily adapted to the changes and freedoms so essential to the dancer's creation.

1. In the Orient, the art of the dance and its association with music developed continuously, and there is no problem in the relationship there; since in all Oriental cultures, both the movements of the dance and the sounds that go with them have been formalized, and certain philosophical meanings are ascribed to them.—HC

New Sounds in Music
for the Dance

FOR USE WITH THE CONCERT DANCE, percussion sounds are recognizably good; nearly all modern dancers have made some use of them. For some uses, melodic sustained instruments are very fine. The piano, which perforce must be the standard concert dance instrument, is partly percussive, partly melodic. However, anyone who is aware of niceties must feel a sense of something being wrong when he hears a perfectly fine piece of music, with complete musical values, used with the dance. It has never worked well yet, in any single case that I can think of. The more complete the music, the less suited for association with the dance.

This is well-known; but there is one connotation of the situation which has not been much investigated. Leaving the piano out of the picture for the time being, let me point out that the standard tone qualities, of well-known instruments such as violins, 'celli, oboes, clarinets, flutes, etc., have been arrived at through a long process of refinement. The present tone, as played by a professional, is the quintessence of refinement and elegance. It is, of its type, a pure melodic tone; musically complete for melody, smooth, and to a certain extent unchanging in tone-quality. All the myriad possibilities of these instruments, tonally speaking, are renounced as uncouth, except the smoothest and slickest. Such a development makes for the greatest musical use of the instruments, and makes them the most complete and well-rounded tonally.

This means that when any standard instruments of the orchestra such as those already mentioned are used with the dance, they may add a great deal of value and color, but have the basic fault of being, tonally, too complete, too entirely adequate and self-reliant. A well-turned phrase on an oboe, violin or flute is a thing of perfection in itself: there is nothing that is necessary for the dance to add, to make a complete coordinated unit. The dance can only add to something which is already complete; or if the dance is composed first, then these lines of perfect instrumental tone add something entirely complete in itself to whatever the dance may be already. There are, as I pointed out before, some cases where this produces a fine result. But in general, I don't think it does; there seems a crying need for the development of something which at present hardly exists—that is a set of highly varied and deliberately rough or incomplete tonal gamuts, for each instrument. Instrument players who wish to specialize in playing with the dance would do well to explore the many extraordinary possibilities of unusual tone-qualities which lie in each sort of instrument. Unfortunately most players, particularly professional ones, have drummed into them so strongly the idea of some one standard of tonal perfection for their instrument that any other sort of tone that can be produced on it, particularly a frankly awkward tone of some sort, seems a sacrilege to them. This may or may not be true from a strictly musical standpoint, but certainly it is not, from the view of what goes best with the dance. Tones which might be discarded as not being purely musical may be awesomely gripping in connection with the dance.

It is possible in the playing of any instrument for there to be a certain amount of irregular vibration mixed with the regular periodic vibration that produces a "pure" or desirable musical tone. The aim, musically, in training instrument players is usually to arrive at a tone with a minimum of irregular vibration. Irregular vibration produces noise or sound; regular periodic vibration produces tone. Contrary to general belief, however, a pure musical tone with no element of irregularity in it is virtually unknown—such a tone can be produced only under laboratory conditions, and when once obtained, it is hopelessly boring musically, and sounds thin and utterly uninteresting. It is the slight irregularities that add color and life to musical tone. Most professional musicians reduce these irregularities to a very fine point, so that their influence is a delicate and refined one. The more refined the irregularities are, the purer the musical tone; but also, the less varied it is. If players were willing to use tone which contains a higher proportion of irregular vibration, and therefore a greater sound content in proportion to the tone, the result would often be incomplete musically, sometimes even sounding fairly discordant. But there would be a great multiplication of the different sorts of tone obtainable on any one instrument. The use of such tones with the dance, where it is highly desirable not to have the music too complete, is ideal. The dance completes and compliments the music, which may be meaningless alone. The types of sound-tones produced on the instruments in this way are actually more suitable and grateful to the dance than the more stereotyped and set tone-qualities.

One great reason why percussion instrument tones are so valuable to the dance is that they contain a combination of sound-noise elements with tone elements. The combined possibilities are almost infinite, and there is lots of variety in tone possible, yet the tones are never perfect enough as pure tones to be entirely complete. It takes the added element of the dance to make a complete whole—or perhaps it would be fairer to put it the other way about, as it is usually the percussion tone which completes the dance. Another value of percussion is its rhythmic incisiveness. It punctuates, makes a rhythmic skeleton which can be moved either with or against by the dancer.

The more purely melodic an instrument is, the less rhythmic. Accentuation brings in the element of noise-sound as opposed to pure tone. The more noise-sounds which are used on the melodic instruments, therefore, the more rhythmically biting they become.

Perhaps all this seems very theoretical. You may say "how can one tell whether these new sorts of tone are going to be of such value to the dance, when they hardly exist?" I can only answer that the reason I am so enthusiastic over the possibilities of such new tones is because I have been spending the fall and winter making experiments with them myself, and even though I am not skilled enough to find all the most exciting possibilities, those I *have* found have proved exhilarating, and have worked out to perfection in the music of the new dance *Trickster Coyote* by Erick Hawkins. The new gamut of tone-values he finds stimulating to such a degree that the movements of the dance are quickened to a new delight. Martha Graham's informal comment, on seeing and hearing a rehearsal was "It is not primitive, but primal; a true 'first-time'."

PART SIX

Musical Craft

Tonal Therapy

SOME INTERESTING EXPERIMENTS in the therapeutic value of tone have been conducted recently in Halcyon with the aid of Dr. Abrams' electronical devices with which, we hope, *Artisan* readers are already familiar. But even though Dr. Abrams' remarkable machines of electronic reactions are understood, it will be well, for an understanding of the tonal experiments, to go over part of the ways of operating the machines.

In order to determine whether a patient has a certain disease, a specimen of his blood is placed in a metal container which is connected with an instrument regulating the current of electricity and from this instrument to the subject, a healthy person from whom a reaction can be obtained if the disease is present. It has been found that each major disease: syphilis, T.B., cancer, etc., has a correspondence in a certain ohmage of electricity, and when the instrument is regulated to the number representing this current, if the patient is diseased, certain reactions can be made evident from the subject, which do not occur if the patient is not afflicted. First, an area of the abdomen, different in different diseases, will give a dull thud when percussed, instead of a resonant sound; second, a rod passed over this area will stick, and move on only under compulsion.

It has been found that if a colored light, a different color for each disease, is thrown upon the blood container, the reactions from the subject are neutralized, and he reacts as though there were no disease present in the patient. And it is further found that owing evidently to some negative relation of the color to the elec-

---

This little text is probably the earliest published article on music which Cowell wrote without collaboration, and it anticipates many notions which have become commonplace in musical therapy. It first appeared in The Temple Artisan *(May 1922) p. 9.*

trical current corresponding to the disease, this color when applied to the patient has curative properties.

The question immediately suggests itself, is there not also a musical tone which will be neutralizing to the disease? And if so, will it not be more potent than colored light? For while the light can only be thrown on the outside of the skin, and then usually only on a certain spot, a tone can penetrate, and will vibrate through the entire body. Inquiry revealed that Dr. Abrams had conducted experiments along this line, but without any great amount of success, with a piano. Now, a tone struck on a piano is not sustained, but begins to die out almost at once; also, the piano cannot easily be placed in direct contact with the blood container. So Dr. and Mrs. Dower decided to hold another experiment in Halcyon. For this a violin was used, since the vibration can be sustained upon it, and the neck was placed directly on the table with the blood specimen in the Dynamizer. Great interest was shown, and Halcyon turned out to witness the results.

The results were surprisingly good, and although not conclusive, open up a remarkable field for investigation.

Dr. Dower used for the experiment blood specimens tested by Dr. Abrams, and known to contain certain diseases. Dr. Dower first established the reactions of the rod sticking on the subject, then the violinist played long sustained tones, going up through every tone in the chromatic scale. The doctor continued to move the rod over the sticking area. When the tone B was sounded, the rod did not stick. And when the octave and double octave of B were sounded, there was no reaction obtained with the rod. The tone E also negated the reaction. These tones, then, when sounded in any octave, though the higher octaves seemed more potent, were negative to the disease, which was cancer in this case, and will probably prove to have a curative effect upon it.

But why two tones? Why E and B? Why, because these two tones a fifth apart, have the closed vibration relation to each other possible to two different tones, and B is the first overtone of E, after the octave. And in other diseases it was found that two tones related a fifth apart would both succeed in removing the sticking reaction from the rod.

The following results were obtained from experiments with other diseases: T.B., B flat and E flat; syphilis, E and B; Strep, C and G. The tone C in altissimo, next highest on the piano, was found to have a general negative effect.

Dr. Abrams was much interested in the experiments and conducted some similar ones in San Francisco afterwards, which to a large extent checked up with those at Halcyon, and it is understood that he is having built an instrument to apply tonal treatment.

There remains a great deal to be done in making sure of the right tones, and checking up, and in working out the reasons of some of the musical relationships; but a wonderful field for research is opened for physicians, musicians, and scientists. It has been known that music has therapeutic value, but if we are able to identify a certain tone with a certain disease, matters will be placed on a much sounder basis; and it is to be hoped that energetic composers may find the idea of writing special music to be used in healing, in which the proper tones will predominate. The overtones are a series of natural super-vibrations from any single musical tone.

The Process of Musical Creation

There are few things more mysterious to the non-musician than the process of musical creation. I rarely pass more than a few days that someone does not ask how I work: "Does it just come to you," people usually ask, "or do you work it out by rules?"

A popular misconception is that in order to be inspired a composition must have been improvised or played on the instrument for which it was written, and that when a composer writes music at his desk, without recourse to his instrument, he does so by means of some cut-and-dried formula or purely intellectual process. I have often wondered how a composer relying thus on improvisation is expected to write an orchestral work, when he could, at best, play only one instrument at a time out of the hundred or more in a symphony orchestra!

The misconception is doubtless caused by a lack of appreciation of the fact that the most perfect instrument in the world is the composer's mind. Every conceivable tone-quality and beauty of nuance, every harmony and disharmony, or any number of simultaneous melodies can be heard at will by the trained composer; he can hear not only the sound of any instrument or combination of instruments, but also an almost infinite number of sounds which cannot as yet be produced on any instrument.

In its original publication in The American Journal of Psychology *XXXVII (April 1926) pp. 233-236, Cowell's text is preceded by a discussion by psychologist Lewis M. Terman who had known and had written about Cowell nine years earlier, when Cowell was only nineteen. Terman is deeply impressed by Cowell's ability to reflect on the process in which music arises within his "sound-mind," and he repeats his hopes from his earlier article that Cowell will become "one of the famous musical composers of his day," adding that this hope seems to be "well on the way toward realization." Terman's discussion is itself analyzed in Lichtenwanger's* The Music of Henry Cowell[:] A Descriptive Catalog *(1986) p. xvi-xviii.*

Each composer, of course, has his own peculiar mental processes and way of working, yet I believe that in order to compose seriously he must have the type of mind that is capable of thinking as accurately in terms of sound as a literary author might think in terms of words.

In this regard one must distinguish between a composer and a performer who writes occasionally; for while the former is an indubitable rarity, nearly all professional instrumentalists write pieces once in a while, some of which contain much charm. There is, however, a great difference of quality between the work of a composer and that of a performer. I have never seen a performer who had developed the particular type of musical imagination described above, although many good performers have it to some degree.

It is doubtful whether any composer can have a well-working "sound-mind" without going through a rigorous process of self-training to make it so. I will give as an example my own development; several other composers have told me they went through a similar progress.

As a child I was compelled to make my mind into a musical instrument because between the ages of eight and fourteen years I had no other, yet desired strongly to hear music frequently. I could not attend enough concerts to satisfy the craving for music, so I formed the habit, when I did attend them, of deliberately rehearsing the compositions I heard and liked, in order that I might play them over mentally whenever I chose. At first the rehearsal was very imperfect. I could only hear the melody and a mere snatch of the harmony, and had to make great effort to hear the right tone-quality. I would try, for instance, to hear a violin tone, but unless I worked hard to keep a grip on it, it would shade off into something indeterminate.

No sooner did I begin this self-training than I had at times curious experiences of having glorious sounds leap unexpectedly into my mind—original melodies and complete harmonies such as I could not conjure forth at will, and exalted qualities of tone such as I had never heard nor before imagined. I had at first not the slightest control over what was being played in my mind at these times; I could not bring the music about at will, nor could I capture the material sufficiently to write it down. Perhaps these experiences constituted what is known as an "inspiration."

I believe, had I let well enough alone and remained passive, that the state of being subject to these occasional musical visitations would have remained, and that I would now be one of those who have to "wait for an inspiration." But I was intensely curious concerning the experiences and strove constantly to gain some sort of control over them, and finally found that by an almost superhuman effort I could bring one of them about. I practiced doing this until I became able to produce them with ease. It was not until then that I began to develop some slight control over the musical materials. At first able to control only a note or two during a musical flow lasting perhaps half an hour, I became able, by constant attempt, to produce more and more readily whatever melodies and harmonies and tone-qualities I desired, without altering the nature of the flow of sounds. I practiced directing the flow into the channels of the sounds of a few instruments at a time, until I could conjure their sounds perfectly at will.

As soon as I could control which sounds I should hear, and turn on a flow of them at will, I was able, by virtue of studying notation, to write down the thought, after going over it until it was thoroughly memorized. I have never tried to put down an idea until I have rehearsed it mentally so many times that it is impossible to forget the second part while writing down the first.

I shall never forget the disappointment I experienced when I first wrote down a composition and played it. Could it be that this rather uninteresting collection of sounds was the same as the theme that sounded so glorious in my mind? I rehearsed it all carefully; yes, it was the same harmony and melody, but most of the indescribable flowing richness had been lost by the imperfect playing of it on the imperfect instrument which all instruments are. Since then I have become resigned to the fact that no player can play as perfectly as the composer's mind; that no other instrument is so rich and beautiful, and that only about ten percent of the musical idea can be realized even at the best performance.

I am able now to produce a flow of musical sounds at will, and to control just what they shall be. I am therefore able to work at any time, as the musical flow would continue indefinitely if I did not shut it off when I have not the time to work. The flow does not merely ramble on ambiguously, but centers about a germinal theme, which it proceeds to enlarge upon. I usually compose around a theme for several months before it develops into its final form as written. Because of devoting so much attention to finding the finest form beforehand, by trying the initial idea over mentally in every conceivable way, I rarely change a note after a composition is written.

Writing in form, I may add, is not a matter of pushing certain sounds into an unyielding mold; crudities of form tend to drop out unconsciously as further experience is gained. The experience of being in the throes of musical creation is distinctly an emotional one; there is a mere semblance of the intellectual in being able to steer and govern the meteors of sound that leap through the mind like volcanic fire, in a glory and fullness unimaginable except by those who have heard them.

The closest observation on my part has failed to reveal what the exact relationship is, if there be one, between my musical creations and the experiences which have preceded it, either immediately or remotely. I can only say that the musical ideas as they run through my mind seem to be an exact mirror of my emotions of the moment, or of moments which I recall through memory.

Our Inadequate Notation

A CERTAIN STANDARD HISTORY of music (I will forbear mentioning which one) makes the following statement: "While musical notation has gone through many changes and improvements, it would appear that the present form will never change, as by its means every shade of musical thought can be expressed."

As a matter of fact, the very opposite is true. The present notation can give the bare details of the pitch and rhythm of conventional modes, but little else. It cannot exactly convey a subtle tonal effect of any description. I have heard many argue that such effects should not be notated but left to the artistry of the performer. This is not safe, however, in even moderately modern music. In older forms there are definite standardized nuances (such as a certain sort of portamento in Italian opera) which are studied and known by performers and consequently hardly need notation; but if a composer today desires a special, new effect and leaves it to the performer, any of a hundred different ones may be produced. Quarter-steps, exact slides and involved cross-rhythms, for instance, cannot be accurately notated without the addition of new means to the current system.

Present notation is not graphically correct. A notation should express the sound to the eye with as great a degree of graphical perfection as possible. The rhythm represents a certain amount of horizontal distance; the pitch, difference of height. But today we have five widely separated pitches (as far as relationship goes) all expressed on the same line or space: for example, D, D-sharp,

"Our Inadequate Notation" (1927) is one of Cowell's earlier 'hands-on' texts, and describes from the point of view of a modernist composer, not a musicologist, some of the limitations a composer must necessarily confront. This appeared in Modern Music *IV/3 (Mar.-Apr. 1927), pp. 29-33.*

D-flat, D-double sharp, and D-double flat. Graphically, these pitches should be on separate degrees of height, and furthermore, being so far apart in acoustical relationship, they should not be called by the same letter; it is too easy to assume a relationship where none exists.

In our notation of rhythm we have different sorts of dots and ovals, some of which represents tones 256 times as long as others. Yet that difference in length is not expressed graphically in any way; one must learn the differences mechanically, by an involved system of stems and hooks. How simple to present the execution of a quarter and two eighth notes to a young student, if the duration of each were indicated by a like duration of the note itself:

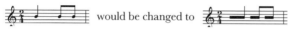

I once copied a simple work using such notation and gave it to a child of six who had not learned to read music. Although there were a number of different note lengths, he gave them the right proportion instinctively, without being instructed as to relative time periods.

Though we have managed to discover, in a large measure, which tones and rhythms the old masters desired, modern composers are forced to invent various appendages to this old system in order to get their work on paper at all. Certain particular effects are often employed by modernists as an integral part of a composition, as for example the so-called "atmospheric" tone quality in some of Debussy's piano works. There is no standard manner of notating such qualities, just as none applies for effects like half pedaling on the piano to bring out desired overtones.

Those interested in collecting native Indian music or writing down any sort of oriental music have had the greatest difficulty in even suggesting the original by means of notation. The printed examples of Indian music published by the Smithsonian Institute if sung purely as written, by one who has never heard Indians, become conventional tunes, no different in type from thousands of our own. An Indian would not recognize them. The yells changing to a tone, the tones which develop into wild cries, the curious wavering sounds, in other words, all that is typically Indian and therefore of interest to preserve, is carefully omitted, as it cannot be put down.

Many contemporary composers use quarter-tones, eighth-tones or lesser divisions, and sometimes sliding pitches in their works, but there is no accepted way of writing them. Certain fractional rhythms at present cannot be notated exactly, as, for instance, if we should have four quarter-tones in one part and desired to place against them a rhythm of two and a third, coming out the same length:

The result of all this is that each composer devises his own improvements which enable him to express his ideas more or less well, but as nothing is standardized a good deal of confusion arises. Many similar effects are notated in an entirely different manner by different composers, while totally separate effects are indicated by the same symbols; and in each instance copious footnotes are offered to the puzzled performer.

For example, a small lozenge shaped note is used by Schoenberg to indicate keys of the piano pressed down without sounding (Opus 11, No. 1). Charles Ives, in the Symphony recently performed in New York by the Pro Musica Society, used similar notes to represent quarter-tones. In my composition, *Fabric,* I employed such notes to indicate a rhythm of seven to the measure. Such a note also has been in use for a long time to show the position for playing artificial harmonics on stringed instruments.

I have seen no less than twelve ways of notating quarter tones in manuscripts of different authors; probably Haba's system will become standard.

It is particularly difficult to indicate to percussion players just what sort of tone one desires to obtain, or just where on their instruments and with exactly which implement they are to strike, let alone how hard. In this respect jazz musicians have been very clever; they have a standard notation for their new jazz instruments and for many of the new effects; these are understood by any trained player.

For example, the ukulele does not use the notation of notes and staff. At the beginning of a chord a formalized picture of the strings and finger positions is shown, with round black dots on the strings where the fingers are to be pressed. Underneath this are written numbers indicating the fingering; over it are letters and numbers naming the resultant chord. Thus E 7 means the dominant seventh chord of the key of A. During the continuation of the chord one horizontal line is maintained, with a vertical dash drawn through it every time the chord is to be repeated. Here is an example, and its translation into familiar notation:

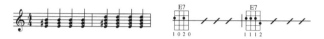

Jazz writers apparently agree without question on their new notations, while the composers of modern "classical" music have been more individualistic.

Improvements on our notation are often suggested, but most of them do not seem to get at the root of the matter, and many substitute one evil for another. Only recently I have received from Paris, Budapest and Los Angeles pamphlets explaining systems independent of each other yet all based on the keyboard of the piano or the organ. The idea, a little differently worked out in each case, is to have a note representing a black key on a line, while a note on a space would represent a white key. Mr. Thompson of Los Angeles uses this staff:

Apparently he does not realize the necessity of a unified system for all music, and that his method has no validity for singers or orchestral players. He eliminates accidentals, but then that is done in a simpler manner by Oboukhov,[1] the Russian composer, who uses crosses as note-heads for sharped tones. In his notation the passage

 will appear thus

Mr. Chilton, of New York, believes that the only notation we have which must of necessity be graphically correct, since it produces the sound itself, is the holes in a player piano roll! He suggests that the rolls be made to play horizontally instead of vertically, and that lines of the staff be drawn through them so that the eye can better distinguish on which pitch the holes occur.

A remarkable system, the best attempt I have yet seen to meet all difficulties, is one devised by Charles Louis Seeger of the Institute of Musical Art in New York. This method I cannot divulge, as his book on the subject has not yet been made public. Here, however, are a few of the things he can notate:

1. Accurate pitch, quarter-tones, third-tones, eighth-tones, or any possible fraction of a whole step, or the exact curve taken by a slide or *portamento*.

2. Accurate rhythm: any irregular as well as regular rhythm, presented graphically to the eye.

3. Accurate dynamics, the exact degree of p*iano* or *forte, crescendo* or *diminuendo*, presented within the very note itself, instead of outside the staff by means of an exterior sign.

4. Tone-color, differences and changes of tone quality which have no present notation, indicated within the note itself.

1. Nikolay Obukhov (1892-1954) was a Russian twelve-tone composer who emigrated to Paris in 1918 where he became a religious mystic. Obukhov developed his notation by 1914, possibly in collaboration with Efin (Jef) Golishev (1897-1970), the Ukrainian composer and dadaist who lived in Berlin until 1933 and may well have known Cowell there.—DH

The Joys of Noise

MUSIC AND NOISE, according to a time-honored axiom, are opposites. If a reviewer writes "It is not music, but noise," he feels that all necessary comment has been made.

Within recent times it has been discovered that the geometrical axioms of Euclid could not be taken for granted, and the explorations outside them have given us non-Euclidean geometry and Einstein's physically demonstrable theories.

Might not a closer scrutiny of musical axioms break down some of the hard-and-fast notion s still current in musical theory, and build up a non-Bachian counterpoint, a non-Beethovenian harmony, or even a non-Debussian atmosphere, and a non-Schoenbergian atonality?

My interest in noise as a musical element began when I discovered my delight on hearing Varèse's *Hyperprism*. Not until I looked at the printed score of it, however, did I realize the depravity into which my musical taste had fallen. This wicked work is recorded for seventeen percussion, and only four melodic instruments. I had been intoxicated by a composition seventeen twenty-firsts noise, yet noise is not a musical element! Although I had often taken and given surreptitious joy with tone clusters, euphometrics, and other concoctions of my own, in which noise was an important element,

In this article Cowell presents his view that pure sound, noise, would be the basis of the next music after the liberation of dissonance. Since the time of Cowell's article a great deal of music for percussion ensemble has been composed and performed. But the music of Edgar Varèse (1883-1965) and of the early George Antheil (1900-1959) seemed to call forth a need for a more thorough investigation of the aesthetic possibilities of noise. Later as a composer, Cowell wrote such works as Pulse *(1939) for John Cage's then newly formed percussion ensemble, and he was thoroughly sympathetic to the percussion music of Cage and Lou Harrison (1917-). This article appeared in* The New Republic, *LIX/765 (31 July 1929), pp. 287-288.*

my musical demoralization was finally completed by Stokowski, who offered the 198-proof noises of Varèse within the pure walls of Carnegie Hall itself.

Having thus become acquainted with Varèse, and later with Antheil, I began an operation, which I shall merely outline in this article—for technical detail would be out of place—calculated to undermine musical standards. Being now beyond reform myself, I shall attempt to show that the noise-makers are developing a little-considered, but natural, element of music, rather than dealing with extra-musical material.

In almost any reliable book on harmony, you will find the axiom that the primary elements of music are melody, harmony and rhythm. If noise were admitted at all, and I doubt if it ever has been, it would unquestionably be classified as part of rhythm. This, however, is a faulty idea of rhythm. Rhythm is a conception, not a physical reality. It is true that to be realized in music, rhythm must be marked by some sort of sound, but this sound is not itself the rhythm. Rhythmical considerations are the duration of sounds, the amount of stress applied to sounds, the rate of speed of as indicated by the movement of sounds, periodicity of sound patterns, and so on.

Sound and rhythm thus are the primary musical elements, sound comprising all that can be heard, and rhythm the formulating impulse behind the sound. Before sound can be divided into melody and harmony, another, and more primary, division must take place: a division into tone—or sound produced by periodic vibration—and noise—or sound produced by non-periodic vibration. Tone may then be divided into melody and harmony; noise remains, a much-used but almost unknown element, little developed from its most primitive usages, perhaps owing to its ill-repute.

The most natural musical expression is to be found in the music of primitives. All primitive music consists in part of beating on percussion instruments, which produces noise-sounds. Without the impelling rhythm induced by these sounds, the backbone of the entrancement of the music would be removed. No primitive can sing comfortably without a flow of beats on some drum-like instrument to support him; and the piling up of the hypnotic spell, which will lift primitives to fanatical ecstasy, is impossible without the ceaseless percussion thuds. When the same rhythm is marked by tones rather than by noises, the force of the music is immeasurably weakened.

Although oriental nations vary greatly in their music, all of them use many percussion instruments; the Chinese not only announce all change in musical form by beats in different gongs—so that one familiar with Chinese music can tell which period of the composition is to be played by which gong precedes it—but the leader of the orchestra is the man who plays the wood-blocks, so important is that position held to be.

We are less interested, however, in primitive and oriental uses of percussion than in our own employment of it, and its power of moving. Noise-making instruments are used with telling effect in our greatest symphonies, and were it not for the punctuation of cymbal and bass drum, the climaxes in our operas would be like jellyfish.

In the search for music based on pure tone, we may turn hopefully to vocal works, only to find that they too are riddled by noises; for it is only while singing a vowel that a singer makes anything like a "pure" tone—the pronunciation of most consonants produces irregular vibrations, hence noise.

But the most shocking of all is the discovery that there is a noise element in the very tone itself of all our musical instruments. Consider the sound of a violin. Part of the vibrations producing the sound are periodic, as can be shown by a harmonic analyzer. But others are not: they do not constantly re-form the same pattern, and consequently must be considered noise. In varying proportions all other instruments yield similar combinations. A truly pure tone can be made only in an acoustical laboratory, and even there it is doubtful whether, by the time the tone has reached our ear, it has not been corrupted by resonances picked up on the way.

As musical sound grows louder, the noise in it is accentuated and the tone element reduced. Thus, a loud sound is literally noisier than a soft one; yet music does not touch our emotional depths if it does not rise to a dynamic climax. Under the best circumstances, the conditions are aroused by musical noise and lulled by musical tone.

Since the "disease" of noise permeates all music, the only hopeful course is to consider that the noise-germ, like the bacteria of cheese, is a good microbe, which may provide previously hidden delights to the listener, instead of producing musical oblivion.

Although existing in all music, the noise-element has been to music as sex to humanity, essential to its existence, but impolite to mention, something to be cloaked by ignorance and silence. Hence the use of noise in music has been largely unconscious and undiscussed. Perhaps this is why it has not been developed, like the more talked-of elements, such as harmony and melody. The use of noise in most music today is little beyond the primitive; in fact, it is behind most native music, where the banality of the thumps often heard in our concerts would not be tolerated.

Men like Varèse, in his *Hyperprism* or *Arcane,* or Bartók, in his Piano Concerto, where he uses percussion noises canonically, render a service by opening a wide field for investigation—although they arrive at nothing conclusive. If we had scales of percussion sounds, with each "key" determined by some underlying quality, such as drum-sound, cymbal-sound, and so on, we could produce music through the conscious use of the melodic steps that would then be at the disposal of the composer. Perhaps this is one of the things music is coming to, and a new chemistry of sound will be the result.

Music of and for the Records

W HAT HAS MECHANICAL RECORDING done for modern music? And further, can a special music be satisfactorily written for records as such?

Records available for player pianos, organs, or gramophones do not cover the field of modern music with any degree of adequacy. They are turned out by commercial companies with the natural object of financial profit and are therefore to a great extent of cheap, salable music. Since, however, there are some people who enjoy and buy music of a better type, a number of "classical" records have also been issued. The purchasers of serious music have been as a whole more interested in who plays than in what is played; so one finds that the recording companies make a great advertising point of the fame of the interpreters. Between the different concerns, almost the entire field of well-known performers is covered, and until quite recently the artists were allowed to play practically anything, provided it was innocuous and pleasurable. The result was that certain time-honored gumdrops were duplicated innumerably by different artists for different companies while some of the world's greatest music went unrecorded. At first no attempt was made to form a record library of the most important musical works. The situation is gradually changing, and some of the companies are covering the ground of the famous classics. Today by combining the American and European productions one finds a good proportion of the best music of the eighteenth and nineteenth centuries recorded, although the player piano rolls are far behind the discs in number.

In this short piece Cowell speculates on music and machine, but also pleads for the issuing of more recordings of modern music. It first appeared in Modern Music *VIII/3 (Mar.-Apr. 1931) pp. 32-34.*

The recording of modern music has just begun. There is no attempt to cover the field, but when a modern work becomes sufficiently popular to insure a record's paying for itself, it is apt to be found on some of the lists. One feels also that some modern works have been included by chance because certain performers or organizations insisted on playing them. At present one cannot form a library of the most important modern works but may obtain some of them when they happen to be popular as well as significant. Stravinsky's *Sacre,* for instance, is duplicated several times, but no composition by Schoenberg can be obtained anywhere. None of his works have ever been recorded except his early *Verklärte nacht,* Opus 4, and even this is now out of stock. Often when well-known modern composers are included, only their early and unrepresentative works are found. Certain foreign companies have published a fair number, for instance the Odeon and Polydor Gramophone Companies, and the Pleyel Player Piano Company. American concerns have done little, and the player piano companies practically nothing. Although it is no more costly to record than to print, about a thousand times as many modern works are published.

Far more interesting than a survey of the few fine records of modern music, is a consideration of the possibilities of writing music specially for a recorded form, music which deliberately utilizes some of the advantages gained by removing the personality of performers from the performance.

A handful of modern composers have written for records, mostly for keyboard player rolls. Respighi makes use of a disc of birdcalls in one of his orchestral works. He used this device, however, not because he was interested in composing for the peculiar tone-quality of the record, but probably because he desired authentic birdcalls. Yet there are possibilities in the phonograph record which would be hard to duplicate. It produces new tone-qualities which might be used in composition. A record of a violin tone is not exactly the same as the real violin; a new and beautiful tone-quality results. Many variations in tone can be artificially produced by different placements of the microphone in recording. Balance of tone in recording a composition of several complex strands can be obtained only if there is a separate microphone for each of the instruments played together.

Stravinsky and many of his followers have written for player piano rolls music which might be played by hand, but which they desired to divorce from the possibility of misconstruction or "interpretation" by performers. By using rolls the composer makes sure that the tempo, notes and duration of notes are right. Antheil used several supposedly synchronized pianos in his *Ballet mécanique* probably for this reason, for the music is nothing that cannot be played by hand. Hindemith, Toch, and others have written for mechanical organ but despite their claims it does not appear that they wrote things impossible to play on an unmechanical organ. Hindemith's *Triadic Ballet* produced at Donaueschingen in 1926 is one of the most elaborate attempts made in this field.

The composer who goes about writing for mechanical instruments in the most penetrating fashion is Nicòlai Lopatnikoff. He has experimented in works for all kinds of recordings, such as mechanical orchestras, organs, violins, and pianos. He writes things which can only be performed mechanically, making the mechanism necessary to the composition. He has player piano passages which are impossibly fast, and combinations impractical for the hands of players, no matter how many should take part in a performance. Lopatnikoff also plans to make phonograph records of various factory and street noises, synchronizing and amplifying them as a percussion background for music written for keyboard recordings.

The field of composition for phonograph records and player rolls is wide and offers many prospects, but the workers have been few and too little has been done to try to summarize the results. Those making attempts in this direction are hampered because the majority of music-lovers misunderstand their efforts.

One excellent line of possible development, which so far as I know has not yet been attempted, would be to work with subtle rhythms. To hear a harmony of several different rhythms played together is fascinating, and gives a curious aesthetic pleasure unobtainable from any other source. Such rhythms are played by primitives at times, but our musicians find them almost if not entirely impossible to perform well. Why not hear music from player piano rolls on which have been punched holes giving the ratios of rhythms of the most exquisite subtlety?

EDITOR'S NOTE

Cowell's unpublished manuscripts include "Rhythm" (?1935) and "The Nature of Melody" (?1938). Neither exists in final form. "Rhythm," to which I have never had access, was described to me by Sidney Cowell as an expansion of some of the ideas in New Musical Resources *(published in 1930 but mostly written much earlier), incorporating other ideas as well derived from HC's experiences working with Leon Theremin (1896-1993) and Percy Grainger (1882-1961) after 1930. "The Nature of Melody" would have been a very radical and ambitious book indeed. Intended for use as a teaching text for composition students, it attempts to relate melody to vocal sounds and speech, more than to the overtone structures from which Cowell derives harmony and musical history. This is one of the most fascinating arguments in the work. Portions of the manuscript are very sketchy, and in other parts the argument seems seriously flawed.*

The first section of Cowell's text, "Why Melodic Study," is a preamble arguing for the importance of the study of melody. The second, "Some General Melodic Considerations," presents, among other things, the melodic theory itself, the relationship of melody to speech. The third, "Scales: Their Science and Grammar," deals with the construction of scales and modes, while the fourth gives concrete examples and a theory of the laying out of melodic lines and discussions of specific compositional problems. Section five (there are discrepancies between sections and chapters), was apparently to be merged into section four. It consists of more examples and analyses paralleling the chapters of section three, mostly with reference to music of the past such as Bach, showing how melodies work together contrapuntally. Also to follow was a glossary (only partly written). Often throughout the work Cowell mentions elements from world music which parallel or differ from western practice, thus enlarging his frame of reference.

The Nature of Melody

SECTION ONE: WHY MELODIC STUDY?

Chapter 5. The Position of Melodic Study in Theory

MELODY IS ONE OF THE THREE most important elements of music; many would say that it is the most important of all. On this account, it would appear to be absolutely necessary for the student to acquire some knowledge of it. If he does not, he cannot compose, nor can he play with proper understanding, nor can he properly appreciate the works of masters on hearing them. Under these circumstances, it would seem obvious that melody should be one of the first and most necessary studies in music; unfortunately, as we have seen, it has not been. A knowledge of it has had to be gathered mostly by inference. These inferences, by which it has been learned, may be found in the studies of harmony, counterpoint, and form. But melody, as practiced in great music, transcends these inferences. The concept of melody which they create is very narrow; the ways by which great composers develop their melodies remain unknown to most students. In fact, this whole vital department of musical knowledge is often a closed book to practicing musicians.

This was not always the case in the study of musical theory. During the time of early ecclesiastical music, melody was the main study; later, when counterpoint was added to musical resources, the study of melody was assumed to be a prerequisite to the study of counterpoint. Still later, when harmony rose, melodic study was more and more ignored, until it was finally discontinued. This was concurrent with the rise of "romanticism," and was bound up somewhat in its ideals. The idea was that a melody, being a pure inspiration, did not need to be studied. Either you were inspired, in

257

which case you did not need to analyze the divine gift; or you were not, in which case there was no hope for you, and it would be useless for you to study! Today, ideas are a bit different. We are able to see that those who have been the most inspired, and who have written the greatest melodies, seem to have been inspired in their magnificent handling of their materials, relationships, and processes, as well as in what was expressed by them. The real inspiration consists of an enthusiasm concerning the means as well as the message which fuses the two. To know the means in a dry-as-dust fashion is not enough. Neither is it enough to have a valuable idea and not know how to set it forth in a telling way: its value may be lost through inability to express it well.

If it is conceded, then, that it would be of value for a composer to know something about the subject of melody, then melody needs to be included among musical theoretical studies. There are any number of facts concerning it which are of value. Its relationships and many ways of developing ideas are of interest, as well as many facts dealing with the scales along which it is built. Some of these facts become well-known to musicians, who perceive them through experience with the works of masters; other facts remain in the dark, so that some musicians are most surprised when simple relationships such as the secondary permutations of melodic motives are shown to them.

SECTION TWO: SOME GENERAL MELODIC CONSIDERATIONS

Chapter 1: The Relation of Melody to Speech

It is useless to speculate on how melody first developed in ancient times. We cannot know with certainty. But, on the other hand, it may be decidedly in order to examine the music of very primitive peoples that still exist today, and to consider some of the facts concerning it. It is highly probable that in ancient times peoples in a similar stage of general development had a somewhat similar musical development as well.

Among the most primitive peoples, speech and song are not as differentiated as among more cultivated peoples. Many sounds are used in speech which have no other purpose than to express feelings in terms of sound; such sounds may not have any meaning as words. Some such sounds are still left in our own speech, but they are comparatively rare. The primitives make very frequent use of them. On the other hand, saying the same words over again on different pitches, or repeating them rhythmically or in sequence are devices often used by primitives to indicate a certain meaning; while among more cultivated peoples, this is almost never a part of speech. The primitive man will often break from speech into song, and back again, unaware that he has entered two different fields. The stronger the feeling concerning what he is relating, the greater his tendency to marshal the forces of rhythm and changing pitch to aid him in expression. Remnants of this may be observed in the preaching in "revival meetings."

Song and speech probably began together, and only became separated after a considerable development had been made in civilization; and after the first stages of the separation took place they still influenced each other very profoundly. Speech is given meaning by its tonal inflections. Melody, in music, rests fundamentally on the same sort of inflections. It is a development from speech, originally was part of speech, and is the offshoot of speech which is used when feeling rather than an intellectual idea is in the ascendancy. Melody's foundation is thus seen to be vocal, and the capabilities of the voice enter into its effectiveness. It comes, in most primitive music, as a prolongation of tones used in speech, and setting them in more definite pitch, instead of the more vacillating pitches of spoken words, and of applying rhythm to them. A very clear history of the procedure by which speech changes into melody may be traced in the case of Irish traditional music. It is recorded that at first the ancient bards of Ireland read poems. In order to make the poems more effective, they chanted them by prolonging the vowels, but still retained the natural pitches which would be used in speech. The old Gaelic, incidentally, was very rich in inflections of pitch. The next step was to exaggerate the differences of pitch, and the chanting changed to singing. The same process has also been recorded in the history of the music of several different peoples whose language is naturally unusually varied in pitch, such as the Swedish and Chinese.

Among the primitive peoples that we were formerly discussing (and this is true of primitive tribes of the same degree of development irrespective of what part of the globe they are from) melodic instruments are used at first simply to go with the singing, and to play the same melody along with the singers, serving to strengthen the melodic unity of the choral groups, such as are common among primitives. When the primitive person cannot sing, he may use the instrument as a substitute. Thus it may be seen that before melodic instruments are used independently, they are used as an extension of the voice, or to take the place of the voice, and their tone-quality is somewhat an imitation of that of the voice. Their primary use was to perform the very same melodies that originate in speech. A sense of the "naturalness" or "melodiousness" of an instrumental melody is often determined by how closely it adheres to what the voice can do. It is only in cultivated music that there has been very much extension of melody beyond vocal possibilities, on account of the technical potentialities of instruments; and most of these extensions become harder for listeners to enjoy in proportion to the distance that they remove themselves from the vocal basis. Meaning is imparted to melodies, very often, through inflections similar to those in speech.

Psychologists have discovered that when a listener is really following a melody, his vocal cords flex and unflex in such a way that if he used them he would be singing the melody. This often does result in the auditor actually singing along with the performance. If there is no physiological reaction on the part of the hearer, it may be said that he is not following the melody to the same extent, and his enjoyment of it cannot be expected to be as great. And if the melody jumps into vocal difficulties that are too great, he will lose its thread, being unable to follow it with his vocal cords. This will result in his becoming at least temporarily confused, and he will probably have the reaction either of finding the melody displeasing, or of simply being uninterested in it.

The negative side of the moral this may point to [for] composers is clear: if you want your melody to be widely appreciated, do not do unvocal things with it. This does not mean that it is wrong to use wide ranges; but it does mean that the wider range you use, the more cultivated your auditors will have to be to really follow it.

The positive construction of this underlying fact of melody is sadly neglected by most composers. By utilizing the inflections which are given meaning through use in speech, melody may be given meaning also. The great Moravian composer, Leo Janachek (who died recently in Brunn)[1] used to go among people, and write down as nearly as possible in notes the rise and fall of their speech in situations of special emotional stress. He used the melodies thus obtained in similar situations in his operas, which are widely performed.

Chapter 2: The Law of Vocal Inertia

It is all very well to caution the composer to consider vocal possibilities when making melody; but he may in turn ask: "What are the most vocal procedures in melody?" This is a very necessary question to consider.

The voice produces tones of a certain pitch through holding to a particular tension of the vocal cords. To change the pitch, it is necessary to alter the tension. The greater the tension, the higher the pitch. To make a wide leap in pitch, it is necessary for the vocal cords to go through a correspondingly great change in tension, which is harder to control than a smaller change. Unless the tone is broken off between pitches, then, during the period of changing from one pitch to another, while the vocal cords are relaxing or tightening, there is a sliding pitch. It is easier for the voice to produce a high tone loudly, because of the necessary tension of the vocal apparatus to gain a high pitch; it is correspondingly easier to produce a low pitch more softly.

It has been universally observed that singers prefer to remain on the pitch that they are already singing—that is, it is more easy for them to remain on it than to make a change.[2] If a change is to be made, then the change which will involve the least shifting of the vocal apparatus is the easiest to make. In terms of the musical scale, this means that the interval of a half-step, its smallest interval, is the easiest to produce, because the smallest shift of tension of the vocal cords is required to make it. As a rule, the wider the jump, the greater and more difficult the required adjustment. In practice this is tempered in the case of some longer jumps by harmonic relationships; thus it is usually easier for a singer to leap an octave, which is a harmonically simple interval, than a seventh, which is shorter but harmonically more complex. The most vocal style, however, is one in which the tones next to each other are related step-wise. During the historical period when the voice was paramount, the rules of counterpoint required that a majority of intervals used in melodies should be steps, either whole or half; and that jumps, when used, should be of small range. In some Oriental vocal music there is no progression except step-wise, and according to the same principle, in systems of music using quarter-tones or other finer intervals, these intervals are the most vocal. In our system, which does not use them officially, such intervals enter as the voice passes from one tone to another. "Good" vocal art in European music requires that the glissando from one tone to another be made as rapidly and unnoticeable as possible; but it is a physical impossibility for it to be entirely absent. It may therefore be pointed out that cut-off steps from one tone of the scale to another are unvocal; the voice will always round off the corners in going from one to another, and the melodies in which these "rounded corners" occur are universally more popular. Another vocal principle is that it is more easy for the voice to proceed downward than upward, as it is easier to remove tension than to add to it—that is, it requires less effort. This principle is not always easy to see applied in modern melody, which often rises to a climax in the middle, or even at the end, for emotional purposes; nevertheless, it is natural for a melody which is sung on one breath to begin high and loud, and during its course to become lower and softer. This is observed almost unfailingly in primitive music all over the world.

Knowledge of the foregoing principles concerning the voice will make it easier for the student to understand why certain melodies seem more natural and less strained than others, and to understand moreover what vocal principles underlie "melodiousness" or "tunefulness" and melodic simplicity. This does not mean that all melodies must be simple; but it does mean that if the student wishes to depart from simplicity in melody writing, he will have the means of knowing just how far the departure will be, and how it relates itself to these fundamental vocal principles.

Chapter 3: The Natural Rectification Curve

There is a tendency for any sudden tension to be followed by the reaction of relaxation. As a matter of balance, when a long leap is taken in melody, there is a tendency for it to be followed by a return toward the direction from which it came. This serves to make the leap easier for the voice to execute, as it supplies a sort of pendulum-swing for it, balancing the difficulty. So strong is this tendency that it has become one of the most-used conventions in melody, and the turn which it gives is sometimes called a "melodic curve," although that term more properly applies to the curve which might be plotted of the whole melody, rather than just this part. But through centuries of association, a return in direction is anticipated by the ear after a leap; the longer the leap, the more it is expected. If the leap is up, the tendency is stronger, since the return down means at the same time a relaxing of the vocal apparatus after the strain of leaping up. But even in the case of a leap downward, the return expectancy is high. This convention is backed by the natural law of reaction following action; the natural tendency of any exaggerated action to rectify itself, and the natural tendency to regard a starting point as a place to return to after making an excursion away from it. Added to this is the greater vocal ease in making skips if they are followed by a return in direction, and the conventions which have been followed during the entire history of European melody. For many centuries it was prohibited in musical theory to follow a skip by anything other than a return in direction. And the reverse rule was also in force—namely, that before a skip, the preceding note should not be in the same line of direction as the skip, but should form a curve into the skip. Thus in the example shown, the skips marked with a circle would be considered correct, while those marked with a cross would have been considered wrong. The smoothest melodies and most vocal ones adhere to this form, and it is recommended to the serious student to practice writing such melodies, in order to attain a technique in smoothness and conventional melodic grace.

In spite of the many points in favor of the curve after a skip, it need not be assumed that it is always necessary to use it. Other considerations often make it desirable to continue in the same direction.

SECTION FOUR: MELODIC CONSTRUCTION

Chapter 47: Modulating Rhythm but not Tone
—Modulating Tone but not Rhythm

Composers often seek a method of retaining a connecting feature which will bind together two otherwise unrelated elements placed in immediate succession. A means of doing this is to change the rhythm while keeping the same melodic motive, or to change the tones while retaining the same rhythmic motive. In either case something new is presented; yet by retaining one of the elements (rhythm and tone) a relation to the past is established, giving the association without which musical logic is not made apparent. In some cases, once the connecting link has thus been established, it may be dropped after serving as an introduction. Here are examples of changes of both rhythm and melody, with one of the two elements retained, after which the new element is continued without retention of the old one:

Rhythm retained:

Here a new motive appears, first using the rhythm of the old one, then repeated with a new rhythm also.

Melody retained:

Here a new rhythm appears, first along the same tones as the first rhythm, then along a new set of tones.

It may be, however, that it is not desired to introduce both a new motive and a new rhythm, in which case the new and old elements may continue together, as in the following examples:

new motive   original rhyth.

A criss-cross may be made, by first changing one element, then returning with it while changing the other. In the following example, first the rhythm is changed, but not the melody; then the melody is changed, while the rhythm goes back to the original form:

Chapter 48: Modulating by Degrees of Rhythm-tone Changes

A more gradual process of carrying out the sort of changes discussed in the last chapter may be found by modulating one tone at a time instead of all at once, or one beat (or other rhythmic element) at a time, instead of the whole rhythmic figure. Where this method is employed, there are usually several near-repetitions of the portion which is being changed, until the change is completed. Sometimes these repeats are on the same level, sometimes in the form of sequences; sometimes with the same rhythm (except for the changed portion), sometimes with the same rhythm in proportion (that is, by substituting throughout longer or shorter tones which keep the same relative values).

Chapter 49: Outlining Several Melodies with One Line of Tone

Owing to the ear's tendency to relate tones which are close together in pitch more readily than those which are wide apart, it is possible to suggest more than one melody, while using only one succession of tones. This is done by the single line of tones skipping back and forth, the upper ones upon which it touches being heard as one melody, the lower ones as another. A third element is formed by the actual succession of tonal skips. This device is very characteristic of J. S. Bach and other polyphonists, who often use it to suggest either harmony or counterpoint in writing for instruments which can play only one tone at a time. The same idea is carried out in some of the works of Paul Hindemith.[3] In writing such passages, the student should bear in mind that the two outside melodies need to be considered in their relation to each other as well as in themselves, since they will be heard as though performed simultaneously, the mind of the listener carrying the tones through and holding them over. Another important factor is that of the size of the steps and skips. In order to achieve the result of suggesting separate melodies from the highest and lowest tones of a line, it is necessary that the intervals between the outside tones themselves shall be smaller than those skipped between the low and high tones. This does not mean that there should never be any skips whatever in the outer melodies, as this would tend to make [a melody] lacking in interest. The art is to be able to introduce skips there, balanced by still greater ones between the lines. Sometimes there may be passing tones introduced in the leap from top to bottom, so that the monotony of too many wide skips may be avoided. In this case, the outside melodic tones may be emphasized by being held, or through being stressed in order to avoid confusion with the inner part.

It is possible to construct a single line in which the central tones form a separate melodic line, as well as the two outside lines of tone; in this way there are three suggested melodies, as well as the actual melody of the succession of all the tones one after the other. Examples of this may be found in the violin solo sonatas of Bach, as well as in other places.

Another method of outlining several melodies with one line, also a favorite with Bach, is not concerned with the position in pitch of the various tones, but with the position in rhythm. Usually this kind of melodic combination is formed in Bach's works by a series of flowing tones, equal in length, or with a steady rhythmical figure always recurring; the tones falling on the same beat in each measure (or each portion of a beat) will form a melody of their own if isolated, so that any succession of tones falling in the same rhythmical position in relation to the measure may be followed as a melody. The first Prelude in the first Book of *The Well-Tempered Clavichord* is an excellent example of this sort of writing. Most often, the whole flow of tones is based on an underlying chord or succession of chords; otherwise all of the melodies would not make perfect classical counterpoint together. What the result would be in case this procedure were applied to modern dissonant counterpoint is nearly unknown, as there have been few such experiments.

Such complexes of several melodies in one offer many problems of relationship. Each of the melodies outlined or actually performed needs to be organized within itself, and also related to the others. The top part may develop one motive, the lower another; or both may develop the same one. Their relation one to the other will call contrapuntal principles into play. There can be only a limited amount of attention given here to these varied problems, which might be made the basis of a protracted study.

1. "Leo Janachek" is Leoš Janáček (1854-1928) and "Brunn" is the German name for "Bruno."—DH

2. This does not mean that it is easy for them to sing an absolutely steady tone; the heartbeats and other bodily disturbances cause certain slight but constant alterations of pitch.—HC

3. Cowell must have in mind the various "Gebrauchsmusik" sonatas which Paul Hindemith (1895-1963) composed prior to coming to the United States.—DH

PART SEVEN

Theory and
Musical History

Harmonic Development
in Music

MUCH OF THE MORE advanced contemporary music appears
to fill the amateur listener with bewilderment and the conservative musician with rage. This is, perhaps, the inevitable result
of a confusion between what is orderly but radical progress on the
one hand, and mere anarchy on the other. In their first appearance these may resemble each other, and as there is so much of the
one in an age which is also characterized by the other, the mistake
is natural enough. The art of music, like the other arts, progresses
by revolutions which break down barriers as well as by rebellions

*This essay is Cowell's first venture into an overview of music history. Written with
Robert L. Duffus, later a well-known journalist who presumably helped Cowell organize his style, the essay presents a historical perspective which Cowell never altered
throughout his career. Summed up, this overview states that western musical history
can be understood as an overall process of constantly correcting and freshening musical experience by the gradual use and acceptance of ever-smaller intervals—chords
and contrapuntal constructions based on fourths and fifths, thirds, seconds, and with
the introduction of dissonant counterpoint and the minor second, tone-clusters. This
puts tone-clusters at stage center, of course, and argues for their inevitability. Later,
speculating on the future of music, Cowell would see noise as the process which lies
beyond the tone-cluster. The text appeared in Van Wyck Brooks's* The Freeman,
III/55 (30 March 1921), pp. 63-65, III/56 (6 April 1921) pp. 85-87 and
III/57 (13 April 1921), pp. 111-113. *However, the original printer left out some
words and phrases at critical points, as a result of which some passages cannot be
interpreted with certainty. The section printed in bracketed italics was garbled by the
original printer. We include it as it stands in the old printed text.*

*The story concerning Guido d'Arezzo (c. 990-c. 1050) is not accurate. Guido
was indeed involved in musical theory, but he was opposed mainly by the Dominican
order of monks. Guido died peacefully in the monastery of another monastic order.
Also, the visual metaphor of the hand, which was often attributed to Guido, does not
appear in any known version of his treatise, and is now ascribed to Bartholomé
Ramos de Pareja (1440-91).*

which are protests, not so much against authority as against the very limitations of life, of art, and of human psychology. There is a nihilism in music as well as a cacophony in politics.

Obviously, the new music must succeed or fail in the end according as it is psychologically correct or false. If it has not some structure or coherence which will eventually be perceived by the listener it cannot give artistic satisfaction. The perception of structure need not, of course, be conscious. With the majority of those who take pleasure in hearing music it probably is not conscious. Nevertheless, it can be predicted that if there does not exist a balance of parts, and even an ascertainable and orderly series of mathematical ratios in the harmony, the music will not be accepted. But this rule must be supplemented by a more definite standard if the relation of contemporary music to what has gone before and to what will probably follow is to be intelligently studied. This relation is to be found, as far as harmonic development is concerned, in the overtones, or partials, of any single tone.

All students of elementary physics are aware that if a taut string is struck or plucked not only will it vibrate as a whole along its entire free length, but each half will begin to vibrate at exactly twice the speed of the whole string, each third at thrice the speed, each fourth at four times the speed, and so on, as far as we know, indefinitely. A vibrating string thus causes an indefinite series of subsidiary vibrations. On a piano string these vibrations will yield successive musical tones—the overtones, or partials—which will be heard, when a key is struck and held, in a series of which each new member is fainter than its predecessor, passing beyond the ordinary range of the human ear after fifteen overtones have been heard. Unless one's ear is very acute and very well-trained, one will not be able to recognize nearly all of these fifteen overtones. The average person hears only three or four. The piano is suggested here only because it is a convenient illustration; the overtones exist, needless to say, in the tones of any musical instrument.

The pitch, which on the piano is indicated by the position of the key played, takes its character from the rapidity with which the whole string vibrates. If a certain number of vibrations a second gives the tone called, on the piano, middle C, twice as many vibrations a second will give the C above middle C. Hence each half of the vibrating string, which vibrates twice as rapidly as the whole string, will produce this upper tone. In the same way, as experiment has shown, each third of the string, vibrating at three times the rate of middle C, will give the next G, five notes above the octave of C, or the musical interval called a fifth; each fourth of the string, vibrating at four times the rate of middle C, will give the next higher C, four notes above the G, or the musical interval called a fourth; each fifth of the string, vibrating at five times the speed of middle C, will produce the next higher E, three notes above the last C, the musical interval of a major third, and so on to the fifteenth overtone, the interval growing progressively smaller. For convenience the whole tone is generally spoken of as the first partial, the octave as the second partial, the G above the octave as the third partial, the C above this G as the fourth partial, and the E above this C as the fifth partial. If the term overtone is used the octave is obviously the first overtone, and so on; but as the octave, mathematically considered, is the second in a series, it is less confusing to use the other terminology. The partials or overtones grow progressively fainter because of the increasing rapidity of the vibrations and the smaller portion of the string in which they originate. These tones are all contained in the single tone, as played upon the piano (or sounded with the voice or with any musical instrument), and indeed, give what we call the single tone much of its character. When the overtones are partially suppressed, as on a tuning fork, the single tone becomes thin and colorless. The second partial, the octave or eighths being nearest in rate of vibration and in volume to the original tone, is the most easily distinguished. For this reason, as will be seen, the use of the interval of the octave was the first step in harmony.

If these familiar facts are borne in mind, the reasons for every step in the progress of harmony are, in fact, obvious. Harmony, which is one of the distinguishing features of Occidental music as opposed to that of the Orient, has evolved by taking the overtones, one at a time, out of their semi-obscurity, their echoing and mysterious sea-caves of sound, and uttering them with the voice or with an instrument simultaneously with the tone or tones with which they are related. The entire harmonic development of music can be summed up as the orderly, though not conscious, employment of one overtone after another until, at the present time, the sixteenth partial is beginning to come into use. What has appeared to be the more or less temperamental growth of an art can be accurately described in terms of the unfolding of an exact mathematical science. New harmonic combinations have been accepted as the ear has been trained to perceive more complex mathematical ratios. As the next partial beyond the sixteenth represents an interval of less than half a tone beyond the sixteenth, or less than the shortest interval in our present scale, further progress in this direction is impossible until the scale has been amplified. The present is, therefore an auspicious moment at which to look back over the successive steps by which this stage has been reached. From a glance at harmonic history it may be possible to make certain deductions as to the future of music, not only harmonically but along other lines.

The first recognizable ancestor of modern Occidental music is the music of Greece, which could boast of at least sixteen scales (a mere nothing, however, compared with the more than five hundred of the musicians of India), but which had no harmony. Both male and female voices, in choral performances, were therefore obliged to sing in unison. The octave, which is so natural to modern ears as often not to be recognized as distinct from the fundamental note, was considered a barbarism, and a singer who sang an octave away from the main body of the chorus committed an offense as reprehensible as that of the member of the modern village choir who sharps or flats. The effect must have been to develop the middle voice—in mixed choirs, the tenors and contraltos—at the expense of the higher and the lower. One musical bolshevist, Aristoxenus, the first of the long series of rash innovators, did indeed happen upon the octave at a late date in Grecian musical history, and the first great musical controversy seems to have arisen. But Aristoxenus did not prevail against the safe and sane musicians of his day, although he had the curious revenge of persuading later generations for a time, that the Greeks had generally used his interval. Rome, which took over so much of the Greek culture, failed to capture the evanescent fragrance of Greek music; and Roman music, as far as can be ascertained, consisted of simple folk melodies, developed without harmonization. For the next step in harmony we must wait until the medieval Church begins to feel the need of organized music in its unfolding ritual; although some authorities are of the opinion that the folk music of the preceding period employed several simple intervals from which the church later borrowed for its harmonies. The first distinct record is that of Brother Ambrose (about 400 A. D.), who revised several of the Greek modes or scales, and took over their musical system, adding to it the octave, which evidently seemed to him so natural that he did not realize that the reputable Greek musicians had rejected it as dissonant. The name of Brother Ambrose, therefore, marks the conquest of the second partial with its simple ratio of one to two, or twice as many vibrations as the single tone from which it was derived. It was now possible to sing two parallel melodies, exactly eight steps apart, or to sing one and play the other on some musical instrument.

The medieval choir of the period consisted of basses, tenors and boy-sopranos, accompanied by a species of organ, of from six to ten keys, which had to be played one at a time by punching them with the clenched fist. A successor of Ambrose thought to have been called Guido d'Arezzo, a monk whose name is in doubt, while experimenting with this Gothic instrument, accidentally pressed two keys at once, was struck by the strangely agreeable nature of the sound produced, and so discovered the use of the interval of the fifth. We may think of him as having struck the C above the middle C with the next G; in fact, this and the discoveries that followed may be visualized as a gradual progress from middle C toward the upper, or right-hand, end of the modern piano. This G would have the relation or vibration-ratio to the preceding C, of two to three. The third partial and the next simplest ratio was thus brought into use.

The monk's fate was that of other innovators. His jarring chord not only set the critics by the ears, but drew down upon him the wrath of the ecclesiastical establishment. Tradition is that he was executed by order of the Pope as an enemy of man and of God. Fifths were thereupon forbidden, and the pious musicians of the day seem to have gone to their rest untroubled by the new dissonance. But the elimination of the innovator did not eliminate his interval, nor the memory of it that lingered in men's ears, nor the mathematical fact, as inescapable as the simple axiom that twice two equals four, upon which it unconsciously rested. Fifty years later the fifth appeared, not only as sanctioned by the Pope of the day, but even as a required feature of all church music. So abundant was the resulting supply of successive fifths that we find them forbidden by later harmonists, not as dissonant but as monotonous and cloying. The ear yearned for yet more complex ratios.

The fifth came to be written five steps below the tenors, but for some reason was given to the boy-sopranos to sing. The latter, unable or unwilling to reach down to this lower level, transposed their song an octave higher. That is to say, they sang four tones above the tenors instead of five tones below. If we consider the tenors as starting on G, the corresponding note for the boy-sopranos became the next C above G. The vibration-ratio of these two tones is three to four; for every three vibrations of the lower tone there are four of the upper. This was the fourth partial. The next step, mathematically inevitable like those which had preceded, was the introduction of the third, of the interval from C to E. The ratio of C to E is four to five, which forms the first partial overtone. This heresy made its appearance in the Vatican itself. It was promulgated by Pope Gregory the Great, despite the protest of the College of Cardinals, who doubted that such a barbaric conflict of tones was a fit thing with which to worship the Almighty. Church music thus came into possession of the whole of the common chord. It was possible to sound at one and the same time the notes C-C-G-C-E, or simply C-G-E, a combination which is sufficiently insipid to the modern ear, but which once was full of wicked thrills.

II

One of the first of the great composers that we still find on our programs is Palestrina (about 1525), who used not only the major third but the minor third, which may be represented by the interval between E and G, or half a tone less than the major third. The ratio here is five to six, and the sixth partial emerges. It had become evident, however, that with the major third the limit of harmonic progress had been reached; and Palestrina, like the unknown monk, found himself in disfavor. Dismissed and banished from the Church, he spent part of his life in exile, being kindly received by the secular barbarians elsewhere. Later his insidious heresy had so far crept into men's minds that he was invited to return to the Church. Far from repenting, he made further use of the musical material at hand, and, by inverting the third, produced the sixth and minor sixth. As these form, not a new ratio, but an inversion of the ratios used in the third, they represent the fifth and sixth partials. These intervals he may have found in folk music evolved long before his time, but he must be given credit for their first conscious artistic use.

In Palestrina also, curiously enough, may be found intervals which are still considered dissonances, but which he employed only in passing from one consonance to another. Each so-called dissonance is prepared for by the prior use of each of its tones in a consonance, and each he immediately resolved into an accepted consonance. As these dissonances are more or less fortuitous, and as he did not use them as independent musical material, Palestrina cannot be considered as having originated them. Had he done so he would have anticipated musical progress by many generations.

Between Palestrina and Bach the only harmonic innovation was the minor seventh, which was probably introduced by Monteverdi. This gives a ratio of four to seven, and may be represented by the interval from D to C. Bach, in whose masterful hands the contrapuntal epoch reached its culmination, was the first to employ the major ninth, or the interval between C and the D above the octave, which, with its ratio of four to nine, is the reverse of the minor seventh. Two more overtones were conquered in this way. It is a curious fact—or possibly not so curious, in view of the traditional attitude toward musical innovations—that although Bach was accepted as a great organist in his own day, he was not so well thought of as a composer. The greater part of his music lay unnoticed until it was brought to the attention of the world by Mendelssohn a century later.

Beethoven's principal contribution to harmony was the minor ninth, with its ratio of six to thirteen, which may be instanced by the combination of C with the D flat above the octave. Wagner shocked the conservatives by using orchestrally the augmented eleventh, or the interval between C and the F sharp above the octave. The ratio here is four to eleven, or, in the chord which Wagner used (for example, C-G-B flat-D-F sharp) 4:6:7:9:11. Wagner also developed, although he cannot claim to have originated, the minor secondary seventh. Since then, Debussy has used major seconds, or the interval of a single tone, both singly and in pairs, and used also major sevenths. The respective ratios here are eight to nine and eight to fifteen. Schoenberg uses consecutive sevenths and minor seconds, with their ratio of fifteen to sixteen; and Ornstein uses consecutive minor seconds as well as more than one minor second at once; although with Ornstein this usage appears to be inspirational, rather than a part of a conscious plan.

By these slow gradations, the more advanced musicians have reached the point where they hear and employ together any two or three of the first sixteen of the innumerable partials which result when a single tone is struck or sounded; and the order in which these combinations appear to have been adopted is, as we have seen, with one exception noted below, exactly the mathematical order in which they occur. We have said "appear to have been adopted," because no absolute proof of the date of the original uses of the new intervals is possible without a complete examination of all musical literature. But a reasonably thorough investigation does indicate that use of the intervals as basic (or unresolved) musical material was made substantially as appears in the following table:

Innovators	Intervals	Notes of intervals	Ratios	New partials represented
Ecclesiastical addition	oct., perfect	(C to C)	1:2	2nd
Guido d'Arezzo's addition	5th, perfect	(C to G)	2:3	3rd
Boy-sopranos' addition	4th, perfect	(C to F)	3:4	4th
Pope Gregory's addition	3rd, major	(C to E)	4:5	5th
Palestrina's addition	3rd, minor	(E to G)	5:6	6th
Monteverdi's addition	7th, major	(D to C)	4:7	7th

Innovators	Intervals	Notes of intervals	Ratios	New partials represented
Bach's addition	9th, major	(C to D 8va)	4:9	9th
Beethoven's addition	9th, minor	(B to C 8va)	5:13	13th
Wagner's addition	11th chord	(C-G-B♭-D-F#)	4:5:7:9:11	11th
Debussy's addition	chord of major 2nds (C-D-A♭-B♭)		8:9:13:14	14th
Debussy's addition	7th, major	(C to B)	8:15	15th
Schoenberg's addition	2nd, minor	(B to C)	15:16	16th
Ornstein's addition	chord of minor 2nds (F#-G-B-C)		11:12:15:16	16th

The mathematical ratio given for the intervals is the simplest that can be given. On the piano, with its "tempered" tuning, the ratios are nearly all extremely complex, being slightly distorted from their overtone position.

The eighth, tenth and twelfth partials do not figure in this series, since they are octaves of the fourth, first and sixth partials, respectively. The only departure from the exact mathematical order of partials, it will be noticed, is in the case of Beethoven's use of the thirteenth partial at a time when the eleventh had not been used, the latter being employed by Wagner later. This extraordinary skip is probably due to the fact that the eleventh partial does not occur in the principal scales which Beethoven used; while Wagner, using the chromatic scale, was able to employ the augmented eleventh, which is only to be found in that scale. It is interesting to notice that while the thirteenth is more complex than the eleventh, Wagner's chord is more complicated than that of Beethoven, because, while Beethoven used only the interval of the minor ninth, with a ratio of 6:13, Wagner used the complete chord of the augmented eleventh with a ratio of 4:6:7:9:11. All these intervals are now commonplaces to musicians, although their mathematical relations are not. The nonmusical reader who has access to a piano may easily identify them for himself. It will be noted that the chords representing the simpler ratios are more acceptable to the unaccustomed ear, and that the more complex the ratio, the more dissonant the combination seems to be. The ratio of one to two represented by the octave, seems identical to many people; and that of two to three, as represented by the fifth, is insipid; but that of fifteen to sixteen, as represented by the minor second (such as C-D flat, or C and the next black note) is at first almost as jarring as a blow, and the listener half consciously waits to hear it resolved into a more consonant interval. But it is undeniable that habituation enables one to perceive, and so find pleasurable, even the most complex of ratios without resolution. What has happened, apparently, has been a gradual increase in the ability to hear the full content of the single tone, to the making of which all the overtones, even when unrecognized, contribute. On this premise it is possible, not only to form a new and more orderly conception of harmony, but to forecast its future.

Dissonance and consonance, as the reader must by this time have concluded, are relative terms with a psychological distinction. Harmonic development may be thought of, to adopt a crude figure, as a rod moving on its axis along a straight line, from the most simple of possible harmonies towards an infinitely complex harmony. Writers on harmony, following the instinctive practice of musicians, have already begun to make rules limiting the use of the simpler consonances, such as the octave, the fifth and even the fourth, on the ground that they are insipid and empty. If this course of procedure continues, the harmony books of the future will limit the use of the third and sixth, since they are the next most consonant. In music, as in philosophy, the heresy of yesterday becomes the dogma of today and the forgotten commonplace of tomorrow. At each stage of development certain harmonies are already falling into disuse and others are just coming into use; but the fact of progress, of the wearing out of old harmonies and the search for new ones, is not to be denied. Our harmony is seemingly destined to become more and more subtle, containing relations more and more remote, calling for, or responding to, a keener perception of the overtones.

An obstacle to such progress is, as has been suggested already, the limitation of our scale. The interval between the fifteenth and sixteenth partials is our half step, of which we have twelve to an octave. The interval between the sixteenth and the seventeenth partial, which is less than a half step, is the interval used in the Arabian scale, there being seventeen tones to an octave, or a little less than three to one of our whole tones. Stringed instruments and voices can now sound this interval, although the piano and other instruments of fixed pitch cannot. It is the natural next interval, which a good musician attempting to sing an interval between two tones of our chromatic (or half-tone) scale can always touch. How far the use of overtones may go is conjectural. It is possible that there is a psychological deadline which will prevent the use of overtones far beyond the limit of our present perceptions.

But before these problems have to be solved, considerable progress along other than the harmonic lines will probably take place. The conception of music as a science as well as an art, standing now upon the threshold of almost limitless expansion, opens up a wide horizon. Certain other possibilities may be reserved for later discussion.

III

In a well-known passage in his autobiography John Stuart Mill confesses to a sense of depression at the thought that the possible combinations of musical sounds in our scale are so limited that they must soon be exhausted, after which music must necessarily be but a repetition of what had gone before. The conservative choir masters, monks and critics of all ages have found in the same apparent limitations a cause for satisfaction, and have strenuously resisted every attempt to overstep them. Music has ever tended to harden into a kind of theology of its own, yet has constantly evolved and even suffered revolution at the hands of heretics and Adullamites.

Harmonic progress (and this is but one of several phases through which music may grow and broaden) may be expected to follow at least three general lines. These are:

1. The use of new overtones, as has been suggested in the preceding discussion.
2. Tone-clusters—a convenient term to indicate two or more minor seconds in juxtaposition, struck simultaneously and used as a unit.
3. Polyharmony, or the simultaneous employment of different chords instead of single tones as harmonic units.

There is an indefinite series of overtones or partials, all of which sound when a single tone is sounded, and which are represented on the piano by the vibrations of any single string, the whole string yielding, let us say, the tone of middle C, each half vibrating twice as fast and yielding the octave above middle C, each third vibrating three times as fast and yielding the G above the octave and so on. The interval between each partial and its successor necessarily diminishes until that between the sixteenth and seventeenth partials (counting the whole tone as the first partial) is less than the smallest interval in our scale—less, that is to say, than a half step. The minor second, or the interval between a given tone and the tone a half step above, is the smallest harmonic unit that can be used with our scale.

The next step would be of necessity the addition of the interval suggested by the distance between the sixteenth and seventeenth partials, and there is no reason to doubt that this step, which is quite in the historic line of musical growth, will eventually be taken. This interval, erroneously described as a third or quarter-tone, is used in the Arabian scale, in which the octave is divided into seventeen equal steps, and that it is readily perceived by the ear is shown by the fact that it is the interval generally hit upon by musicians who endeavor to make use of the quarter step. It can be easily played upon stringed instruments, especially upon the 'cello. The richness and variety that this addition alone might give our music is more easily imagined than described. Nor need this be the final interval to be added to the scale. The limit is fixed only by the delicacy of our hearing and the flexibility of our tastes.

It will be natural to use the new interval somewhat tentatively at first, and no doubt its original employment, together with the use of the large number of new harmonies that will become possible through the combination of this with other tones, will be in passing from one accepted harmony to another, by means of a chromatic passing tone between the half steps.[1] In this way our ears will become accustomed to it and like other harmonies which have come into use those formed on the new tone will finally be used unresolved.

The purely technical difficulties in the adoption of a new interval will be plain to anyone who considers the matter for a moment. We should be compelled to expand the piano keyboard to about double its present length, or to introduce some system of double-decking similar to (though more complex than) that already in use on the organ. This mechanical difficulty would be lacking on the stringed instruments and in vocal music, but even here a new system of musical notation and a new technique would be essential. Such obstacles cannot permanently hold back progress in this direction, but they are certain to dam it up for a time. Musical development will follow the paths of least resistance.

One of these paths leads to what we have called, for convenience, tone-clusters. The tone-cluster is simply a group of two or more minor seconds; that is, it is a cluster of three or more tones, each a half step from its neighbor, sounded simultaneously. If we drop a book flat on the piano keys we may achieve a tone-cluster, although, not forming part of a musical structure, the result will be nothing but noise. The cluster obviously differs from any other musical chord in being incapable of internal movement, for there is no room in which to shift or add to any of the component tones. One of the characteristic qualities of harmony is this very shifting of tones within fixed limits. The tone-cluster, consisting of two or more minor seconds in juxtaposition, thus differs from any other harmony. Psychologically it is a unit, although really a group of chromatic tones. The only movement of which it is capable is movement up and down the scale, as in a melody, or an expanding or contracting movement in which the outer limits vary.

An unstudied and incidental use of combinations which might be said to be tone-clusters may be found in the work of such modernists as Ornstein. Ornstein has, for instance, used such groupings as C-C sharp-D-D sharp, but only as part of a complicated chord. [*Neither he nor any other of the tone-cluster. Experiment shows that clusters as a melodic or harmonic unit.*][2] We may say, accordingly, that it is a new musical medium. It is by no means difficult to comprehend (still using the piano keyboard as a handy means of visualizing the principles involved) the possible uses of the tone-cluster. Experiment shows that clusters of which the outside limits form a consonant interval are more pleasing than those which form a dissonant interval. A cluster of twelve semi-tones, the outside notes of which are an octave apart, seems less dissonant than one of two semitones, the outside notes of which are a major apart; and the ear seems readily to recognize consonance in clusters formed by filling in the fourth, third, and other very consonant intervals. The reader may easily determine this for himself by trying the effect, first, let us say, of filling in all the black and white notes between C and B and then of filling in those between C and G; or he may note the difference between two adjacent semitones played at once and twelve played at once.

The significance of the tone-cluster, like that of the single tone, is to be found in its possibility of combinations with other tone-clusters or with other tones. In general, all that can be done with single tones can also be done with tone-clusters. We may take a simple melody and parallel it with a series of tone-clusters of which the lowest or highest notes shall carry the original theme. We may accompany a melody with tone-clusters. We may combine tone-clusters with tone-clusters. We may produce a harmony in tone-clusters or counterpoint of tone-clusters.

A given cluster may be varied in a number of ways. Movement up and down the scale may be secured by leaving off notes at one end and adding an equal number at the other end. A cluster may be expanded by adding the same number of notes simultaneously at both ends, or by adding a different number of notes simultaneously at both ends. In the latter case, obviously, the nature of the cluster would change, since its outer limits would change: and something like counterpoint would result, each outer note making a path or melody of its own. A cluster may be built up by filling in the interval between two or more clusters, and in the same way a large cluster may be broken up. In the use of two or more clusters at once one cluster may remain stationary, while another moves; one may expand and contract while another preserves its original limits; or the movements, contractions and expansions may vary in speed and extent.

All this is sufficiently complicated when put into words and sufficiently simple when translated into terms of the black and white keys of a piano. Enough has been accomplished, perhaps, if it has been made clear that the tone-cluster is an elastic medium, capable of producing a great number of absolutely new musical effects, and is therefore the potential parent of a wide and varied musical literature.

The acceptability of the tone-cluster depends, of course, upon its appeal to the ear. Considered as a series of dissonances, a composition built upon tone-clusters might at first thought appear totally unmusical, but experiment shows that it is not, in fact, difficult to perceive structure in such a composition. In considering the nature of dissonance in tone-clusters it might be borne in mind that the dissonance of the semitones forming the cluster is not felt if the cluster be considered as a unit, real dissonance being obtained only when the outer limits of the cluster form a dissonance. Structure, the principal element of the musical art, indeed of all art, is just as readily found in a composition of tone-clusters as in one of single tones and consonant chords. The ear quickly learns to test tone-clusters, as it tests the single tones and accompanying chords of a melody, by their progress up and down the scale and by their relations to one another.

Polyharmony develops even more naturally out of the accepted musical material than does the tone-cluster. Just as harmony grows out of the series of overtones produced by a single tone, polyharmony is produced by the combination of the overtones of at least two different tones. Each single tone, it must be noted, produces not only the single overtone series, but each overtone sets in motion a series of overtones of its own and so on infinitely. That this must be so is evident from a consideration of what happens when a tone is sounded, let us say, on a piano. The first overtone—or second partial—is formed by each half of the string vibrating at twice the speed of the main string and independently of the main string. Each half, acting in all respects as an independent string, sets in motion its own series of overtones, and so does each successive fraction of the string as it divides into smaller and smaller units vibrating at greater and greater speeds. Let us take the common chord of C, C-E-G. If the three tones are sounded simultaneously the three series of overtones develop at the same time, each overtone starting a new series that branches off from the main series, and so we have a series of overtone chords based upon the original common chord, C-E-G. The third partial, or interval of a fifth, would be represented by the chord G-B-D, the fifth, or interval of a third, by E-G sharp-B, and so on, the intervals between the tones remaining exactly the same, but the interval between each original tone and each successive overtone diminishing. The chord C-E-G, however disguised in the overtone series, would retain its substantial identity.

But it is possible to play simultaneously a chord formed on C, another chord formed on E, and a third, formed on G. If this is done the overtones of the three chords, which are really heard as units, will bear throughout a relation corresponding to the relations of the tones C-E-G. The combination of these chords produces what may be called a polychord or polyharmony. Each consonant combination of single tones has its counterpart in a combination of chords formed upon these tones. In making use of them we are simply exploiting still further the infinite riches of the overtones from which harmony has already been evolved. As every tone may be made the basis of two chords, a major and a minor, and as we may use not only the overtone series but the undertone series, which, though unheard, furnishes a mathematical basis for a curve corresponding to that of the overtones, the diversity of the material available is apparent.

The similarity of the processes of harmony to the use of polyharmony is very close. We have grown so accustomed to simple harmonies, like that of the common chord, that we hear them as a unit, instead of several tones. Likewise a single tone, which owes its richness to its content of overtones, may be regarded, in conjunction with these overtones as a chord. The boundary between a single tone and a chord is not, in short, acoustically distinct; they overlap and shade into one another.

If chords are regarded as units, in the same way in which we have just been regarding tone-clusters, it at once appears that they, too, may be employed as single notes have been. Some limited use of that which might really be called polyharmony has already been made, although by rule of thumb, with no conception of the underlying principles. Pedal point, in which a chord may be held in the bass while the treble performs independently, is such an approach to polyharmony, and pedal point, elaborated by Beethoven, was in use long before his time. But polyharmony soon outruns the capacities of the piano, at least of the solo piano, and for its development we must look to the orchestra, to which it is admirably suited.

Viewed as a single harmony, there is no polychord which does not form a dissonance. The reason for this is easily understood if it is remembered that what our ears regard as consonance is a simple ratio between the rate of vibrations of notes sounded simultaneously, and that which we regard as dissonance is merely a more complex ratio. In sounding a series of overtones, each with its branching series of overtones, as we do in polyharmony, we inevitably introduce a series of ratios more complex than any now commonly in use in music—so complex that they cannot at present be thought of as consonances.

The tone-cluster, as has been seen, is more acceptable to the ear if its outer limits form a consonant interval. Similarly, the polyharmonic chord, or polychord, is more acceptable if it is based on a consonant interval. A polychord based on C-G would be the most easily understood of any, one based on the minor second C-D flat would prove the least comprehensible. Another element also enters into the employment of polychords. If they overlap one another, or are not widely enough spaced, they are heard only as a confusion of sound. To be heard as units they must be separated by a considerable interval. This is easily possible with the orchestra.

Let us again imagine a simple composition, made up of a melody and a consonant accompaniment. We have seen that the structure of such a composition could be copied, by way of variation, in tone-clusters. Similarly, it could be copied in polyharmonic chords. Any musical form adapted to single tones may also be used in compositions employing the tone-cluster and the polychord. We may have polyharmonic counterpoint and tone-cluster counterpoint. We may relate our tone-clusters and polychords in all the ways in which we relate single tones, and musical development may take them through all the harmonic stages from the simplest down to the most complex.

Once the possibilities of musical progress are thoughtfully examined other avenues than those that have been mentioned appear to open out. Time, meter and tempo, for instance, are all capable of variations far beyond the accepted practice, as a simple mathematical analysis will show. The common factor of music is vibration, into which tone as well as time, meter and tempo may all be resolved, and from which there emerges a vast number of possible combinations and recombinations. These potentialities are beyond the scope of this discussion. Music, far from being subject to the limits dreaded by John Stuart Mill, still contains its undiscovered continents. As an art and as a science the work of exploration has just begun; and this, for a jaded world, is perhaps a sufficient moral.

1. Thus (calling the new interval, for convention, ¼) C½ sharp would resolve to C sharp, D¾ flat to D.—HC

2. The bracketed passage was badly garbled by the original printer.—DH

The Impasse of Modern Music

SEARCHING FOR NEW AVENUES OF BEAUTY

FIVE HUNDRED YEARS AGO the composer who attempted to enrich the simple music of his day by introducing what is now called the common chord, was roundly denounced by the critics of his day. Modern, they stigmatized his work, as if modernity in itself was necessarily evil, as if out of the modern music of yesterday had not come the classical of today.

Of the great works of music, nine-tenths were criticized unfavorably when first produced. They offered something new that the ear—hearing is the most conservative of our senses—at first refused to consider pleasing, sometimes refused to consider even bearable. The denunciations of Strauss and Stravinsky were only echoes of the storms of protest against Wagner and Beethoven by an earlier generation of critics, and the people who today term modern music a "development of twentieth-century bunk," a "complete departure from the classics," "plotted nonsense," "world insanity," and "the embodiment of the spirit of ugliness"—I quote from present-day critics—are only repeating the criticisms of a century, or five centuries, ago.

It is not to be inferred that all the innovations which have been

---

This is Cowell's first attempt to bring non-western music into the picture of modern and western music; it appeared in Century Magazine *CXIV/6 (Oct. 1927) pp. 671-7. He includes some ideas from "Harmonic Development in Music," written earlier. The legend of the excommunication of Guido d'Arezzo, noted in an earlier text, has now been transferred to an anonymous monk. Alois Haba (1893-1973) was a Czech who wrote microtonal music. Leo Ornstein (1892-) is a composer-pianist. Carlos Salzedo (1885-1961), mentioned elsewhere, became primarily a harpist.*

denounced as modern in their day, have been accepted later as legitimate enrichments of the field of music. Far from it. Of the many innovations offered, only a small fraction have emerged from the test of time. Why some music has lived and some died has been sensed but vaguely until recent times when, with a more accurate knowledge of acoustics, we have begun to perceive that acceptance or rejection has not been haphazard but that through the maze runs a thread of logic.

The development of European music has been chiefly the development of harmony. To trace its progress it may be clearer if we think of music as having dimensions—harmony as perpendicular and counterpoint as horizontal. The notes that are sounded at one time come under the subject of harmony, and melodies, whose notes follow one another to form tunes, make up counterpoint when played simultaneously.

The earliest European music of which we know had only melody, a single note played or sung at a time, and harmony made its modest beginning in the playing of notes an exact octave above or below this melody. At that early stage in the development of the sense of hearing, any other combination of notes was considered unpleasantly discordant.

An unknown monk gave the world a new idea: he punched two keys which did not form an octave; the sound pleased him and he trained his choir boys to sing, not with the notes of the crude instruments that carried the tunes, but a fifth above. For a time his innovation passed unnoticed, then the cry of heresy was raised. In vain did the monk try to explain that the sound was beautiful. His act was considered not only ugly but a matter of desecration and for this he was excommunicated and exiled. Many, however, had heard his music and the sounds which at first shock seemed so repellent, by familiarity grew tolerable and then fascinating. Fifty years from the date of his excommunication the Church itself issued an edict that all church music be sung a fifth above the notes, and thus gave official sanction to the tenor's traditional propensity for embroidering the pattern of music by singing above and below the written notes.

⁝⁝⁝⁝⁝⁝⁝⁝⁝⁝

So began the development of European music whose leading innovators—Palestrina, Monteverdi, Bach, Haydn, Mozart, Beethoven, Wagner and Debussy, the modernists of their day— have given to the present generation of modernists the inspiration of innovation as well as of beauty. Through five hundred years the principal developments have been to make harmony more and more complicated, while melody has remained comparatively simple and rhythm has atrophied.

Western music has taken one road and Oriental another, going in exactly the opposite direction. In contrast with our complicated harmony and simple melody and rhythm, they have not developed harmony but have complicated melody and rhythm. A cultured Chinese derives no pleasure from our greatest symphonies; our harmony only confuses him and the simplicity of our melody and rhythm seems to him childish and uninteresting. We retaliate, of course, by looking in vain for harmony in Chinese music and by having the complicated melody and rhythm fall upon our unattuned ears with little meaning. So, too, with the music of Indians, Africans and other primitive peoples. I once heard four Indians beating different rhythms on their tom-toms while the native audience sat entranced for hours listening to the harmonic variations of rhythm—with no melody and no harmony—to our ears, a meaningless and monotonous sound.

In the development of harmony we began by considering as pleasing only octaves, but gradually we have accepted smaller and smaller intervals between the notes. What to one generation was discordant has been accepted by the next as concordant, and the concords of earlier generations have been dismissed as insipid and flavorless. At first dissonances were passed over swiftly and the ear was allowed to rest on safely concordant notes, but gradually the ear has become trained to listen with zest to dissonance. Not, however, to all dissonance. Some was accepted and some rejected, but only now are we beginning to understand the determining principle behind this test of time.

Physics has offered so many rival fields of interest that acoustics has been virtually deserted since the time of Helmholtz. Recently, however, interest has been revived and scientists have given to the musical world corrections of our older theories of sound which will help us—not to create music scientifically, but to understand the steps of progress in the past and the possibilities and limitations with which we are now confronted.

As to the nature of sound itself, we have learned that what distinguishes sound from mere noise is that sound is produced by a periodic vibration, and noise by an irregular vibration. If a string is held at both ends, the complete vibration from one bridge to the other produces a fundamental tone. The string vibrates first as a whole and then divides and vibrates in sections. It divides first into halves and this vibration of the halves produces a tone exactly an octave above the first tone, thus creating the first overtone. The string then subdivides into smaller and smaller divisions, each new length producing a new vibration and a new overtone. When you hear a single tone, what you think is a unit is actually a combination of many parts, all of which can be registered accurately by scientific instruments and some of which can be distinguished by the unaided ear. Professor Miller of the Case Institute of Applied Science, who probably has the most acutely trained ear in the world, can hear as many as forty-four overtones without the aid of instruments, an extraordinary achievement, as most persons can distinguish only the first few overtones and even trained musicians can rarely hear more than a dozen.

As the overtones rise, they form a regular series and this overtone series constitutes a measure of harmony itself. If we start with C the first overtone is C, an octave higher, then G, C, E, G, F sharp, G, A flat, B flat, B natural, and C, at which point we return to the third octave above our original tone. This series of overtones is according to the natural pitch of tones, and may be played on a violin but cannot be picked out accurately on a piano as our pianos are tuned by an equalized scale, not by natural pitch.

The first intervals between the overtones are farther apart, but the distance between the notes grows less and less as one progresses up the series. The first notes we readily class as concords and the latter ones as dissonants, but there is no definite point at which we can say that concord stops and dissonance begins. We often hear it said that a person whose ear is acute cannot bear dissonance, but exactly the reverse is true. A keen ear hears more of the overtones which are a part of all sound, and the person who hears the higher, more dissonant intervals, grows accustomed to them and accepts them with enthusiasm. The great composers have steadily given us more and more dissonance. Each new interval has been denounced, usually with the extreme bitterness which critics feel toward the person who deliberately violates beauty. Time has taught us to accept certain of the intervals and to reject others. The important truth which is demonstrated scientifically by acoustics, is this: that the intervals which have been accepted have been accepted in the order in which they occur in the overtone scale—first the octave, then the perfect fifth, then the fourth, then the third, and so on. The innovations in harmony which time has refused, were out of that order. By this discovery science helps us to grasp intellectually the principle behind the beauty toward which we have groped slowly, blindly, yet surely through our emotional responses. The great masters who have developed our music step-by-step, have done so because their ears were keen enough to hear the harmony of the overtones and to play in outward notes the combinations which they heard.

The harmony of Schoenberg marks the interval between the fifteenth and sixteenth overtones, and the acceptance of Schoenberg brings music to a crisis, for the next step in the overtone scale cannot be played on the instruments which Western music knows. If the past is to be taken as a foreshadowing of the future, we should say that the next development in music would be to utilize the next steps in the overtone scale. Doubtless our ears would be ready to accept these new sounds, but we are confronted by the barrier of our own instruments and will be forced either to invent new ones or depart from the path of our historical development. Of course music can still be written with the materials which we now have in hand, but in the past each generation has added to the field of possibilities, and the impetus for the expansion of the barriers of sound has been part of the beauty of the great music of the past. Nothing more perfect than Beethoven could be written, but Beethoven was a fundamental innovator and to write, limiting one's self to the materials which Beethoven used and lacking entirely the impetus for a wider expression of beauty, would be only to produce more of the Beethoven-and-water school of music which has fallen flat even on the ears of those who object to any innovations since the master's.

¦¦¦¦¦¦¦¦¦

We stand today at music's crossroads. The impetus for widening the possibilities of beauty, so integral a part of the creative genius, will force us to break the barriers. We are forced to depart from the historic tradition of development, but exactly where the barriers are to be broken, is the problem which confronts us today. The conservative critic says that the modernist writes outside of the old rules from ignorance and laziness; that he writes dissonance from ignorance of harmony, and breaks rules because he has no theory. Of a small minority this is doubtless true, but never have so much thought and study been put into music as by the modernists of today and never have men set themselves such extraordinarily difficult tasks. There are theories without end; some scientific, some aesthetic, some based on nothing at all, but the hopeful thing about the modernists is that each has a theory and is willing to let time slip while he devotes his energy to proving he has a method.

If we must depart from the historic development of harmony we can either make the jump which our instruments can be adjusted to permit, that is, to the quarter-tone, or we must abandon further steps in harmony and develop other elements in music. Haba, the Czech composer, is the foremost figure in the development of quarter-tones, but it remains to be seen whether this quarter-tone will be accepted. If it is accepted it will break all Western precedent by skipping over, by completely omitting, a field as vast as all the fields which we have explored step by step in five hundred years. Haba is primarily a musical creator although he brings to his music an amazing grasp of the science behind the art. He writes in quarter-tones because his music demands this closer, dissonant interval—not merely to demonstrate the use of quarter-tones. He has a piano constructed like two grand pianos, one above the other, the hammers of the upper striking downward and those of the lower striking upward, tuned to quarter-tones. He has invented a notation for quarter-tones and has published works on the acoustics and also on the psychology of the quarter-tone; and his classes at the Conservatory of Prague are the only places in the world where the quarter-tone can be studied.

If we are blocked by the limitation of our instruments from further steps in harmony, we can only turn for progress to the other elements of music, to counterpoint, rhythm, tempo, tonality, tone-clusters, and the addition, perhaps, of the sliding tones which characterize primitive music. Along all of these lines the modernists are searching for new avenues of beauty and expression.

Carl Ruggles, foremost of American composers, is devoting himself exclusively to the development of dissonant counterpoint. His theory is one of the conspicuous theories of present-day music. Since the time of Bach and Handel no composer has given counterpoint such exclusive attention. His musical conscience is as straightlaced as his Puritan ancestors—Ruggles is the one American composer of genuine Yankee lineage—and his style is watertight. The task which Ruggles has set himself to accomplish is well-nigh impossible; he often spends an entire day in developing a single chord, and his compositions, whose clarity of melodic line is stripped of all dross, are polished perfection.

:::::::::

To Stravinsky the world owes more, perhaps, for his introduction of rhythmical variations than for all his other unique and colorful additions to music. From 1700 to 1900 rhythm had atrophied. It was expected, even demanded, that a composition should continue throughout in one rhythm and the first attempts to alternate rhythms were denounced as monstrous. Stravinsky rose above this first storm of criticism, Scriabin broke down more barriers with his simple cross rhythms, and, in America, Varèse, who occupies a high place among the moderns, has narrowed the interest of his compositions to rhythm and the tone-quality of the percussions. Rhythm is as essential a part of music as melody, but we have never made any attempt at developing rhythmic harmony or combining rhythmic meters. Gross accenting, of course, approaches this effect and in a halting and unacknowledged fashion, all music teachers make some effort to get their pupils away from the obvious accents which would otherwise become unbearably monotonous. At the moment we have a loosening up of meters for the reason that modern music changes meter, but we have not attempted to harmonize different meters at one time. We have limited ourselves to half notes, quarters, eighths, and further division by halves, but we do not divide by thirds, fifths, sevenths or ninths and we have no means of notating such divisions. We look askance at the very suggestion, yet, when we have developed rhythm one-tenth as far as we have developed harmony, we shall be using rhythms in chords and shall have added enormous interest to music.

‡‡‡‡‡‡‡‡‡

In orchestral music we may very practically evolve combinations in musical tempo which cannot well be written for any single instrument. As a matter of musical feeling a slow note in allegro is very different from a fast note in adagio, and music which is to convey more than a simple emotion, can be written far more effectively by using different tempos in its different parts. The effort of conveying different emotions in the same tempo is a tremendous handicap to a composer, and is largely responsible for the stilted and artificial quality of most opera. Take, for example, the quartet from *Rigoletto,* where Verdi attempts to portray the emotions of four different characters. It would be far more realistic if each part were written in the tempo called for by the emotion of the character. The contralto part should be sung in allegro, the tenor in allegretto, the baritone in adagio and the soprano in andante. Instead, all are sung in the same tempo, the conflict of emotions is reduced to an average and the standardized tempo reduces, rather than advances, the dramatic action.

Another of the long accepted rules of music which is being questioned today, is that of tonality, the homing sense of music which demands that a composition be ended in the same key in which it began. Schoenberg has made experiments in not returning to any key, and a whole group of composers, known as atonalists, now urge the logic of not returning to the original key. Most persons experience a disagreeable sense of incompleteness if a composition does not return home, particularly if the composer builds up the feeling of tonality and then disappoints the expectation, but the abler atonalists, such as Schoenberg, do not build up that expectation. The polytonalists return, not to one key, but to several keys at once, and between different keys which synchronize one experiences strange, peculiar emotion with great subtleties of feeling. Béla Bartók plays one hand in one key and a different key with the other hand which demands that the composer write in polyharmony, an innovation first suggested by Strauss. Polyharmony, with doubtless a widening future ahead, demands a very keen sense of acoustics as the chords, if put together ignorantly, are extraordinarily discordant, but when combined sensitively become a most effective means of creating atmosphere and emotion.

The tone-cluster, the use of an aggregate of sound, of all the major or minor tones within an octave or more, has not been worked out at all. It is not a hit or miss striking of notes, but a very definite construction of sound, with a thousand possibilities for the piano as well as for orchestral handling. Against the background of sound, the melody, carried higher or lower, takes on a new richness of tone and overtone values, and the shifting of tones within the cluster has possibilities of great subtlety. Once the public is willing to accept the cluster seriously and not regard it merely as a gymnastic method of piano playing, its acoustic soundness will be understood and its use as a means of obtaining strength and character of tone will undoubtedly be seized on by the large body of musicians who are seeking more adequate sound production.

There is a whole category of sounds used by primitive peoples in their music, which are highly expressive—the sliding tones, wails and other tones which do not maintain pitch. At the present time when our singers attempt to gain emotional effects by slipping and wailing, we are properly disgusted because this violation of pitch is not a part of our music and its use is due either to lack of technique or deliberate "cheating" for emotional effect. In old Italian music the sliding tone was a recognized musical device, very lovely in its place, but its use was discontinued. Seeger terms the sliding pitch "inarticulate" in distinction to articulate pitch, and recognizes the possibility of legitimately adding the inarticulate tones to our idiom. The idea is in the air. Weisshaus, in Budapest, is adapting it to his compositions and many other composers are working with the principle.

These are a few of the means whereby modern music is seeking to break the barrier with which Western music is now confronted, to break the barrier which otherwise threatens to balk its historic tradition of innovation and development. Modern music is distinctly not attempting to disregard the classics but rather to do exactly what those same classics accomplished in their day—to add new principles to what had been established before. The traditional line of development has brought us to the limitations of our instruments, the further development of harmony is halted, and from this impasse we must strike out in other directions through the development of those other elements in music which the classicists passed over in their race for more and more complicated harmony. Never have composers taken their task more earnestly, and never before has America—with Ruggles, Varèse, Rudhyar, Ornstein, Salzedo, Aaron Copland and a host of other young composers—stepped to the forefront in music with compositions that are not mere echoes and imitations of Europe, but alive with the vitality of new growth from new soil.

1. Imre Weisshaus is mentioned by HC elsewhere also, but I can find no mention of him by others.—DH

Towards Neo-Primitivism

Loosely speaking, every one interested in modern music realizes there is some resemblance between certain aspects of primitive and of contemporary music. But there is no group of deliberately neo-primitive composers with formulated ideas that have been made public, similar, for example, to the painters of this school. Yet primitivistic tendencies exist in modern music, none the less, and give every evidence of growing stronger.

It is now more than twenty years since those adventures in dissonance and rhythm, loosely called modern music, were launched by Schoenberg, Ives and Stravinsky and their contemporaries. Some of the changes they inaugurated did release certain primordial elements; but as a whole their music was a further step in cultivating complexity, with its delicate harmonic complexes, shades of tone coloring, wider melodic skips, and frequent use of a very large orchestra. Only the rhythm revealed a closer kinship to the primitive than did the music of the preceding period; because rhythm is more complex in aboriginal than in classic music. A growth of complexity in rhythm would necessarily take music in this direction and it would be absurd to say that this new rhythmic freedom represented a deliberate return to the primitive by the modern composers. Stravinsky was of course influenced by Russian peasant rites which were somewhat barbaric in character, but

Attacking neo-classicism as a rehashing of old materials, HC favors a "Neo-Primitivism" based on an intuitive linking of world musics and contemporary materials. One sees an affinity here with Friedrich Schiller's "Naive and Sentimental Poetry," written 150 years before, which helped clear the path for romanticism. Cowell's piece appeared in Modern Music *X/3 (Mar.-Apr. 1933) pp. 149-153. This short essay was enormously important in the musical controversies of the thirties as it summed up much of the skepticism which greeted the imitators of Stravinsky. Most of the composers HC mentions are today unknown.*

his use of these elements was comparatively slight and highly sub-limated. The "primitiveness" which the public associates with the pioneers of modernism is the result of a most casual impression, often based on unfamiliarity with both the modern and the primi-tive idiom. The general conception of savage music is that it is something wild, confused, with raucous cries and noisy instruments all bound together by powerful rhythm—an impression associated also with the more experimental type of modern music. But the primitive is often soft, melodious and soothing—and modern mu-sic is, after all, a highly organized, involved and sophisticated art.

Following the Schoenberg-Ives-Stravinsky innovations by ten or fifteen years came a new counter-tendency, neoclassicism. This has had far greater ramifications than is usually conceded. The neoclassical writings of Stravinsky are known; but Schoenberg has made as many experiments in this field. Schoenberg kept his har-mony and intervals in counterpoint modern but has worked in classical forms. Some almost forgotten, very rigorous ones, such as retrograde, much used by early Flemish composers, are character-istic of his style since about 1920. With Stravinsky, the return to the old is easier to hear, for he began to use old types of chords and tunes. It is safe to say that one can find the neoclassic influence in nearly all important European composers in form, melody, har-mony or general polyphonic line. Its popularity may be partly due to the fact that a composer who adopts it may still be considered "up-to-date" and yet run no risk of being misunderstood. He may deal with simple familiar materials which none will find too hard to digest. Even the conservative can take up neoclassicism and find himself seriously considered by the progressives.

Neoclassic music is not, of course, just like classical music; it contains new elements. But these are easy to understand since the background is familiar. The result is far too comfortable. Easy to compose, easy to understand, easy to forget. This preoccupation with the external aspects of a short period of musical history has resulted in some stagnation of creative work in Europe and even here. Nor is the effect on the public stimulating to its musical devel-opment.

Now the time has come for a strong new counter-movement, full-blooded and vital. The tendency already exists, and shows signs of steady growth. It reacts against the over-complexity of the earlier modern music but not against experiment; against the sentimentality and pomp of later romantic music but not against feeling; against the supercilious formalism of a return to the particular style of some past century but not against the use of primary musical elements.

This tendency is obviously neo-primitive in its drive for vitality and simplicity. It is not an attempt to imitate primitive music, but rather to draw on those materials common to the music of all the peoples of the world, to build a new music particularly related to our own century.

Today the connection between primitive and contemporary music is clearer and more definite, not only because the newest music is far more genuinely related to this source, but also because we have learned a great deal more about primitive art itself within the past few years. Many of the customary generalizations can no longer be made in the face of this wider knowledge. There is, of course, no aboriginal music to be found anywhere which corresponds to the common conception of an uncontrolled expression of wild, unbridled, savage feeling. Nor can primitive music be lumped into one group. The music of various tribes is as different as the music of the various cultivated nations. A tribe may have a scale of its own, certain rhythms or instrumental color, or its own special vocal curve. The North Siberian tribes and the Mongolians for instance, use sharp angular lines of tone and rhythm, while the Maoris of New Zealand and other South Sea Islanders never use a straight line of sound but curve every tonal edge and even employ a rhythm which has no beats but only a curved dynamic line. Our Indians lean to vocal music; they have few melodic instruments; the Pygmies of the Belgian Congo, on the other hand, use panpipes of great complexity and refinement as a standard, and their vocal music actually imitates the instrument. There is also a wide difference in scales. The same Pygmies use a scale built on their panpipe overtones, sometimes running a gamut from the fifth to the thirteenth partial in the overtone series, a highly developed medium. There are others, in Tierra Del Fuego, for instance, who in some songs use only one pitch.

This list of differences could of course be extended indefinitely; it is given here to dispel the idea of uniformity. The primitives nearly always have certain musical conventions that demand strict adherence. In some places, among certain tribes in Hawaii, for example, to sing a tone out of the proper scale is an offense punishable by death. Elsewhere certain rhythms, scales, tone-qualities and melodies are taught as sacred, never to be altered or defiled.

However there are some general characteristics which nearly all primitive music shares. Most of it is sung to the accompaniment of percussion; melody and rhythm are thus the main elements. Where several different voices sing together they are either in unison or heterophonic, making a free polyphony in which each part is quite independent except that it must come out with the others at the end. Further, nearly all primitive music has rapid rhythmical changes, syncopations, polyrhythms and cross-rhythms. In the melody there may be a wide range of different sorts of pitch curves as well as straight lines of sound. The tones either wobble back and forth or slide up or down—not carelessly, but as a vital part of the musical scheme.

Let us now examine our contemporary music to determine in what direction its characteristics tend. If we look at the larger proportion of new music in Europe we will find the dominant aspect on the whole still neoclassical. There are major and minor scales and modes; many scales and other passages in unvaried meters and a running series of quarter, eighth or sixteenth notes—all the signs of a cultivated music. Furthermore, the structure is usually built on harmony, either dissonant or consonant, and the form is some version of the classic.

There is however in the music of some American and some Russian composers today enough material to justify us in pointing out a new movement that is primitivistic.

Soviet Russia is developing a new musical art. Modern, sophisticated, experienced composers write works which are interesting to serious musicians and yet may be sung by proletarian choruses. This music is characterized by a melody standing on its own feet and getting little support from harmony; if there is any harmony at all it is a secondary consideration. There is often an accompaniment on drums and a single line of melody as in primitive music. The songs are often neither major nor minor, nor even modal, but they may have a melodic line with some free intervals suggested by the words. There is considerable use of vocal slides which are actually written into the score. The rhythm is apt to change frequently and to be vigorous and direct.

The well-known composers Mossolov, Shostakovitch and Vladimir Vogel, for example, write a great deal in this vein; Szabo and Weisshaus of Hungary are following suit, as well as Hans Eisler of Germany. In this country, Lahn Adomyhan has written successfully in the same manner, and there are about a dozen young composers working with him. Their music is being sung by proletarian choral groups all over the country.

Among the more radical works written by non-proletarian American composers recently, there may not be anything so very definitely primitive in style, but there are strong tendencies to use primitive means in creating new sorts of structures. Up to this year, in my experience as a music publisher I have never been offered any work for percussion instruments alone. This season I have been offered fifteen different works for such combinations, the two most interesting being Varèse's *Ionization,*[1] and William Russell's *Fugue for Eight Percussion Instruments.*

Then there is the tendency of many of the young composers to emphasize vocal slides, as in the work of Irwin Heilner, Lehman Engel and Jerome Moross of the Young Composers' Group. Primitive rhythms are extremely noticeable in Moross' *Those Everlasting Blues.* In all such works, there is also a tendency to use chords percussively and for emphasis rather than to exploit them in a harmonic connection. This too is a sort of primitive simplification. Tone clusters, which are a simplifying into one unit of otherwise complex dissonances also represent a return to such direct, primary modes of expression. Primitive elements may of course be utilized in many ways. One may be rather literal in their use, as in the case of Soviet musicians, or one may make a sublimation of direct and primary, musical materials, unhampered by ecclesiastical rules, scales or rhythms. The latter course is being followed by many of the young American composers who have recently made a bid for attention.

1. The spelling of Varèse's *Ionization* (Eng.) is often given as *Ionisation* (Fr.). Varèse and HC, the latter of whom played one of the pianos at its world premiere, use both spellings. The original New Music Orchestra Series edition of the work (1934) spells it *Ionisation,* and its composer's first name as "Edgard."—DH

Shaping Music for Total War

T HE MAIN PURPOSE of the Overseas branch of the Office of
War Information has been and still is to wage psychological
warfare against the enemy, thus shortening the war and saving
American lives. It does this in many ways including dissemination
of information to Allied and neutral countries.

One of the few ways of reaching into enemy and occupied
countries is by radio, which was soon found to be of paramount
importance in OWI's scheme of things. It was at first assumed that
music would have little or no part in a program whose objective
was to present information. As it turned out, however, this view
proved to be fantastically incorrect.

This then is an account of the gradual evolution of the present
clear-cut policy for the use of music in the Radio Program Bureau
of the OWI. It is not too much to say that music's very precise
exploitation has frequently been the deciding factor in our ability
to reach hundreds of millions of foreign peoples with Allied news
and American views.

The necessity for such a vital and accurate use became evident
in the spring of 1943, when the enemy radio turned two slips against
us. First, it appeared that one of a series of broadcasts addressed
to an important ally made use of works by the most noted composer of a country which was our ally's traditional enemy,[1] engaged in war against it at the time. Second, the German radio
began ridiculing America, claiming that we were incapable of pro-

---

*During World War Two Cowell was employed by the Overseas Branch of the Office
of War Information to wage psychological warfare against the enemy. Cowell's impressions of the project, discussed here and in a separate lecture, "Music as Propaganda," are vivid and interesting, although Cowell digresses into the hybridization of
world musics. This article appeared in* Modern Music *XXIII/3 (Summer 1946)
pp. 226-228.*

ducing a native culture and had to fall back on German tunes as part of our national music. This was traced to the innocent broadcast of *Maryland, My Maryland* by an OWI producer to illustrate American folksongs. Unfortunately he based his selection on the words alone; the melody happens to be the famous German Christmas carol, *Tannenbaum, O Tannenbaum.*

At about this time I was asked by Macklin Marrow[2] (then music chief) to advise on serious works, American pieces, and music especially selected to go out to particular districts, such as Persian music for Persia. When the Allies invaded Italy, the Germans realized perfectly that Italians would not listen to broadcasts which did not contain a great deal of music; so, as they retreated, they destroyed every record which could possibly be used on our broadcasts to the Italians. Within a few hours of the landings in Italy I was asked to gather a stockpile of Italian music large enough to equip all the radio stations we might need to cover Italy for a year's programs.

Surveys show that radio listeners all over the world assume *a priori* that a speech will be a bore. If they tune in on talk over the air, casually, they are likely to keep spinning the dial. But the same listeners make just the opposite assumption in the case of music, and will almost universally listen for several seconds, to discover whether they want to hear the piece through. This has resulted in the employment of two or three measures of music for station identification almost all over the world; music catches and holds listeners as nothing else will do. Also it saves time. In broadcasting to enemy-held territory, the first few notes of *Yankee Doodle* have identified the programs as ours more quickly than you could say "This is the United States of America, one of the United Nations," words often spoken where there has been time. The vital news can be told and the radio beam cut before the enemy can tell who is listening.

II

Music plays its most vital part in programs where we have been in competition with enemy broadcasts, that is, in neutral and occupied countries which the enemy tries to convert to his views. To direct listeners away from radio Tokyo, our newscasters find that it is especially the *music* we offer which must be more attractive than that on Japanese programs. If music were really a sufficiently international language so that likes and dislikes elsewhere in the world could be measured by our own, the problem would be simplified. Many of us have had enough experience with the larger European cities to make a guess as to how to reach their audiences with music, but we also had to reach the rest of the world! We used art music, old and new, from all countries, and found that pieces by modern Americans whose style is not too complex were well received. (We did not try to force American music on foreign audiences but we saw to it that it was always included in the international picture. We used commercial popular music—the latest song hits, jazz and swing, show pieces, European cabaret tunes—wherever it was needed, though we did not want even the people who request and like it to form the opinion that this is the only music in America. (There are more "Hot Jazz" clubs in Turkey than in the U.S.A.) We need folk and traditional songs of all peoples, for country music comes closest to being international. We often play, for example, the love songs adored by the Japanese people but forbidden by their government, which fears they will make their soldiers homesick.

Hybrid forms, sometimes distasteful to musicologists, have sprung up everywhere and proved helpful. Our popular tunes are to be found in every Oriental country played and sung on native instruments in the style of the land. These adaptations are liked much more than the straight American versions, just as we may prefer *Sheherazade* to the product of a real Oriental orchestra. Performances in our broadcasts of songs like the Chinese *Chee Lai,* which is in westernized style, establish the bond between East and West. Yet, to allay the fear of conservative Orientals that we are trying to force Western culture on them, it is very necessary to show that we know and appreciate their old traditional music too.

In the use of religious pieces also, we must exercise great care. Old and loved Catholic music was sent to the people of Italy, Lutheran hymns to the Icelanders, but we had to be careful not to play Christian music to the Mohammedans. To them we could not even mention the year 1940 A.D.—instead we said "five years ago." In the Far East, where Japanese propaganda claims we will make everyone a Christian if we win, we particularly avoid any

music, either Oriental or Occidental, with strong religious connotations.

<h2 style="text-align:center">III</h2>

For all except the large European countries a great body of
indigenous pieces had to be found to supplement the standard repertory. In some cases we found natives here who played and sang.
The only Annamite in this country who sings was located in San
Francisco with the aid of the Indo-China branch of OWI. He
made records for me as did some members of the Royal Thai
legation in Washington who were excellent singers and players on
their own instruments. Then we had to find record collections of
native music, to borrow and copy them, after tests for musical worth,
surface noise, and meaning of words.

The most exciting feature of my work with OWI was the speed
with which material from abroad could be obtained when vitally
needed. At the time of the Indo-China problem, for instance, I
remembered the recordings made in Paris during the Colonial
Exposition in the early thirties. I sent a cable to our representative
in France; within five days a collection had been located at the
University of Paris and I had copies in my New York office! A
cable to New Delhi produced a list of over two thousand records
which we were able to purchase there.

The OWI collection thus built up over a period of years contains more folk music of the world's peoples and more symphonic
works by serious American composers than any other I know, besides being remarkably complete in other fields too; I understand
that the Library of Congress has negotiated to obtain it after the
War.

While accomplishing the primary objective of gaining worldwide audiences for our radio programs of news and views, we have
succeeded in introducing American music to many people who
had never heard it before. They will inevitably now give serious
consideration to our place in the international field of art.

---

1. Since the anecdote which follows does not refer to any particular composer, there
may be a lost reference here.—DH
2. Mr. Daniel Saidenburg later succeeded Mr. Marrow in this post, and more recently
Mr. Roy Harris has assumed the duties of chief.—HC

On Programing American Music

I BELIEVE THAT WE ARE ALL in agreement that in making plans for a Music Club program season, American music should be included. The question of what to choose and how to place it is therefore of interest to all of us.

There could never be any objection to having a program or even a season of American music, if it is chosen wisely to give the widest possible contrast, especially since we have an extensive variety from which to select.

We do not have a great living composer who writes in the classical style; but more and more early American music is being made available, and some of this is quaintly and beautifully eighteenth century. We as music-lovers need to know the music by American composers that was liked and played by George Washington and Benjamin Franklin. Many publishers offer collections of music of this period—songs, piano pieces, choral works. An excellent one is that edited by Richard Franko Goldman, published by G. Schirmer. For early choral works that have a distinctive American flavor, there are easy-to-sing ones by the doughty Bostonian, William Billings. Those edited by Oliver Daniel, published by C. C,. Birchard Co. of Boston, are also to be recommended.

For piano pieces in nineteenth century drawing-room style there is no composer better than Louis Gottschalk, of New Orleans and points South. Edward MacDowell is, of course, the most representative of the latter part of the same century. For other examples of music belonging to the "romantic" style, without relapsing into sentimentality, one thinks at once of our early twentieth century

---

HC, ever the promoter, was unceasing in his activities on behalf of American, world and modern music. Presented here is the second of three brief articles he wrote for Music Clubs *magazine, this one from XXXI/5 (May 1952) p. 23.*

composers, such as Chadwick, Foote and Converse of Boston, Horatio Parker of New Haven, and the still-living Daniel Gregory Mason of New York and Arthur Shepherd of Cleveland. The impressionistic style is represented in music by Charles Griffes.

This is historical: but after all, America's position as a composer-producing country is based mainly on its contemporary music, and the composers of today. For biographies and lists of works, there are Claire Reis's book *Composers in America,* with shorter biographies and many composers, and David Ewen's book, *American Composers Today,* with more data on the composers, but with fewer included.

In selecting program material, it is of interest to make sure that no important trend in American music remains unrepresented. American music has made its greatest name in the field of modern music, and this should always be included, even if it creates a controversy—this only makes for greater life and interest. In a surprising number of cases, individual American composers have written some things in a "modern" style, others in more conventional styles: so it is not enough to choose a work by a certain composer because he is called a modernist—if you wish a work of his to represent modernism, you must be sure that the right type of work is chosen. This is why, form time to time, we offer suggested lists, with annotations as to the musical styles. Charles Ives, for example, was ahead of the famous European modernists in his innovating with new musical resources in nearly every field: yet some of his songs are as simple as the simplest folk songs or lieder.

The modern style includes the highly dissonant atonal-chromatic style of such men as Wallingford Riegger in his string quartets and Symphony #3; the simpler modal and mildly polytonal style of Aaron Copland in his *Appalachian Spring;* the more rigidly neo-classical styles of Irving Fine or Arthur Berger; the integrated contemporary styles of many of the younger men such as Peter Mennin, Robert Ward, Elliott Carter, etc.

Last, but not least, let us not exclude those men who choose America as their country. Many of us are Americans through accident of birth. How proud we should be that the opportunities and principles of America have attracted many of the world's greatest composers to become citizens! All too often they are forgotten in American programs; yet they ARE Americans, and have no other country. And they represent every sort of music. We think of the warm romanticism of Ernest Bloch, Swiss-American; the great innovator, Arnold Schoenberg, Austrian-American; the unique Igor Stravinsky, Russian-American; the leader of the "gebrauchsmusik" (music for use) school, Paul Hindemith, German-American. And there are such others who prefer America as Milhaud, of France; Reite,[1] of Italy; Martinu, of Czechoslovakia, etc.

Unless we devote our entire program-time to Americans, we can hardly hope to cover all the important composers, native or naturalized. But we can draw constantly on their works, whether we wish to devote a season or a single program to American composition, or whether we follow the method which many of us prefer—namely, to incorporate American works in larger quantities on general programs. If we are careful never to select any American music unless it is of sufficiently fine quality to compare favorably with music from anywhere in the world, and then place it in general programs, there can be no possible doubt.

1. Cowell surely means Vittorio Rietti.

A Composer's World

I MUST BEGIN BY SAYING that I am a composer, not a musicologist. So I am more concerned with the future of musical traditions than with their past.

It is true that I have devoted more time to the study of non-European musical systems than other Western composers, but that is because I took it for granted that a twentieth century composer (particularly one who grew up on the Pacific Coast of North America, halfway between Europe and Asia, as I did) would need to know and to choose from among many kinds of musical inheritance in the world, not just the French and German ones alone. It seemed natural for an American to stretch his mind beyond the limitations of European traditions, and to welcome the infinite variety and vitality of the human imagination as it has expressed itself in the music of the world.

I soon found, of course, that every continent has developed literally dozens of musical styles, all of which had beauty and meaning for their practitioners. This great sea of musical imagination seemed to me my natural inheritance, within which I must find my own music. The multiplicity of musical experience to which I subjected myself seemed to me to be a fact of modern life—useless to try to turn one's back on it.

Today every composer is faced with the problem I embraced

In this late text (1961), written after his heart condition had returned, Cowell attempts to synthesize many of his ideas into a whole. He speaks here of his own development, of the creative process (it is interesting to see how close this article is to Cowell's very early "The Process of Musical Creation," published some thirty-six years before), and of the education of composers in general. World music is, for Cowell, a big part of that education. This text, originally delivered as a speech at Teheran in April, 1961 and first published in Music in Ghana *2 (May 1961) pp. 36-49, is one of the few in which Cowell talks about himself in relation to his work.*

for myself in my youth: How may one learn to live in the whole world of music—to live and to create? No single technique, no single tradition is any longer enough.

Perhaps because I was fortunate enough to hear so many different kinds of music from childhood, music has always seemed to me a single worldwide art, because its basic elements (rhythm, melody, polyphony, form, and so on) are basic everywhere. They have simply been given different emphasis in different places, and this has led to different degrees of development and different combinations and relationships for identical musical elements, in different parts of the world.

Of course, if one should attempt to learn a thousand traditions as separate cultural entities, one sees that this is impossible, at once. But a thousand permutations for rhythm or melody, which may be found in different places but which can be grouped in the student's mind in a kind of family tree of relationships, growing perhaps in many directions but always in systematic and understandable ways—these it is possible to grasp and to appreciate as a fund of musical possibilities for use. Such a concept is simple enough to enable a composer to examine any kind of music that appeals to him in an orderly way, and to understand it. The limitations of his music will then be due only to his own capacity for absorption and use of new ideas; they will not be imposed by the past.

My early interest was in discovery, and in the organization of my "discoveries" for my own use as a composer. I was not looking for origins nor for national styles, but to discover what different *types of organization* one could find in the world for the materials of my own craft: melody, rhythm, and multi-voiced music, for instance. One always tends to begin regionally or nationally with such studies, but I soon found that this approach was of little use to me.

When I first began to write music, around 1908, the romantic harmonies of the nineteenth century seemed to me thoroughly tiresome and old-fashioned, and I thought I should find out what new possibilities there might be for rhythm and melody instead. I found great numbers of such new possibilities in natural acoustic phenomena, but this interest soon carried my music far beyond any possibility of performance in those pre-electronic days. So I turned to explore rhythm and melody in actual musical traditions, and was surprised to discover that these aspects of music were not given the same orderly historical study in the West that polyphony and harmony were. Eventually I learned that to train myself in handling rhythmic and melodic possibilities systematically, I must go to Oriental teachers, and this I did. I was not planning to write Oriental music, of course, partly because I do not think a Westerner can completely abandon the multi-level; music which is so impressive a part of music in the twentieth century. But I felt I must learn more about general melodic and rhythmic concepts and principles of development, and these were too unconscious still, and rudimentary, in the West.

In the days when a man's musical experience came chiefly or wholly from a long undisturbed tradition, whether in Vienna or Peking, he composed his music out of an unconscious experience of organized sound which had developed gradually into an integrated style so that a composer's conscious studies were related to his total experience of music in an almost effortless and inevitable way.

On the other hand, at the moments in the world history when many different cultures have crossed, mankind seems to be shocked into enlarging areas of conscious thought. Unconscious practices, along with the suggestions for new art forms implicit in them, become conscious, and can be organized in an orderly way for study by anyone who needs to develop skill in their use. Artists then carry forward what they have learned in this way in fresh integrations, and later, of course, the resulting works of art become a new starting-point for other men's creative thought. There are a thousand possibilities for the application of the personal creative impulse by combining new techniques with old traditions. These make good music when the composer is sufficiently aware of the relationships between the aspects of music he is handling, to reject those that are unsuitable (either because they are beyond his personal ability to integrate, or else because their relationships are so distant that nobody could hope to make a unified work of art from them). The one thing one cannot demand of a creative artist is that he leave a tradition exactly where he found it. This he is really unable to do.

A great increase in awareness, an extension of conscious knowledge and the necessity for understanding has marked the twentieth century all over the world, and in many ways: Everyone knows how Einstein and the Curie family, in science, and Sigmund Freud in psychology, struggled to formulate complex concepts that they had first perceived and begun to use intuitively. I think the same effort to bring unconscious control is required of us in music today.

This is true whether one is concerned with the preservation and continuity of old traditions in their earliest surviving forms, or with their continuity in new forms and new relationships in the hands of composers. No one here, for instance, believes that old Iranian traditions can be perpetuated any longer by the same process of oral transmission within a protected culture that enabled these traditions to survive until our day—much though we all regret the fact, we cannot change it. Today's multiple influences can no longer be excluded, and collectors and archivists are discovering that they must have conscious knowledge of the traditions they touch, as they accept, reject, identify and select from the music offered [to] their microphones. Consider also the elaborate conscious organization of musical elements that was achieved hundreds of years ago in India; I do but think that this would have taken place in a country where a single people remained isolated from any culture other than its own.

Whether peoples migrate carrying their music with them, or the music itself migrates by air as it does today, makes no difference. Faced with great contrast and variety, the human spirit is forced to *think,* not only to *feel* or to *dream.*

Thought is a technique for examining, accepting or rejecting and then recombining *ideas,* and since its bearing on composition is so little understood because of the nineteenth century emphasis on romantic expression of personal emotion, I should like to describe how a composer works.

A man who sits down to write a piece of music starts with a musical idea which he proposes to develop. This idea is the result of "taking thought," as we say in English, of a conscious choice from among the innumerable musical germs that inhabit the unconscious levels of his mind, out of which he decides to make the subsequent musical composition grow.

Ideas in this sense have nothing to do with words, but are purely a matter of sound: a fragment of melody, or an attractive rhythm, or some polyphonic interplay of differently-colored melodic lines, or a harmonic sequence. Many such things float to the surface of the composer's mind, and he chooses the one that he feels at the moment like building into a piece of music. Its expansion will the depend on his skill in applying musical logic to this initial musical idea—one cannot just add anything at all to make the music longer or livelier. (By logic in music, a composer means consistency and clarity in setting forth the musical relationships within the piece as it grows.)

Conscious decisions may affect the initial choice of musical ideas somewhat: the instruments available, the tastes of a particular audience as to length or complexity, degree of dissonance, and so on. But if he is wise he will not undertake to write a piece of music unless something about it really appeals to him, because the unconscious side of his musical talent will not come into play otherwise. There cannot be too many requirements imposed from outside, particularly in connection with work of great scope, because it is fatally easy to inhibit the organic growth of the music, which depends in all the subsequent stages upon the free interplay of unconscious mental powers. From time to time in the course of a composition certain other decisions may have to be made consciously, of course, but whether conscious or unconscious, the creative act is the free act of choice. The more skillful the composer is in bringing the conscious and unconscious levels of his music[al] invention to bear on his music at the same time, the more deeply integrated will the music be.

The creative act is also an act of faith. One must trust one's self, and be unaffectedly willing to be whatever one *is* at this moment of creativity. The philosopher Ralph Waldo Emerson understood the state of mind in which any artist must invite the creative spirit: "To speak adequately one must speak wildly, with the flower of the mind, abandoning himself to the nature of things and letting the tides roll through him."

Absurd as it may sound, everyone has this experience in a small way when he writes a letter. One knows in advance, in a general way, what one wants to say, and the general tone one must take in order to be understood by the reader. We all have inherited conventions for opening and closing a letter, which today we are inclined to vary according to circumstances when we [*are answering writing. If we are*]¹ clear about these few things to begin with, it all goes very easily and with little or no conscious thought.

What one often forgets, however, is the long conscious effort that we all once made to form letters, and then to learn to spell, and to use grammar and syntax and, finally, literary form. Then we spent years using these tools consciously and carefully in different ways, practicing with them in school and at home and so gradually making the choices which, if persevered in, will establish a personal literary style. Eventually all such techniques become a part of one's unconscious wealth, to be used creatively whether one writes letters or novels.

Nobody believes that the study of other writers and other literatures will cripple an author's ability to express himself. On the contrary, this variety of artistic and technical experience is recognized as a great conscious enrichment, which gradually reaches the unconscious levels of the personality, and in time it serves to increase the skill with which the writer sets down even the simplest thing. A composer trains himself in the same way, and as he writes he is no longer aware of the effort he had to make to acquire the concepts and skills that shape and unify his music.

Such preparation for creative expression in music is no more artificial than any other kind of learning. One simply makes as many such things one's own as one finds one can, by exposure and study and practice. Little by little one discovers what materials and techniques will attract to themselves one's unconscious powers of assimilation, growth and integration. And then one must surrender all one has learned to those unconscious powers.

This process is repeated many times in a composer's lifetime. It offers the possibility of musical contagion from more than one carefully observed national tradition, as well as from several of the elaborately cultivated techniques in and out of those traditions. It gives some conscious control from the much-needed protection of the composer against random influences when he wishes to write music in close relation to some single tradition. He may stay within that tradition entirely if he understands what it is, and when he carries his music forward into fresh developments, he will understand how to discover the techniques which can fruitfully be applied to the traditional elements for this purpose.

Today the aspiring composer must analyze carefully for himself several of the musical styles that appeal especially to him, whether they be Asian or American or African or European, old or new, traditional or "experimental." If he does this he will come to understand the principles of modal melody that offer such immense numbers of attractive possibilities for tonal music, and he will learn how a tonal melody has been defined and enlarged, and how its own fitting counterpoint and harmony have been derived from it. By inquiring into more than one traditional culture he may discover fresh techniques for using rhythm: India, Africa, Persia and Indonesia all have wonderfully imaginative different concepts for the rhythmic organization of music, both for monodic and multilinear music.

As to the various polyphonic techniques, he must learn to use sixteenth century modal counterpoint and twentieth century dissonant counterpoint really well, and thoroughly. He should understand the theoretical basis of the various historical types of harmony—harmony based on thirds, on fourths, on seconds; the several types of dissonant harmony; polytonality; polyharmonic writing. From these he should choose two or three which he will learn to handle really skillfully. Only then will he understand how to derive new harmonic systems for use with the rapidly expanding variety of modal music. And if he is to live in the contemporary world of music, he must be familiar with the principles, at least, of the main types of electronic music.

These are the basic skills required for literacy in musical composition today, without which a young composer's music will sound weak, or limited, or thin. It is very hard work, and the longest lifetime, I am sorry to say, cannot suffice to encompass all of it. Music's ultimate reconciliation and unity will always be just out of reach of any one man. But a composer has no choice but to make the ever-renewed attempt to achieve it.

There is no reason to feel that a composer is in danger of losing his musical personality by working to enrich it in the way I have described. In the time of Bach, for example, composers habitually wrote deliberately in more than one national style—one recalls Bach's Italian Concerto and the English and French Suites.

Today we find this music much more characteristic of Bach than it is of the national cultures whose music he must have studied —after all, Bach's unconscious choices were inevitably the man himself, the result of a profound fusion and reorganization which selected, and eliminated, and shaped fresh ideas for his music in relation to older ones.

Nineteenth century romanticism, on the other hand, reacted against the intellect, feared conscious study, and its composers declared in favor of expressing *themselves*. There were of course historical reasons for this in the cultures of Central Europe, France and Russia at that time. The romantic personal approach resulted in many beautiful and original small pieces of music in the hands of Schubert, as later with Franck and Tchaikovsky, who essayed the larger forms. But we have come to realize that these pieces do not wear as well, they will not stand as much repetition today, as does the music of the baroque and classic period (and of later men like Brahms and Stravinsky), where musical ideas and personal musical expression were encouraged to broaden and deepen each other, and were better balanced.

I used to be afraid that the pressures from commercially circulated music would produce one single musical style that would be the same everywhere—a dreadful prospect! But I stopped worrying about this when it became evident that the most energetic efforts to establish one single "international" style of fine-art music (in Vienna, following Schoenberg), could not succeed in creating a style that would sound the same in the hands of any composer in the world. The style would somehow not stand still, and after a few years it was apparent that regional and national musical characteristics has crept into the most atonal music, in spite of the most determined efforts to avoid them.

When one realizes, then, that neither commercial popular music nor dodecaphonic "internationalism" have been able in fifty years to reduce the world's music to monotony, one comes to have more confidence in the creative human spirit. It is still today as strong as it ever was, and as various, and as determined to give ever-renewed form to each art. So one can trust it, I think. None of us here can decide which old traditions will last comparatively unchanged and which will form new hybrids rapidly. This is a process that must have taken place many times in the world, and it must always have been lamented as we lament it here. But no one has ever discovered how to stop it.

What we *can* do, perhaps, is to see to it that children hear first of all the best that their own culture has to offer, not from books but from authentic performers and authentic recordings. Then if they are also encouraged to join in, to make music themselves while they are young, as amateurs, they will not be likely to spend much time listening passively to the mediocre music of other people.

One of the marvels of the music of the entertainment world has always been its carefully built-in obsolescence. It is designed for the taste of the present moment, and nobody expects it to last. This was true of English music-hall music, and vaudeville, and all the many French popular styles; it is true of Broadway and film music today. Most such songs disappear from the radio within a few weeks; the more popular they are at first, the sooner the audience will get tired of them. The music's success is judged only by its immediate popularity, and by a kind of majority vote about it that is expressed in commercial listings like the Hit Tune Parade. It is hard to imagine what would happen to the music of the world if some one night-club style were to last as many years as Beethoven's Fifth Symphony has, but fortunately such a thing seems to be impossible!

Composers of fine-art music, on the other hand, write out of some inner compulsion that is a law unto itself, so that they are often quite incapable of conforming to the immediate expectations of other people, most of whom tend to prefer what they have heard before. If a composer is truly creative, this is because he really hears something new. He hopes that people will learn in time to like his music, of course, and that his music will last beyond his own lifetime because it fulfills a need for its hearers. But there is no way for him to make sure of this. All he can do is to dedicate himself to the cultivation of his garden, and to render thanks for the many beautiful living things in music that have been preserved for him by the efforts of others.

I should like to end by saying again: No matter how deliberately initial ideas and techniques have been acquired, it is still true today that the complex expansions and integrations necessary to create a lasting work, in any of the possible styles of cultivated fine-art music, can only be given their ultimate form on a profound level of unconscious organization within a composer's mind. At that profound level everything the composer is or has been, all he has experienced or known or felt, will play its part. Only then will his music, however national, be *more* than national, so that he is able to speak freely, as man and artist, in personal accents but of universal things.

1. In the text itself, which is printed in typewritten form in *Music in Ghana*, there is a line missing here. In the photocopy from which I worked text has been added in, evidently by HC, but it is illegible and the original manuscript was not available.–DH

Selected Bibliography

Cowell, Henry. *American Composers on American Music*. Stanford, CA: Stanford University Press, 1933. 2nd ed.—New York: Frederick Ungar, 1962.

_____. *New Musical Resources*, ed. David Nicholls. Cambridge: Cambridge University Press, 1996. [Original edition 1931.]

_____and Sidney. *Charles Ives and his Music*. New York: Oxford University Press, 1955.

Cowell, Sidney. "The Cowells and the Written Word." In Richard Crawford, R. Allen Lott and Carol J. Oja. *A Celebration of American Music: Words and Music in Honor of H. Wiley Hitchcock*. Ann Arbor: University of Michigan Press, 1990. Pp. 79-91.

Hitchcock, H. Wiley and Sadie, Stanley, eds. *The New Grove Dictionary of American Music*. 4 vols. New York: Grove's Dictionary of Music, 1986. [Entry on Cowell is by Bruce Saylor (text) and William Lichtenwanger (work list) with Elizabeth A. Wright, vol. 1, pp. 520-529.

Lichtenwanger, William. *The Music of Henry Cowell[:] A Descriptive Catalog*. I.S.A.M. Monographs, 23. Brooklyn: Institute for Studies in American Music, Conservatory of Music, Brooklyn College of the City of New York, 1986.

Manion, Martha L. *Writings about Henry Cowell: An Annotated Bibliography*. I. S. A. M. Monographs, 16. Brooklyn: Institute for Studies in American Music, Conservatory of Music, Brooklyn College of the City of New York, 1982.

Mead, Rita. *Henry Cowell's New Music[:] 1925-1936. The Society, the Music Editions and the Recordings.* Ann Arbor, MI: UMI Research Press, 1981.

Nicholls, David. *American Experimental Music, 1890-1940.* Cambridge (UK): Cambridge University Press, 1990.

Rich, Alan. *American Pioneers: Ives to Cage and Beyond.* London: Phaidon, 1995.

Saylor, Bruce. *The Writings of Henry Cowell[:] A Descriptive Bibliography.* "I. S. A. M. Monographs," 7. Brooklyn: Institute for Studies in American Music, Conservatory of Music, Brooklyn College of the City of New York, 1977.

Soares, Janet Mansfield. *Louis Horst: Musician in a Dancer's World.* Durham, NC: Duke University Press, 1992.

Tick, Judith. *Ruth Crawford Seeger: A Composer's Search for American Music.* New York: Oxford University Press, 1997.

Ziffrin, Marilyn. *Carl Ruggles: Composer, Painter and Storyteller.* "Music in American Life." Champaign: University of Illinois Press, 1994.

A Discography of the Music of Henry Cowell

COMPILED BY DICK HIGGINS

This discography is based on record catalogs and on the database in the New York Public Library at Lincoln Center, Rodgers and Hammerstein Collection. Thus, some of these could be blind listings. I have also checked against Carol J. Oja's American Music Recordings: A Discography of 20th-Century U.S. Composers *(Brooklyn, NY: Institute for Studies in American Music, 1982). Valuable corrections and additions were also made by Akihiro Taniguchi of Florida State University, by Kevin Holm-Hudson of Northwestern University, by John Frisch, and by Carol J. Oja.*

Adagio for Cello and Thunder Stick.
See Ensemble for String Quintet with Thunder Sticks (1924)

Advertisement (1917; =Third Encore to Dynamic Motion)
(78 RPM) Henry Cowell, piano. 4-discs. Concert Hall B9.
(LP) Henry Cowell, piano. Composers Recordings CRI-109.
(LP) Henry Cowell, piano. Circle L-51-101 and Folkways FM3349.
(LP) Doris [=Sorel] Hays, piano. Finnadar Records SR-1096 and SN-9016.
(LP) "American Composers." Roger Shields, piano. 3 discs. Vox SVBX-5303.
(CD) Henry Cowell, piano. Smithsonian/Folkways SF 40801.
(CD) "American Composers." Roger Shields, piano. 3 discs. Vox CD 3X 3027.
(CD) Steffen Schleiermacher, piano. Hat Hut "Now" series, Hart Art CD 6144.1

(CD) Chris Brown, Sorrel Hays, et al. New Albion 103.
(Cassette) Henry Cowell, piano. Composers Recordings CRI ACS 6005.

The Aeolian Harp (ca. 1923)
(78 rpm) Henry Cowell, piano. 4-discs. Concert Hall B9.
(LP) Henry Cowell, piano. Composers Recordings CRI-109.
(LP) Henry Cowell, piano. Circle L-51-101 and Folkways FM3349.
(LP) Henry Cowell, piano. Folkways FX 6160.
(LP) Doris [=Sorel] Hays, piano. Finnadar Records SR-1096 and SN-9016.
(LP) Robert Miller, piano. New World NW 203.
(LP) "American Composers." Roger Shields, piano. 3 discs. Vox SVBX-5303.
(CD) Henry Cowell, piano. Smithsonian/Folkways SF 40801.

(CD) Alan Feinberg, piano. 436 925-2.

(CD) Robert Miller, piano. New World 80203-2.

(CD) Steffen Schleiermacher, piano. Hat Hut "Now" series, Hat Art CD 6144.

(CD) Henry Cowell, piano. Composers Recordings CRI-670.

(CD) "American Composers." Roger Shields, piano. 3 discs. Vox CD 3X 3027.

(CD) "Gay American Composers," vol. 2. HC, piano. Composers Recordings CRI CD 750.

(CD) Chris Brown, Sorrel Hays, et al. New Albion 103.

(CD) Anthony de Mare, piano. Composers Recordings 837.

(Cassette) Henry Cowell, piano. Composers Recordings CRI ACS 6005.

Air for Violin and Strings (1952)

(CD) "Music for Strings." Marjorie Kransberg Talvi, violin; Alun Francis, conductor; Northwest Chamber Orchestra, Seattle. Classic Produktion Osnabruck CPOLC 8492 & CPO 999 222-2.

(CD) Richard Auldon Clark, conductor; Manhattan Chamber Ensemble. Koch International Classics KIC 7220.

Air and Scherzo for Saxophone and Chamber Orchestra (1961)

(LP) "Dimension 5." Robert Black, alto saxophone; Patricia Black, piano; ensemble. Brewster Records (no number).

(CD) Richard Auldon Clark, conductor; Manhattan Chamber Orchestra. Koch International Classics KIC 7282.

Air and Scherzo for Saxophone and Piano (1961)

(CD) Lawrence Gwozdz, alto saxophone. Lois Leventhal, piano. Crystal Records CD652.

American Melting Pot (1940)

(CD) Richard Auldon Clark, conductor; Manhattan Chamber Ensemble. Koch International Classics KIC 7220.

Amiable Conversation (1917; =Second Encore to Dynamic Motion)

(LP) Henry Cowell, piano. Circle L-51-101 and Folkways FM3349.

(LP) Doris [=Sorel] Hays, piano. Finnadar Records SR-1096 and SN-9016.

(CD) Steffen Schleiermacher, piano. Hat Hut "Now" series, Hart Art CD 6144.2

(CD) Henry Cowell, piano. Smithsonian/Folkways SF 40801.

(CD) Chris Brown, Sorrel Hays, et al. New Albion 103.

Ancient Desert Drone (1940)

(78 rpm) Werner Janssen, conductor; The Symphony Orchestra of Los Angeles. Artist 2404 (1401-04?).

(LP) Werner Janssen, conductor; The Symphony Orchestra of Los Angeles. 4 discs. Artist 100, reissued as Everest 3118/S 2455 & LPBR-6118/SDBR-3118.

Andante for Violin and Cello (1962)

(CD) "Trio America" Vol. III. Kenneth Goldsmith, violin; Terry King, cello; John Jensen, piano. Music and Arts 934.

Anger Dance (1914)

(LP) Henry Cowell, piano. Circle L-51-101 and Folkways FM3349.

(LP) Doris [=Sorel] Hays, piano. Finnadar Records SR-1096 and SN-9016.

(CD) Henry Cowell, piano. Smithsonian/Folkways SF 40801.

(CD) Steffen Schleiermacher, piano. Hat Hut "Now" series, Hart Art CD 6144.

Angus Og (The Spirit of Youth, 1917)

(CD) Mary Ann Hart, voice. Jeanne Golan, pianist. Albany Records 240.

Anniversary Pieces (1941-1965; =Cleistogamy)

(LP) "Miniatures for Three Players." Mirecourt Trio. TR Records TRC 110

(CD) Mirecourt Trio: Kenneth Goldsmith, violin, Terry King, cello. Music and Arts CD 635.

Wedding Hymn (1941)

Wedding Tune (1941)
Seventh Two Part Invention
Duet (1959?)
Andante (1962)
Allegro "August Duet" (1963)
Moderato
Family Cowell (1946)
Andante
Allegro
Two Part Invention (1950)

Anniversary Pieces: Duet for Our Anniversary Sept. 1958 love Henry (1965)
(CD) "Trio America" Vol. III. Kenneth Goldsmith, violin; Terry King, cello. Music and Arts CD 934.

Antinomy (1917; =Fourth Encore to Dynamic Motion)
(LP) Henry Cowell, piano. Circle L-51-101 and Folkways FM3349.
(LP) Doris [=Sorel] Hays, piano. Finnadar Records SR-1096 and SN-9016.
(CD) Henry Cowell, piano. Smithsonian/Folkways SF 40801.
(CD) Steffen Schleiermacher, piano. Hat Hut "Now" series, Hart Art CD 6144.5
(CD) Chris Brown, Sorrel Hays, et al. New Albion 103.

April (1918)
(CD) Mary Ann Hart, voice. Jeanne Golan, pianist. Albany Records 240.

Ballad and Dance. *See* Symphony No. 4

Ballad for String Orchestra (1954)
(LP) F. Charles Adler, conductor; Vienna Symphony Orchestra. Unicorn 1011 and UN 1045.
(LP) Jorge Mester, conductor; Louisville Symphony Orchestra. Louisville LOU-682/LS-682.

Ballad for String Orchestra (1954): transcribed by Cowell in 1956 as Ballad for Woodwind Quintet
(LP) Performers unknown. Churchill Films 5-113.
(LP) "The Flute in American Music."

The New York Flute Club; Eleanor Lawrence, flute; William Arrowsmith, oboe; Irving Neidich, clarinet; Richard Vrotney, bassoon; Books Tillotson, horn. Musical Heritage MHS 3578.
(CD) Boehme Woodwind Quintet. Premiere Recordings PRCD 1023.

The Banshee (ca. 1923)
(LP) Henry Cowell, piano. Composers Recordings CRI-109.
(LP) Henry Cowell, piano. Circle L-51-101 and Folkways FM3349.
(LP) Henry Cowell, piano. Folkways FX6160.
(LP) Robert Miller, piano. New World NW 203.
(LP) Doris [=Sorel] Hays, piano. Finnadar Records SR-1096 and SN-9016.
(CD) Henry Cowell, piano. Smithsonian/Folkways SF 40801.
(CD) Robert Miller, piano. New World 80203-2.
(CD) Steffen Schleiermacher, piano. Hat Hut "Now" series, Hart Art CD 6144.6
(CD) Henry Cowell, piano. Composers Recordings CRI-670.
(CD) "Gay American Composers," vol. 2. HC, piano. Composers Recordings CRI CD 750.
(CD) Chris Brown, Sorrel Hays, et al. New Albion 103.
(CD) Anthony de Mare, piano. Composers Recordings 837.
(Cassette) Henry Cowell, piano. Composers Recordings CRI ACS 6005.
(Cassette) Cheryl Seltzer, piano. Musical Heritage Society MHC 9370Z.

Because the Cat (1951-5?)
(CD) Mary Ann Hart, voice. Jeanne Golan, pianist. Albany Records 240.

Casual Developments (1933).
See Six Casual Developments

Celestial Violin (1942).
See How Old is Song?

Cleistogamy. *See* Anniversary Pieces

Concerto Grosso for Flute, Oboe, Clarinet, Cello, Harp, and Strings (1963)
(CD) Richard Auldon Clark, conductor; Manhattan Chamber Orchestra. Koch International Classics KIC 7282.

Crane (1956). *See* Three Songs on Poems by Padraic Colum.

Curley Locks (1937).
See Mother Goose Rhymes.

A Curse and a Blessing (1949; A Blessing; =The Blessing of Lugh)
(LP) William D. Revelli, conductor; University of Michigan Symphonic Band. Golden Crest CR5-4214.

Daybreak (1946)
(CD) Mary Ann Hart, voice. Jeanne Golan, pianist. Albany Records 240.

Daydreams (1946).
(CD) Mary Ann Hart, voice. Jeanne Golan, pianist. Albany Records 240.

Deep Color.
See Two Movements for Piano (1938)

Demand (1964).
See Three Poems of Langston Hughes.

The Donkey (1946, lyric by G.K. Chesterton)
(LP) "Songs by American Composers." John McCollum, tenor. Edwin Biltcliffe, piano. 2 discs. Desto (monaural); 6411/6412 and (stereo) SLP 664411/12; also Stand (monaural) 411/412 and (stereo) 7411/7412.
(CD) Mary Ann Hart, voice. Jeanne Golan, pianist. Albany Records 240.
(CD) "Love's Sacred and Other Songs." John McCollum, tenor. Edwin Biltcliffe, piano. Vox Box 5129, 2 discs.

Dr. Foster Went to Gloucester (1937).
See Mother Goose Rhymes.

The Dream Bridge (1915).
(CD) Mary Ann Hart, voice. Jeanne Golan, pianist. Albany Records 240.

Duet for Our Anniversary Sept. 1958
(=Duet for Violin and Cello).
See Anniversary Pieces

Duet for Violin and Cello.
See Anniversary Pieces.

Dynamic Motion (1916)
(LP) Henry Cowell, piano. Circle L-51-101 and Folkways FM3349.
(LP) Doris [=Sorel] Hays, piano. Finnadar Records SR-1096 and SN-9016.
(CD) Henry Cowell, piano. Smithsonian/Folkways SF 40801.
(CD) Steffen Schleiermacher, piano. Hat Hut "Now" series, Hart Art CD 6144.
(CD) Chris Brown, Sorrel Hays, et al. New Albion 103.
(CD) Anthony de Mare, piano. Composers Recordings 837.

Elegie.
See Six Casual Developments (1933-4)

Ensemble for Chamber Orchestra (1925; arranged 1928 as Sinfonietta).
(CD) "Music for Strings". Alun Francis, conductor, Northwest Chamber Orchestra, Seattle. Classic Produktion Osnabruck CPO LC 8492 & CPO 999 222-2.

Ensemble for String Quintet with Thunder Sticks (1924): Adagio for Cello with Thunder Stick
(CD) "Cello America" Vol. 2. Terry King, cello. Music and Arts CD 685-1.
(CD) Richard Auldon Clark, conductor; Manhattan Chamber Ensemble. Koch International Classics KIC 7220.

Episode No. 3 in G-sharp Minor (1921)
(LP) Herbert Rogers, piano. Composers Recordings CRI SD 281.
(CD) Herbert Rogers, piano. Composers Recordings CRI CD 281.

Euphoria (1929)
(Cassette) Cheryl Seltzer, piano. Musical Heritage Society MHC 9370Z.

Exaltation (1921)

(LP) Henry Cowell, piano. Circle L-51-101 and Folkways FM3349.

(LP) Bradford Gowan, piano. New World NW-304.

(LP) Mirecourt Trio. "Miniatures for Three Players?" TR Records TRC 110.

(LP) "American Composers." Roger Shields, piano. 3 discs. Vox SVBX-5303.

(CD) Henry Cowell, piano. Smithsonian/Folkways SF 40801.

(CD) Alan Feinberg, piano. Argo 436 925-2.

(CD) "American Composers." Roger Shields, piano. 3 discs. Vox CD 3X 3027.

(CD) Bradford Gowen, piano. New World 80304

(CD) Chris Brown, Sorrel Hays, et al. New Albion 103.

Fabric (1920)

(LP) Henry Cowell, piano. Circle L-51-101? and Folkways FM3349.

(CD) Henry Cowell, piano. Smithsonian/Folkways SF 40801.

(LP) Doris [=Sorel] Hays, piano. Finnadar Records SR-1096 and SN-9016.

(CD) Joel Sachs, piano. Musical Heritage Society 513109Z.

(CD) Louise Bessette, piano. SNE. 553-CD.

(CD) Chris Brown, Sorrel Hays, et al. New Albion 103.

The Fairy Answer (1929)

(LP) Henry Cowell, piano. Circle L-51-101 and Folkways FM3349.

(CD) Henry Cowell, piano. Smithsonian/Folkways SF 40801.

(CD) Joel Sachs, piano. Musical Heritage Society 513109Z.

Fanfare to the Forces of the Latin American Allies (1942)

(CD) Jorge Mester, conductor; London Philharmonic Orchestra. Koch International Classsic 3-7012-2.

Fiddler's Jig for Violin and Strings (1952)

(LP) F. Charles Adler, conductor; Vienna Orchestral Society. Unicorn UNLA 1008 & UNLP-1045.

(CD) Richard Auldon Clark, conductor; Manhattan Chamber Orchestra. Koch International Classics KIC 7282.

(CD) "Music for Strings." Marjorie Kransberg Talvi, violin; Alun Francis, conductor; Northwest Chamber Orchestra, Seattle. Classic Produktion Osnabruck CPO LC 8492 & CPO 999 222-2.

Firelight and Lamp (1962. Lyric by Gene Baro)

(CD) Mary Ann Hart, mezzo; Dennis Helmrich, piano. Albany Records 118.

(CD) Mary Ann Hart, voice. Robert Osborne, pianist. Albany Records 240.

For Unaccompanied Cello (1919)

(CD) "Cello America" Vol. 2. Terry King, cello. Music and Arts CD 4685.

Four Casual Developments.

See Six Casual Developments (1933-4)

Four Combinations for Piano, Violin, and Cello (1924; =Four Combinations for Three Instruments)

(LP) Mirecourt Trio. TRC Records 110.

(CD) Hartley Trio. Gamut GAM 536.

(CD) Mirecourt Trio. Music and Arts 635.

(CD) Trio Phoenix: Josephine Gandolfi, piano; Kay Stern, violin; Sarah Fiene, cello. Koch International Classics KIC 7205.

Four Declamations with Return (1949)

(78 rpm) Seymour Barab, cello; William Masselos, piano. Paradox 10001.

(LP) Terry King, cello; John Jenson, piano. Mirecourt Trio. Composers Recordings CRI SD 386.

Four Irish Tales.

See Tales of Our Countryside

Fulfillment (1964).
See Three Poems of Langston Hughes.

Goosey Goosey Gander (1937).
See Mother Goose Rhymes.

Gravely and Vigorously (In Memory of JFK) (1963)
(LP) Terry King, cello. Mirecourt Trio. Composers Recordings CRI SD 386.

Grinnell Fanfare (1948)
(CD) Christopher Larkin, conductor; London Gabrieli Brass Ensemble. Hyperion 55018.

The Harp of Life (1924)
(LP) Henry Cowell, piano. Circle L-51-101 and Folkways FM3349.
(LP) Doris [=Sorel] Hays, piano. Finnadar Records SR-1096 and SN-9016.
(CD) Henry Cowell, piano. Smithsonian/Folkways SF 40801.

The Hero Sun.
See Three Irish Legends

Homage to Iran (1957)
(LP) Leopold Avakian, violin; Mitchell Andrews, piano; Basil Bahar, Persian drum. Composers Recordings CRI 173.

How Old Is Song? (Lyric: Harry Cowell.1931)
(CD) Mary Ann Hart, mezzo; Dennis Helmrich, piano. Troy 118.
(CD) Mary Ann Hart, voice. Jeanne Golan, pianist. Albany Records 240.

How Old Is Song (1931; arranged for violin and piano as Celestial Violin, 1942)
(78 rpm) Joseph Szigeti, violin; Henry Cowell, piano. Columbia MM-920.

Hymn and Fuguing Tune No. 1 (1943): symphonic band arrangement73
(LP) Peter Todd, conductor; Leeds Concert Band. Columbia ML 4254.

Hymn and Fuguing Tune No. 2 [for Strings] (1944)
(78 rpm) Serge Koussevitsky, conductor; Boston Symphony Orchestra [recorded 1944)] RCA Victor, number unknown..
(LP) F. Charles Adler, conductor; Vienna Orchestral Society.. Unicorn UNLP 1011.
(LP) Serge Koussevitsky, conductor; Boston Symphony Orchestra [recorded 1944)] CRI-248.
(LP) Jorge Mester, conductor; Louisville Symphony Orchestra. Louisville LOU-682 LS-682.
(CD) Richard Auldon Clark, conductor; Manhattan Chamber Ensemble. Koch International Classics KIC 7220.
(CD) "Music for Strings." Alun Francis, conductor; Northwest Chamber Orchestra, Seattle .   C l a s s i c Produktion Osnabruck CPO LC 8492 and CPO 999 222-2.
(CD) Serge Koussevitsky, conductor; Boston Symphony Orchestra (1944). CRI ACS 6005.
(Cassette) Serge Koussevitsky, conductor; Boston Symphony Orchestra. CRI ACS 6005.

Hymn and Fuguing Tune No. 3 (1944)
(LP) Jorge Mester, conductor; Louisville Symphony Orchestra. Louisville LOU-682 LS-682.

Hymn and Fuguing Tune No.5 (1945-6)
(LP) David Randolph, conductor; David Randolph Chorus (a capella vocalise version). Concert Hall Society CHC 52
(CD) "Music for Strings." Alun Francis, conductor, Northwest Chamber Orchestra, Seattle. Classsic Produktion Osnabruck CPO LC 8492 and CPO 999 222-2.

Hymn and Fuguing Tune No. 7 (1947)
(LP) Philip Clark, viola; Bryan Sayer, piano. Ode 150.

Hymn, Chorale and Fuguing Tune No. 8 [for Strings] (1947)

(CD) "Music for Strings." Alun Francis, conductor, Northwest Chamber Orchestra, Seattle. Classic Produktion Osnabruck CPO LC 8492 and CPO 999 222-2.

Hymn and Fuguing Tune No. 9 for Cello and Piano (1950)

(LP) Terry King, cello; John Jenson, piano. Mirecourt Trio. Composers Recordings CRI SD 386.

(CD) Sarah Fiene, cello; Josephine Gandolfi, piano.. Koch International Classics KIC 7205.

Hymn and Fuguing Tune No. 10 for Oboe and Strings (1955)

(LP) Neville Marriner, conductor; Academy of St. Martin-in-the-Fields. Argo ZRG-845.

(LP) F. Charles Adler, conductor; Vienna Orchestral Society.. Unicorn UNLP 1011.

(CD) Richard Auldon Clark, conductor; Manhattan Chamber Orchestra. Koch International Classics KIC 7282.

(CD) "Music for Strings". Frank Avril, oboe; Alun Francis, conductor, Northwest Chamber Orchestra, Seattle. Classic Produktion Osnabruck CPO LC 8492 and CPO 999 222-2.

(CD) Neville Marriner, conductor; Academy of St. Martin-in-the-Fields. Uni/Argo 17818.

Hymn and Fuguing Tune No. 12 (1958)

(CD) Christopher Larkin, conductor; London Gabrieli Brass Ensemble. Hyperion 55018.

Hymn and Fuguing Tune No. 16 (1963; published 1968)

(LP) David Sackson, violin; Dwight Peltzer, piano. Folkways FSS 37450 A.

Hymn for Strings (1946)

(CD) "Modern Masters" No. 2. D.

Amos, City of London Sinfonia, Harmonia Mundi HMU 90601.

I Heard in the Night (1956). *See* Three Songs on Poems by Padraic Colum.

"...if He please" (1954)

(LP) William Strickland, conductor; Norwegian Choir of Solo Singers; Oslo Philharmonic Orchestra. Composers Recordings CRI 217 USD.

Invention (1950?; =Two-Part Invention in Three Parts)

(LP) Herbert Rogers. Composers Recordings CRI SD 281.

(LP) "American Composers." Roger Shields, piano. 3-discs. Vox SVBX-5303.

(CD) Herbert Rogers, piano. Composers Recordings CRI CD 281.

(CD) "American Composers." Roger Shields, piano. 3-discs. Vox CD 3X 3027.

Iridescent Rondo in Old Modes (1959)

(LP) William Schimel, accordion. Finnadar 90234-1.

The Irishman Dances (1935)

(LP) Charlotte Martin, piano. Educo 3121.

(LP) "Piano Music for Children." Marga Richter, piano. MGM E 3147.

Jig (1916)

(78 rpm) Henry Cowell, piano. Concert Hall B9.

(LP) Henry Cowell, piano. Circle L-51-101 and Folkways FM3349.

(CD) Henry Cowell, piano. Smithsonian/Folkways SF 40801.

Jubilation (?)

(LP) William Strickland, conductor; Vienna Symphony. MGM E 3084.

Lamentations (?)

(LP) "Miniatures for Three Players." Mirecourt Trio. TR Records TRC 110.

The Lilt of the Reel (1928)
(LP) Henry Cowell, piano. Composers Recordings CRI-109.
(LP) Henry Cowell, piano. Circle L-51-101 and Folkways FM3349.
(LP) Doris [=Sorel] Hays, piano. Finnadar Records SR-1096 and SN-9016.
(CD) Henry Cowell, piano. Smithsonian/Folkways SF 40801.
(CD) "Gay American Composers," vol. 2. HC, piano. Composers Recordings CRI CD 750.
(CD) Gloria Cheng-Cochran, piano. Telarc 80549.
(CD) Chris Brown, Sorrel Hays, et al. New Albion 103.
(CD) Anthony de Mare, piano. Composers Recordings 837.
(Cassette) Henry Cowell, piano. Composers Recordings CRI ACS 6005.

The Little Black Boy (1952-4)
(CD) Mary Ann Hart, voice. Jeanne Golan, pianist. Albany Records 240.

Little Concerto for Piano and Band (1942)
(LP) Alcides Lanza, piano. Robert Gibson, conductor; McGill Wind Ensemble. McGill University Records 79008.

Luther's Carol for his Son (1948; text is from Martin Luther's Geistliche Lieder via the Brothers Wedder-burn's 1767 Compendious Booke)
(LP) Greg Smith, conductor; Columbia University Men's Glee Club. 3 discs. Vox SVBX-5353.

Maestoso (1926)
(LP) Doris [=Sorel] Hays, piano. Finnadar Records SR-1096 and SN-9016.

Manaunaun Birthing (1924)
(CD) Mary Ann Hart, voice. Jeanne Golan, pianist. Albany Records 240.

Mice Lament (1940)
(CD) Mary Ann Hart, voice. Jeanne Golan, pianist. Albany Records 240.

Moonlight Night (1964). *See* Three Songs by Langston Hughes.

The Morning Pool (1918)
(CD) Mary Ann Hart, voice. Jeanne Golan, pianist. Albany Records 240.

Mother Goose Rhymes (Curley-Locks, Three Wise Men of Gotham, Dr. Foster Went to Gloucester, Goosey Goosey Gander and Tommy Trot, 1937)
(CD) Mary Ann Hart, voice. Jeanne Golan, pianist. Albany Records 240.

Movement for String Quartet (1921)
(78 rpm) Dorian String Quartet. New Music Recordings M-388. Reissued on Columbia 69747 D.

Music [for Orchestra] (1957)
(LP) Akeo Watanabe, conductor; Japan Philharmonic Symphony Orchestra. CRI SD 132.
(CD) Akeo Watanabe, conductor. Japan Philharmonic Orchestra. Citabel CTD 88122

Music I Heard (1961).
(CD) Mary Ann Hart, voice. Robert Osborne, pianist. Albany Records 240.

Music When Soft Voices Die (1922)
(CD) Mary Ann Hart, voice. Jeanne Golan, pianist. Albany Records 240.

Night Fliers (1956). *See* Three Songs on Poems by Padraic Colum.

Nine Ings (1917-1922) *See also* Six Ings.
(CD) Chris Brown, Sorrel Hays, et al. New Albion 103.

Old American Country Set (1937-1939)
(CD) Richard Auldon Clark, conductor; Manhattan Chamber Ensemble. Koch International Classics KIC 7220.

Ongaku (1957)

(LP) Robert Whitney, conductor; Louisville Orchestra. Louisville LOU-59-5.

Ostinato Pianissimo (1934)

(LP) Raymond DesRoches, conductor; New Jersey Percussion Ensemble. Nonesuch H-71291.

(LP) Siegfried Fink, conductor; Percussion Ensemble. "Drums in Concert." Thorofon Capella MTH 149 [different from and better than that listed below].

(LP) New Music Consort. New World NW 319.

(LP) Paul Price, conductor; Manhattan Percussion Ensemble. Time Stereo S/8000 and Mainstream MS-5011.

(CD) Siegfried Fink, conductor; Wnrzburger Perkussions-Ensemble. Thorofon CTH 2003.

(CD) Raymond DesRoches, conductor; New Jersey Percussion Ensemble.. Nonesuch 79150.

Paragraphs. *See* Seven Paragraphs

Party Pieces (composed jointly by Cowell, Virgil Thomson, John Cage, and Lou Harrison ca. 1945)

(LP) Arr. Flute, Clarinet, Bassoon, Horn and Piano by Robert Hughes. Lukas Foss, conductor; Brooklyn Philharmonic Symphony Orchestra. Gramavision Records GR 7006.

The Pasture (1944).

(CD) Mary Ann Hart, voice. Jeanne Golan, pianist. Albany Records 240.

Persian Set for Piccolo, Clarinet, Tar, Drum and Piano (1956-57)

(LP) Leopold Stokowski, conductor; "Members of his orchestra." Composers Recordings CRI-114.

(CD) Richard Auldon Clark, conductor; Manhattan Chamber Ensemble. Koch International Classics KIC 7233.

(CD) Leopold Stokowski, conductor; "Members of his orchestra." CRI ACS

6005.and Citadel CTD 88123.

(Cassette) Leopold Stokowski, conductor; "Members of his orchestra." CRI ACS 6005.

[Piano Music]

(LP) Doris Hays, Piano. *See* individual entries.

(LP) Jorge Zulueta, piano. Centro Argentino por la Libertad de la Cultura. LP 501—no listing of contents available.

(CD) Henry Cowell, piano. Circle 51-101, reissued as CRI C 109. *See* individual entries.

(CD) Doris Hays, piano. Finnadar CS 9016. *See* individual entries.

Piece for Piano (1924)

(LP) "Adoration of the Clash." Doris [=Sorel] Hays, piano. 2 discs. Finnadar Records SR 2-720.

(LP) Robert Miller, piano. New World NW 203.

(Cassette) Cheryl Seltzer, piano. Musical Heritage Society MHC 9370Z.

Polyphonica for Small Orchestra (1930)

(CD) Joel Sachs, conductor. Musical Heritage Society 513109Z.

Prelude for Violin and Harpsichord (1925)

(LP) Robert Brink, Violin; Daniel Pinkham, Harpsichord. CRI 109.

(CD) Robert Brink, Violin; Daniel Pinkham, Harpsichord. C 1209.

Processional (1942)

(LP) "Organ Music by Modern Composers." Richard Elsasser, organist. Organ of John Hays Hammond Museum, Gloucester, Massachusetts. MGM E 3064.

Pulse (1939)

(LP) Kroumata Percussion Ensemble. BIS LP-232.

(LP) New Music Consort. New World Records NW 319 stereo.

(CD) Kroumata Percussion Ensemble. BIS CD 232.

(CD) New Music Consort. New World 80405-2.

Quartet No. 2: "Movement for String Quartet" (1928)

(LP) Beaux Arts Quartet. Composers Recordings CRI-173.

(CD) Beaux Arts Quartet. CRI ACS 6005.

(Cassette) Beaux Arts Quartet. Composers Recordings CRI ACS 6005.

Quartet No. 3: "Mosaic" (1935)

(LP) Beaux Arts Quartet. Composers Recordings CRI-173.

Quartet No. 4: "United Quartet" (1936)

(LP) Beaux Arts Quartet. Composers Recordings CRI-173.

(LP) Composers String Quartet. Musical Heritage MHS Stereo 4823H.

Quartet No. 5: for Strings (1956 rev. 1962)

(LP) Performer information not available. Columbia ML 5788/ MS 6388.

Quartet Euphometric (1916-1919)

(LP) Composers String Quartet. Golden Crest Records NEC-115.

(LP) Emerson Quartet. New World. NW 218 stereo.

(CD) Emerson Quartet. New World. 80453-2.

(CD) Kronos Quartet. Electra/Nonesuch 979310-2.

(Cassette) Kronos Quartet. Electra/Nonesuch 79310-4.

Quartet for Flute, Oboe, Cello and Harpsichord (1954)

(CD) Joel Sachs, director. Continuum. Musical Heritage Society 513109Z.

Quartet Romantic for Two Flutes, Violin and Viola (1915-1917)

(LP) Paul Dunkel, conductor. Speculum Musicæ. Paul Dunkel, flute; Susan Palma, flute; Ralph Schulte, violin; John Graham, viola. New World Records NW 285 stereo.

(CD) Paul Dunkel, conductor. Speculum Musicæ. New World Records 80285.

Rest. *See* Sunset/Rest.

Rondo (1958)

(CD) Christopher Larkin, conductor. London Gabrieli Brass Ensemble. Hyperion 55018.

Rumor (?)

(CD) Neville Marriner, conductor. Academy of Saint Martin in the Fields. Argo 417 818-2.

Sailor's Hornpipe (1949)

(CD) Roth Saxophone Quartet. Pan Extra 510 529.

Saint Agnes Morning (ca. 1914)

(CD) Mary Ann Hart, mezzo; Dennis Helmrich, piano. Troy 118.

(CD) Mary Ann Hart, mezzo; Robert Osborne, piano. Albany Records 240.

Saturday Night at the Firehouse (1948)

(LP) F. Charles Adler, conductor. Vienna Philharmonia Orchestra. Spa Records SPA-47.

(CD) Lukas Foss, conductor. Milwaukee Symphony Orchestra. Intersound 3502.

Scenario (1915).

(CD) "Trio America" vol. III. Kenneth Goldsmith, violin; Terry King, cello; John Jensen, piano. Music and Arts CD 4934.

Set of Five for Violin, Piano and Percussion (1952)

(LP) Anahid Ajemian, violin; Maro Ajemian, piano; Bailey, percussion. MGM E3454.

(CD) Abel-Steinberg-Winant Trio. New Albion NA 036.

(CD) Josephine Gandolphi, piano; Kay Stern, violin; Rick Kvistad, percussion. Koch International Classics KIC 7205. (Cassette) Joel Sachs, Conductor. Musical Heritage Society MHC 9370Z.

Set of Four (1961)
(LP) Carole Terry, harpsichord. CRI SD 533.
(CD) Ralph Kirkpatrick, harpsichord (recorded 1961). Music and Arts DDD CD-977.

Set of Two: Prelude. *See* Prelude for Violin and Harpsichord (1925).

Seven Paragraphs (1925)
(LP) New World Consort. Evan Paris, violin; Lois Martin, viola; Madeleiner Shapiro, cello. New World NW 319.
(CD) New World Consort. Evan Paris, violin; Lois Martin, viola; Madeleiner Shapiro, cello. New World Records 80285.

Shoonthree (The Music of Sleep) (1939)
(LP) Acton Ostling, conductor. University of Maryland Symphonic Band. Franco Colombo [no number but dated 1968].

Sinfonietta (1928)
(LP) Robert Whitney, conductor. Louiville Symphony Orchestra. Louisville 681.

Sinister Resonance (ca. 1930)
(LP) Henry Cowell, piano. Composers Recordings CRI-109.
(LP) Henry Cowell, piano. Circle L-51-101 and Folkways FM3349.
(LP) Doris [=Sorel] Hays, piano. Finnadar Records SR 1096 and SN-9016.
(CD) Henry Cowell, piano. Smithsonian /Folkways SF 40801.
(Cassette) Henry Cowell piano. Composers Recordings CRI ACS 6005.
Six Casual Developments for Clarinet and Piano (1933)

(LP) John Russo, clarinet; Lydia Walton Ignacio, piano. Capra Records USR 1204.
(CD) John Russo, clarinet; Lydia Walton Ignacio, piano. CRS Master Recording CRS 9561.

Six Ings (1917-1922) *See also* Nine Ings.
(LP) Doris [=Sorel] Hays, piano. Finnadar Records SR 1096 and SN-9016
(LP) Herbert Rogers. Composers Recordings CRI SD 281
(CD) Herbert Rogers, piano. CRI CD 281

Slow Jig (1925)
(CD) Chris Brown, Sorrel Hays, et al. New Albion 103

The Snow of Fuji-Yama (1924)
(78 rpm) Henry Cowell, piano. Circle L-51-101
(LP) Henry Cowell, piano. Folkways 3342
(CD) Henry Cowell, piano. Smithsonian/Folkways SF 40801

Sonata for Cello and Piano (1915)
(CD) "Cello America," Vol. 2. Terry King, cello; John Jensen, piano. Music and Arts 4685
(CD) Gilbert Kalish, piano; Joel Krosnick, cello. Arabesque 6709

Sonata [No. 1] for Violin and Piano (1945)
(LP) David Jackson, violin; Dwight Peltzer, piano. Folkways FSS 37450 A
(LP) Joseph Szigeti, violin; Carlo Busotti, piano. Columbia ML 4841. Reissued ca. 1974 as "AML 4841-2" and CML-4841.
(CD) Cameron Grant, piano; Zina Schiff, violin. 4-Tay 4005.

Square Dance Tune (1942)
(LP) Gerson Yessin, piano. Jacksonville University [no number but date,1968].

Suite for Violin and Piano (1925)
(LP) David Jackson, violin; Dwight Peltzer, piano. Folkways FSS 37450 A stereo.
(CD) Fritz Gearheart, violin; Paul Tardif, piano. Koch International Classics 3-7268-2.
(CD) Mia Wu, violin; Cheryl Seltzer, piano; Joel Sachs, director. Musical Heritage Society 513109Z.

Suite for Wind Quintet. *See* Six Casual Developments.
(78 RPM). Barrere Woodwind Ensemble. New Musical Quarterly Recordings NMQR 1111A-B (1935).
(LP) New Art Wind Quintet. "An American Woodwind Symposium." Classic Editions 2-LP 2003

Sunset/Rest: "Two songs for low voice" (1933, poems by Catherine Riegger)
(Cassette) Raymond Murcell, baritone; Cheryl Seltzer, piano. Musical Heritage Society MHC 9370Z
(CD) Kansas City Chorale. Nimbus 5413
(CD) Mary Ann Hart, voice. Jeanne Golan, pianist. Albany Records 240

Symphonic Set, Opus 17 (1938-39)
(CD) Linda Hobenfeld, soprano. Stephen Somary, conductor. Nürnberg Symphony Orchestra [Switzerland] Claves CD 50-9806

Symphony No.4 "Short Symphony" (1946)
(LP) Howard Hanson, conductor. Eastman-Rochester Symphony Orchestra. Mercury MG 40005, MG 50078 and SRI 75111.
Symphony No. 4 (1946), "Ballad" and "Dance" only
(45 rpm-EP). Howard Hanson, conductor. Eastman-Rochester Symphony Orchestra. Mercury EP-1-5063.

Symphony No. 5 (1948)
(LP) Dean Dixon, conductor. Vienna Symphony Orchestra. American Recording Society ARS-2.

(LP) Dean Dixon, conductor. Vienna Symphony Orchestra. American Recording Society ARS-112.
(LP) Dean Dixon, conductor. Vienna Symphony Orchestra. Desto D405.
(CD) Dean Dixon, cond. Vienna Symphony Orchestra. Bay Cities BCD 1017.

Symphony No. 6 (1952)
(LP) William D. Revelli, conductor. University of Michigan Symphony Band. Franco Colombo BP 112.

Symphony No. 7 (1952)
(LP) William Strickland, conductor. Vienna Symphony Orchestra. CRI SD 142.
(Cassette) William Strickland, conductor. Vienna Symphony Orchestra. CRI ACS 6005.
(CD) William Strickland, conductor. Vienna Symphony Orchestra. Composers Recordings 740.

Symphony No. 8 (1952)
(LP) Thor Johnson, conductor. All-Ohio High School Chorus and Orchestra. Wilmington College 1.

Symphony No. 10 (1953)
(LP) F. Charles Adler, conductor. Vienna Orchestral Society. Unicorn UN LA 1008.

Symphony No. 11: "Seven Rituals of Music" (1953)
(LP) Robert Whitney, conductor. Louisville Symphony Orchestra. Louisville 545-2. Also Columbia "American Classics" ML 5039.
Symphony No. 15: "Thesis" (1961)
(LP) Robert Whitney, conductor. Louisville Symphony Orchestra. Louisville LOU-622.

Symphony No. 16: "Icelandic" (1962)
(LP) William Strickland, conductor. Icelandic Symphony Orchestra. CRI-179.
(CD) William Strickland, conductor. Icelandic Symphony Orchestra. Composers Recordings 740.

Synchrony (1930)

(LP) William Strickland, cond. Polish National Radio Orch. CRI 217 USD. (CD) William Strickland, conductor. Polish National Radio Orchestra. Citadel CTD 88122.

Tales of Our Countryside (=Four Irish Tales, 1940)

(78 RPM) Henry Cowell, piano; Leopold Stokowski, conductor. All-American Orchestra. 2 discs. Columbia Masterworks Set X-235.

Tall Tale (1947)

(CD) Christopher Larkin, conductor. London Gabrieli Brass Ensemble. Hyperion 55018.

Three Anti-Modernist Songs (1938)

(CD) Ellen Lang, soprano; Cheryl Seltzer, piano; Joel Sachs, director. Musical Heritage Society 513109Z.

Three Anti-Modernist Songs: "Who Wrote this Fiendish Rite of Spring?"

(LP) Paul Sperry, Baritone; Irma Vallecillo, piano. Troy 051. (CD) Paul Sperry, Baritone; Irma Vallecillo, piano. Albany Records 81.

Three Irish Legends (1922)

(LP) Doris [=Sorel] Hays, piano. Finnadar Records SR-1096 and SN-9016. (CD) Steffen Schleiermacher, piano. Hat Hut "Now" series. Hat Art CD 6144.

Three Irish Legends: The Hero Sun (1922)

(LP) Doris [=Sorel] Hays, piano. Finnadar Records SR-1096 and SN-9016. (CD) Steffen Schleiermacher, piano. "The Bad Boys." Hat Art CD 6144. (CD) Chris Brown, Sorrel Hays, et al. New Albion 103.

Three Irish Legends: The Tides of Maunaunaun (1922)

(LP) Henry Cowell, piano. Composers Recordings CRI-109.

(LP) Henry Cowell, piano. Circle L-51-101 and Folkways FM3349. (LP) Doris [=Sorel] Hays, piano. Finnadar Records SR-1096 and SN-9016. (CD) Henry Cowell, piano. Smithsonian /Folkways SF 40801. (CD) Steffen Schleiermacher, piano. "The Bad Boys." Hat Art CD 6144. (CD) Chris Brown, Sorrel Hays, et al. New Albion 103. (Cassette) Henry Cowell, piano. Composers Recordings CRI ACS 6005.

Three Irish Legends: The Voice of Lir (1922)

(LP) Doris [=Sorel] Hays, piano. Finnadar Records SR 1096. (LP) Henry Cowell, piano. Circle L-51-101 and Folkways FM3349. (CD) Henry Cowell, piano. Smithsonian /Folkways SF 40801. (CD) Steffan Schleiermacher, piano. "The Bad Boys." Hat Art CD 6144.

Three Ostinati, with Chorales for Oboe and Piano (1937)

(CD) H. Sargous, oboe; R. Conway, piano. Crystal CD 326.

Three Ostinati, with Chorales for Oboe and Piano: one ostinato and two chorales

(78 RPM) Joseph Marx, oboe; Vivien Fine, piano. New Music Quarterly Recordings NMQR 1413. (78 RPM) Norbert McBride, oboe; Lionel Novak, piano. Yaddo 1104.

Three Ostinati, with Chorales for Oboe and Piano: arrangement for flute and piano (1937)

(LP) Eldred Spell, flute; Lydia Ignacio, piano. Columbia(?) CRS 8528.

Three Songs on Poems by Padraic Colum

(CD) Mary Ann Hart, voice. Albany Records 240.

Three Songs on Poems by Langston Hughes
  (CD) Mary Ann Hart, voice. Jeanne Golan, pianist. Albany Records 240.

The Tides of Maunaunaun. (1912)
  See Three Irish Legends (1922).

Tiger (1928)
  (LP) Henry Cowell, piano. Circle L-51-101 and Folkways FM3349.
  (LP) Doris [=Sorel] Hays, piano. Finnadar Records SR 1096 and SN-9016.
  (CD) Henry Cowell, piano. Smithsonian/Folkways SF 40801.
  (CD) Joel Sachs, piano. Musical Heritage Society 513109Z.
  (CD) Steffen Schleiermacher, piano. Hat Hut "Now" series. Hat Art CD 6144.
  (CD) Louise Bessete, piano. SNE. SNE 553-CD.
  (CD) Anthony de Mare, piano. Composers Recordings 837.

Time Table (1914/15)
  (CD) Steffen Schleiermacher, piano. Hat Hut "Now" series. Hat Art CD 6144.
  (CD) Chris Brown, Sorrel Hays, et al. New Albion 103.

Toccanta (1938)
  (LP) Helen Boatwright, soprano; Carleton Sprague Smith, flute; Aldo Parisot, cello; John Kirkpatrick, piano. Columbia AML 4986.
Triad
  (CD) David Kuehn, trumpet; Persis Pershall Vehar. Fleur De Son 57934.

Trio in Nine Short Movements for Violin, Cello and Piano (1965).
  (LP) Philharmonia Trio. Composers Recordings CRI 211.
  (CD) Hartley Trio. Gamut GAM 536.
  (CD) "Contemporary American Piano Trios." Mirecourt Trio. Music and Arts CD-686-1.
  (CD) Trio Phoenix (Josephine Gandolfi, piano; Kay Stern, violin; Sarah Fiene,

cello). Koch International Classics KIC 7205.

Triple Rondo for Flute and Harp (1961)
  (LP) Claire Polin, flute; Phyllis Schlomowitz, harp. Educo (M) 4031.

The Trumpet of Angus Og (1918, = The Spirit of Youth)
  (LP) Henry Cowell, piano. Circle L-51-101 and Folkways FM3349.
  (LP) Doris [=Sorel] Hays, piano. Finnadar Records SR 1096 AND SN-9016.
  (CD) Henry Cowell, piano. Smithsonian/Folkways SF 40801.

Twilight in Texas (1965)
  André Kostelanetz, conductor. André Kostelanetz Orchestra. Columbia MG 33728.

Two-Bits (1941)
  (LP) Carol Winenc, flute. With ensemble. Nonesuch 79 114.

"Two Chorales and Ostinato." *See* Three Ostinati...

Two Movements for Piano: Deep Color (1938)
  (CD) Joel Sachs, piano. Musical Heritage Society 513109Z.
  (CD) Brown, Hays, et al. New Albion 103.

Two-Part Invention in Three Parts (1950)
  (LP) Herbert Rogers, piano. CRI-281.
  Roger Shield, piano. Vox SVBX 5303.

Two Songs for Low Voice. *See* Sunset/Rest.

Two Woofs (for Piano). *See* Woof I and Woof II.

The Universal Flute (1946)
  (CD) Fachel Radich, flute. Music and Arts CD 1012.

Variations for Orchestra (1956)
(LP) William Strickland, conductor. Polish National Radio Orchestra. CRI 217 USD.
(CD) William Strickland, conductor. Polish National Radio Orchestra. Composers Recordings 740.

Variations on Thirds for 2 Violas and Strings (1960)
(CD) "Music for Strings." Eileen Swanson and Ruth Sereque, violas; Alun Francis, conductor, Northwest Chamber Orchestra, Seattle. Classic Produktion Osnabruck CPO LC 8492 and CPO 999 222-2.

Vestiges (1920)
(CD) Alan Feinberg, piano. Argo 436 925-2.
(Cassette) Cheryl Seltzer, piano. Continuum. Musical Heritage Society MHC 9370Z.

Vocalise (1936)
(78 RPM) Ethel Codd Luening, soprano; Otto Luening, piano. Yaddo M-1.
(LP) Da Capo Players. "Da Capo in Song." New World Records NW 317.
(LP) Da Capo Players. "Voices from Elysium." New World Records 80543.

The Voice of Lir (1920).
See Three Irish Legends (1922).

Wedding Anniversary Music (1957)
(CD) "Trio America" vol. III. Kenneth Goldsmith, violin; Terry King, cello; John Jensen, piano. Music and Arts CD 4934.

What's This [="First Encore" to Dynamic Motion] (ca. 1915)
(LP) Henry Cowell, piano. Circle L-51-101 and Folkways FM3349.
(LP) Doris [=Sorel] Hays, piano. Finnadar Records SR 1096 AND SN-9016.
(CD) Henry Cowell, piano. Smithsonian/Folkways SF 40801.
(CD) Steffen Schleiermacher, piano. Hat Hut "Now" series. Hat Art CD 6144.
(CD) Chris Brown, Sorrel Hays, et al. New Albion 103.
(Cassette) Cheryl Seltzer, piano. Continuum. Musical Heritage Society 9370Z.

Where She Lies
(CD) Mary Ann Hart, voice. Jeanne Golan, pianist. Albany Records

Woof I and Woof II (1928)
(CD) "Fascinatin' Rhythm." Alan Feinberg, piano. Argo 444 457 2.

Publisher's note: Higgins' listings have been brought current to 2001.

Index

Credits and Acknowledgments

ADDITIONAL permission to reprint texts by Henry Cowell is gratefully acknowledged for the following works. Effort has been made to locate and identify all original sources: any omissions are inadvertent and the publisher respectfully requests that additions or corrections be directed to its attention for crediting in future printings.

Musical credits are printed beneath the passages of works to which they apply.

The frontispiece photograph is reprinted by permission of the Archives of the Peabody Institute of Johns Hopkins University, copyright © 1964 by Peabody Institute.

"Music Is My Weapon" is reprinted by permission of Simon & Schuster from *This I Believe* by Edward Murrow, edited by Raymond Swing. Copyright © 1952 by Simon & Schuster, Inc. Copyright renewed 1980 by Edward P. Morgan.

"John J. Becker," "Charles E. Ives," "Charles Seeger," and "Edgar Varèse" are reprinted from *American Composers on American Music*, edited by Henry Cowell, by permission of Stanford University Press. Copyright © 1933 by the Board of Trustees of the Leland Stanford Junior University. Copyright renewed 1961 by Henry Cowell.

Reviews of Antheil, Becker, Cage, Busoni, Harrison, Ives, McPhee, Thomson, Ruggles, Sessions, Stravinsky, and Varèse originally appeared in *New Musical Quarterly*'s regular feature, "Current Chronicle: New York": XXXIV/3 (July 1948, McPhee and Thomson), XXXVI/1 (January 1950, Sessions), XXXVI/2 (April 1950, Ruggles), XXXVI/3 (July 1950, Harrison), XXXVIII/1 (January 1952, Cage and Busoni), XXXIX/2, Stravinsky), XXXIX/3 (July 1953, Becker), XXXIX/4 (October 1953, Antheil), XLI (January 1955, Ives) and XLI/3 (July 1955, Varèse). They are copyright their respective years and were originally published in New York by Schirmer Books. Printed by permission of Oxford University Press.

"Drums Along the Pacific" [on Lou Harrison] and "Roldan and Caturla of Cuba" originally appeared in *Modern Music*, copyright 1940 and 1941 respectively and are reprinted by permission of The League of Composers, c/o American Music Center, New York. All rights reserved.

Reviews of Ives, Sessions, and Slonimsky from the Music Library Association's *Notes* V/3 (June 1948), VIII/1 (December 1950), and IV/2 (March 1947) are copyrighted 1950 and 1947 respectively and are reprinted by permission.

"43-Tone Minstrelsy" [on Harry Partch] first appeared in *Saturday Review of Literature* XXXII/48 (26 November 1949). Reprinted by permission The Saturday Review, © 1949, SR Publications, Ltd.

The essay on Béla Bartók's recordings appeared in *Musical Quarterly* XXXIX/4 (October 1953), copyright 1953 and originally published by Schirmer Books, New York. Printed by permission of Oxford University Press.

"Carl Ruggles[:] A Note" first appeared in a chapbook by Lou Harrison, *About Carl Ruggles: Section Four of a Book on Ruggles*, copyright 1945 by the Alicat Book Shop, Yonkers, New York.

"Overture to the Schillinger System" is from *The Schillinger System of Musical Composition* by Joseph Schillinger. Copyright © 1941, 1942, 1946 by Carl Fischer, Inc. Copyrights renewed. International copyright secured. Reprinted by permission. All rights reserved.

"The Schillinger Case: Charting the Musical Range" appeared in *Modern Music* XXIII/3 (Summer 1946). Reprinted by permission of The League of Composers, c/o American Music Center, New York. All rights reserved.

"The Scientific Approach to Non-European Music" first appeared in *Music Vanguard* 2 (1935).

"Folk Music," coauthored with Sidney Robertson Cowell, first appeared as "The American Scene, Part 3" in *Listen* VIII/1 (May 1944), copyright 1944.

"Music of the World's Peoples" reprints the introduction and notes from *Music of the World's Peoples*, Volume 1, edited by Henry Cowell (Ethnic Folkways Library Albums P504, P505 and P506), copyright © 1951, 1953 and 1955 by Folkways Records and Service Corp. Reprinted by permission.

"The World's Vocal Arts" reprints the notes to *The World's Vocal Arts*, edited by Henry Cowell (Ethnic Folkways Library Album FERR 4510). Copyright © 1955 by Folkways Records and Service Corp. Reprinted by permission.

"Music of Indonesia" reprints the notes to *Music of Indonesia*, edited by Henry Cowell (Ethnic Folkways Library Album FE 4537 A/B and C/D). Copyright © 1960-61 by Folkways Records and Service Corp. Reprinted by permission.

"Music of the Orient" first appeared in *Music Journal* and was reprinted in *Peabody Notes* XVII/2 (February 1964). Copyright © 1964 by Peabody Institute. Reprinted by permission of the Archives of the Peabody Institute of Johns Hopkins University.

Cowell's notes on *Persian Set*, *Quartet Romantic*, *Quartet Euphemetric* and *United Quartet* are copyright © 1974 by C. F. Peters Corporation. Used by permission. All rights reserved.

"Vocal Innovators of Central Europe" first appeared in *Modern Music* VII/2 (February-March 1930); and "The League's Evening of Film" in *Modern Music* XVIII/3 (March-April 1941), copyright 1930 and 1941 respectively. Reprinted by permission of The League of Composers, c/o American Music Center, New York. All rights reserved.

"How Relate Music and Dance," "Relating Music and Concert Dance," and "New Sounds in Music for the Dance" were published by *Dance Observer*, copyright 1934, 1937, and 1941 respectively.

"Tonal Therapy" appeared in *The Temple Artisan* in 1922 and is reprinted by permission of The Temple of the People.

"The Process of Musical Creation" first appeared in *The American Journal of Psychology* XXXVII (April 1926).

"Our Inadequate Notation" and "Music of and for the Records" first appeared in *Modern Music* IV/3 (March-April 1927) and VIII/3 (March-April 1931), copyright 1927 and 1931 respectively. They are reprinted by permission of The League of Composers, c/o American Music Center, New York. All rights reserved.

Selections from *The Nature of Melody* are printed by permission of the David and Sylvia Teitelbaum Fund.

"The Joys of Noise" first appeared in *The New Republic*, LIX/765 (31 July 1929).

"Harmonic Development in Music," coauthored with Robert L. Duffus, appeared in three parts in *The Freeman*, III/55 (30 March 1921), III/56 (6 April 1921) and III/57 (13 April 1921).

"The Impasse of Modern Music" first appeared in *Century Magazine* CXIV/6 (October 1927).

"Towards Neo-Primitivism" and "Shaping Music for Total War" appeared in *Modern Music* X/3 (March-April 1933) and XXIII/3 (Summer 1946), copyright 1933 and 1946, respectively. Reprinted by permission of The League of Composers, c/o American Music Center, New York. All rights reserved.

"On Programming American Music" was published in *Music Clubs Magazine* XXXI/2 (May 1952) p. 23, copyright © 1952; it is reprinted here with the permission of the National Federation of Music Clubs.

"A Composer's World" appeared originally in *Music in Ghana,* © 1961. Reprinted by permission of The International Centre for Music and Dance, University of Ghana, Legon, Ghana.

AUTHOR'S NOTE

I had three useful bibliographies—Bruce Saylor's *The Writings of Henry Cowell: A Descriptive Bibliography*, Martha L. Manion's *Writings about Henry Cowell: An Annotated Bibliography*, and William Lichtenwanger's *The Music of Henry Cowell: A Descriptive Catalog*—to help direct my editing of this book. I was fortunate also in having the advice and guidance of H. Wiley Hitchcock, Professor Emeritus in Music at Brooklyn College, a friend of the Cowells who had helped Sidney Cowell handle rights and permissions for years. Special thanks are due to Richard Teitelbaum of the Department of Music at Bard College. His long-term interest in Cowell and his friendship with Sidney Robertson Cowell have placed him in a unique position of knowledge and interest in the Estate of Sidney Cowell, and without his efforts on its behalf this book would not exist. I also want to give special thanks to Don Gillespie and Susan Orzel of the C. F. Peters Corporation, one of the main publishers of Cowell's music, who helped not only with permissions but with the finding of much needed information. Wiley Hitchcock in turn put me into contact with George E. Boziwick of the New York Public Library at Lincoln Center, who was very helpful in finding obscure items. Jeffrey Katz of the Stevenson Library at Bard College, and his excellent staff, helped immeasurably in the endless process of tracking down rights. Thanks also are due to Elizabeth Schaaf, Archivist at the Archives of the Peabody Institute of Johns Hopkins University, who found and printed the photograph used as the frontispiece; and to Andy Harp of San Luis Obispo, California, who told me about "Tonal Therapy," Cowell's hitherto unknown earliest published text. [1998]

Publisher's Colophon

ORIGINALLY, this book was commissioned to appear in a series of volumes presenting writings by American composers. It was a natural project for Dick Higgins, who was a lifelong advocate for Henry Cowell's centrality to American music, and he had finished all but the final editing of the fifth draft when that series and this book were abruptly cancelled by their publisher in 1997. That fall Dick proposed that I take over the project. By midsummer 1998 I had agreed, and over the next two months we discussed the book in greater detail when, to the shock of his family and friends, Dick died suddenly in October at the age of 60. We had been good friends for twenty-five years, and had worked closely together on various publishing projects. Over the next three years my completion of *Essential Cowell* became, therefore, a more personal undertaking, and, I now hope, a tribute to that friendship.

I am indebted beyond measure to many persons for their direct assistance in realizing this publication. Higgins family members—Alison Knowles, Hannah Higgins, Jessica Higgins, and Elizabeth Higgins Null—provided much needed moral support, as well as access to Dick's files pertaining to this book and help with matters concerning the Higgins Estate. Likewise, Richard Teitelbaum smoothed the way with the Cowell Estate, directing me to the very capable Laura Mankin, Esq. Brian McHugh located the computer files of the manuscripts. Kyle Gann, who had been Dick's choice to author a preface, very graciously complied. Joan Tower helped with an appeal for funding. Joan K. Davidson and M. J. Gladstone took particular interest in the book, which resulted in needed financial support from Furthermore... Pauline Oliveros sent me to Scott Smallwood, who reset the musical examples, which were then expertly proofread by Malcolm Smith. Keir Littlebird and Jorge Santana produced the index and helped proofread the final version of the text, which, incidentally, restores some short essays of Cowell's that Dick had reluctantly cut at the request of the commissioning editor, and incorporates minor corrections and some changes in ordering and titling. To everyone involved in this project I extend my utmost gratitude.

—BRUCE R. McPHERSON

347